PENGUIN BOOKS

PORTUGUESE PHRASE BOOK

OTHER PENGUIN PHRASE BOOKS

Dutch

French

German

Greek

Italian

Russian

Spanish

Turkish

PORTUGUESE
PHRASE BOOK

THIRD EDITION

JILL NORMAN

ANTONIO DE FIGUEIREDO

PENGUIN BOOKS

PENGUIN BOOKS

Published by the Penguin Group
Penguin Books Ltd, 27 Wrights Lane, London W8 5TZ, England
Penguin Books USA Inc., 375 Hudson Street, New York, New York 10014, USA
Penguin Books Australia Ltd, Ringwood, Victoria, Australia
Penguin Books Canada Ltd, 10 Alcorn Avenue, Toronto, Ontario, Canada M4V 3B2
Penguin Books (NZ) Ltd, 182 190 Wairau Road, Auckland 10, New Zealand

Penguin Books Ltd, Registered Offices: Harmondsworth, Middlesex, England

First published 1971
Second edition 1979
Third edition 1988
11

Printed in England by Clays Ltd, St Ives plc
Filmset in Linotron 202 Ehrhardt

CONTENTS

TRAVEL 15

DIRECTIONS 32

DRIVING 35

CYCLING 49

HOTELS & GUEST HOUSES 52

CAMPING 63

INTRODUCTION

In this series of phrase books, only those words and phrases that might be called essential to a traveller have been included, but the definition of 'traveller' has been made very wide, to include not only the business traveller and the holiday-maker, whether travelling alone, with a group or the family, but also the owner of a house, an apartment or a time-share. Each type of traveller has his or her own requirements, and for easy use the phrases are arranged in sections which deal with specific situations.

Pronunciation is given for each phrase and for all words in the extensive vocabulary. An explanation of the system used for the pronunciation guide is to be found on pages xiii–xvii. It is essential to read this section carefully before starting to use this book.

Some of the Portuguese phrases are marked with an asterisk* – these attempt to give an indication of the kind of reply you might get to your question, and of questions you may be asked in your turn.

For those who would like to know a little more about the Portuguese language, a brief survey of the main points of its grammar is provided at the end of the book (pages 197–204).

We have tried to add new words and phrases to take into account recent social and technological developments. However, there is a tendency to use original English words; words such as 'stress', 'babysitter', 'jet lag', 'hovercraft' and 'hydrofoil' are still better known than their Portuguese equivalents. But you will always be rewarded for, and helped in, your efforts to speak Portuguese.

PRONUNCIATION

The pronunciation guide is intended for people with no knowledge of Portuguese. As far as possible the system is based on English pronunciation, but as Portuguese has an infinitely more complex sound structure, complete accuracy will sometimes be lost for the sake of simplicity. However, the reader should be able to understand Portuguese pronunciation and to make himself understood if he reads this section carefully. Each word and phrase has a transcription into English symbols according to the rules set out below.

VOWELS

Pronounce:	**a** as **a** in father	symbol **ah**	fábrica – factory (fah-bree-ka)
	as **a** in about or as **u** in put	symbol **a**	amigo – friend (a-mee-goo)
	e, é as **e** in bet	symbol **eh**	serra – mountain (seh-ra)
	e, ê as **ay** in stay or as **ey** in they	symbol **ay a ai**	fazer – to do (fa-zair)

	e, i as **e** in open or as **i** in bit (occurs only in an unstressed syllable, and as a final letter it is almost silent)	symbol **e**	antes – before (an-tesh)
	i as **i** in machine	symbol **ee**	mil – thousand (meel)
Before a, e, o or u in unstressed syllables **i** resembles **y** in yes		symbol **y, ee**	férias – holiday (fe-ree-ash)
	o as **o** in olive	symbol **o**	bola – ball (bo-la)
	o, ou, ô, final **oa** as **o** in so, most	symbol **oh**	ôvo – egg (oh-voo)
	o as **oo** in boot (used in most unstressed syllables)	symbol **oo**	dormir – to sleep (door-meer)
Before stressed a, e, i, **o** resembles **w** in wet		symbol **w**	Coimbra (kwee^{n}-bra)
	u as **u** in rule or **oo** in boot	symbol **oo**	usar – to use (oo-zar)
Before a, e, i, and after o the **u** sound resembles **w** in wet		symbol **w**	água – water (a-gwa)

DIPHTHONGS

Pronounce			
Pronounce	**ai** as **ie** in tie	symbol **i, y**	pai – father (py)
	au as **ow** in how	symbol **ow**	causa – cause (kow-za)
	oi, ói, as **oi** in oil or **oy** in boy	symbol **oy**	lençois – sheets (lay^n–soysh)

The other double vowels – **ei, éi, éu** – do not really have special sounds. They are very close to the sounds of the separate parts as listed above, and the same symbols are used.

e.g. comeis – you eat (koo-may-eesh); céu – sky (seh-oo).

NASALS

These sounds should be made through the nose, but without pronouncing the 'n'. Nasalization is shown in spelling by a tilde over the vowel, or by an **m** at the end of a word, or by **m** or **n** before a consonant.

ã, am, an	symbol **a^n**	maçã – apple (ma-sa^n)
ẽ, em, en	symbol **ay^n e^n**	cento – hundred (se^n-too)
im, in	symbol **ee^n**	cinco – five (seen^n-koo)
õ, om, on	symbol **o^n**	bom – good (bo^n)
um, un	symbol **oo^n**	um – one (oo^n)
ão	symbol **ow^n**	pão – bread (pow^n)
ãe, ãi	symbol **y^n**	mãe – mother (my^n)
õe	symbol **oy^n**	limões – lemons (lee-moy^{n}sh)

CONSONANTS

b, f, l, m, p, q, t, v are pronounced as in English, but note the following:

c before a, o, u or a consonant is pronounced **k**	symbol **k**	casa – house (kah-za)
c before e, i and **ç** are pronounced **s**	symbol **s**	certo – certain (sair-too)
ch is pronounced **sh** as in ship	symbol **sh**	chave – key (shahv)
d is softer than in English		
g before a, o, u is pronounced **g** as in got	symbol **g**	garfo – fork (gahr-foo)
gu in combination gue and gui the u is not pronounced; its purpose is to keep the **g** hard, as above		
g before e, i is pronounced as **s** in pleasure	symbol **zh**	gente – people (zhe^{n}t)
h is always silent		
j is pronounced as **s** in pleasure	symbol **zh**	laranja – orange (lar-a^{n}zha)
lh is like **lli** in million	symbol **lly**	toalha – towel (too-a-llya)
nh is like **ni** in onion	symbol **ny**	vinho – wine (vee-nyoo)
rr is strongly trilled		
s, ss at the beginning of a word or after a consonant is pronounced **s**	symbol **s**	saber – to know (sa-bair)
s between two vowels is pronounced **z**	symbol **z**	mesa – table (may-za)

s is pronounced as **sh** at the end of a word, and in certain other places as	symbol **sh**	luvas – gloves (loo-vash)
s in pleasure	symbol **zh**	
x is pronounced **sh** at the end of a word or when **ex** is followed by a consonant	symbol **sh**	excelente – excellent (esh-say-le^{n}t)
as **z** when **ex** is followed by a vowel	symbol **z**	exacto – exact (ez-a-too)
as **s** between two vowels	symbol **s**	auxilio – help (ow-see-lyoo)
and occasionally as **ks**	symbol **ks**	táxi – taxi (tak-see)
z is pronounced as **z**	symbol **z**	azul – blue (az-ool)
as **sh** at the end of a word	symbol **sh**	faz favor – please (fash fa-vor)
and sometimes as **s** in pleasure	symbol **zh**	

STRESS

Words ending in the single vowels **a**, **e**, **o** or in **m** or **s** are stressed on the last syllable but one: **falo** – I speak; **casas** – houses; **vestido** – dress. In other words the stress usually falls on the last syllable: **falar** – to speak; **maçã** – apple; **nação** – nation; **animal** – animal. Note that nasal vowels and double vowels at the end of words do carry stress. Exceptions to these rules are indicated by a written accent: **café**, **bebé**. Stressed syllables are printed in **bold type** in the pronunciation guide.

ESSENTIALS

FIRST THINGS

Yes	**Sim**	See^n
No	**Não**	Now^n
Please	**Por favor/faz favor**	Poor fa-**vor**/fazh fa-**vor**
Thank you	**Obrigado**	O-bree-**ga**-do
You're welcome	**De nada**	De **nah**-da

LANGUAGE PROBLEMS

I'm English	**Sou inglês (inglesa)**	Soh ee^n-**glaysh** (ee^n-**glay**-za)
American	**americano (americana)**	a-me-ree-**ka**-no (a-me-ree-**ka**-na)

South African	**sul-africano (sul-africana)**	sool a-free-ka-noo (sool a-free-ka-na)
Do you speak English?	**Fala inglês?**	Fa-la ee^{n}-glaysh
Does anyone here speak English?	**Há aqui alguém que fale inglês?**	Ah a-kee al-ge^{n} ke fa-le ee^{n}-glaysh
I don't speak much Portuguese	**Não falo (muito) português**	Now^{n} fa-loo (moo-ee-to) poor-too-gaysh
Do you understand me?	***Compreende (me)?**	Ko^{n}-pre-ay^{n}d (me)
I don't understand	**Não entendo/ compreendo**	Now^{n} ay^{n}-tay^{n}-doo/ko^{n}-pre-ay^{n}-doo
Would you say that again, please?	**Repita isso por favor?**	Re-pee-ta ee-soo poor fa-vor
Please speak slowly	**Fale lentamente por favor**	Fa-le lay^{n}-ta-may^{n}t poor fa-vor
What does that mean?	**O que quer dizer isso?**	Oo ke ker dee-zayr ee-soo
Can you translate this for me?	**Pode traduzir-me isto?**	Po-de tra-doo-zeer-me eesh-to
Please write it down	**É favor escrever**	Eh fa-vor esh-kre-vayr
What do you call this in Portuguese?	**Como se chama isto em português?**	Ko-moo se sha-ma eesh-too ay^{n} poor-too-gaysh
I will look it up in my phrase book	**Eu vou ver no meu livro de frases**	Ay-oo vo vayr noo may-oo lee-vroo de fra-zesh
Please show me the word in the book	**Por favor mostre-me a palavra no livro**	Poor fa-vor mosh-tre-me a pa-la-vra noo lee-vroo

QUESTIONS

English	Portuguese	Pronunciation
Who?	**Quem?**	Kay^n
Where is/are ...?	**Onde está/estão ...?**	O^n-de esh-ta/esh-tow^n
When?	**Quando?**	Kwa^n-doo
How?	**Como?**	Ko-moo
How much/many?	**Quanto/Quantos?**	Kwa^n-too/kwa^n-toosh
How much is/are ...?	**Quanto é/são ...?**	Kwa^n-too eh/sow^n
How long?	**Quanto tempo?**	Kwa^n-too tay^n-poo
How far?	**Qual é a distância?**	Kwal eh a deesh-ta^n-see-a
What's that?	**O que é aquilo?**	Oo ke eh a-kee-loo
What do you want?	**O que deseja?**	Oo ke de-ze-zha
What must I do?	**O que devo fazer?**	Oo ke day-voo fa-zayr
Why?	**Porquê?**	Poor-kay
Have you ...?	**Tem ...?**	Tay^n
Is/Are there ...?	**Há ...?**	Ah
Have you seen ...?	**Viu ...?**	Vee-oo
Where can I find ...?	**Onde posso encontrar ...?**	O^n-de po-soo ay^n-ko^n-trar
What is the matter?	**Que se passa?**	Ke se pas-sa
Can you help me?	**Pode ajudar-me?**	Po-de a-zhoo-dar-me
Can I help you?	***Posso ajudá-lo?**	Po-soo a-zhoo-da-loo
Can you	**Pode**	Po-de
tell me?	**dizer-me?**	dee-zayr-me
give me?	**dar-me?**	dar-me
show me?	**mostrar-me?**	moosh-trar-me

USEFUL STATEMENTS

It is ...	**É ...**	Eh
It isn't ...	**Não é ...**	Now^n eh
I have ...	**Tenho ...**	Tay^n-nyoo
I don't have ...	**Não tenho ...**	Now^n tay^n-nyoo
I want ...	**Quero ...**	Ke-roo
I would like ...	**Gostaría ...**	Goosh-ta-ree-a
I need ...	**Preciso ...**	Pre-see-zoo
I like it	**Gosto disto**	Gosh-too deesh-too
OK/That's fine	**OK!/Está bem**	O.K./Esh-ta bay^n
I'm lost	**Estou perdido**	Esh-toh per-dee-doo
We're looking for ...	**Estamos à procura de ...**	Esh-ta-moosh ah pro-koo-ra de
Here it is	**Aqui está**	A-kee esh-ta
There they are	**Ali estão**	A-lee esh-tow^n
There is/are ...	**Há ...**	Ah
It's important	**É importante**	Eh ee^n-poor-ta^{n}t
It's urgent	**É urgente**	Eh oor-zhay^{n}t
You are mistaken	**Está enganado/a**	Esh-ta ay^n-ga-na-doo/a
I like it	**Gosto**	Gosh-too
I don't like it	**Não gosto**	Now^n gosh-too
I'm not sure	**Não tenho a certeza**	Now^n tay^n-nyoo a ser-tay-za
I don't know	**Não sei**	Now^n say-ee
I didn't know	**Não sabía**	Now^n sa-bee-a

I think so	**Penso que sim**	Pe^{n}-soo ke see^{n}
I'm hungry/thirsty	**Tenho fome/sede**	Tay^{n}-nyoo fom/sayd
I'm tired	**Estou cansado/a**	Esh-toh ka^{n}-sa-doo/a
I'm in a hurry	**Estou com pressa**	Esh-toh ko^{n} pre-sa
I'm ready	**Estou pronto**	Esh-toh pro^{n}-too
Leave me alone	**Deixe-me por favor**	Dayee-she-me poor fa-vor
Just a minute	***Um minuto**	Oo^{n} mee-noo-too
This way, please	***Por aquí/siga-me**	Poor a-kee/see-ga-me
Take a seat	***Sente-se**	Se^{n}-te-se
Come in!	***Entre**	E^{n}-tre
It's cheap/expensive	**É barato/caro**	Eh ba-ra-too/ka-roo
It's too much	**É demasiado**	Eh de-ma-zee-a-doo
That's all	**É tudo**	Eh too-doo
You're right	**Tem razão**	Tay^{n} ra-zow^{n}
You're wrong	**Não tem razão**	Now^{n} tay^{n} ra-zow^{n}

GREETINGS

Good morning/good day	**Bom dia**	Bo^{n} dee-a
Good afternoon	**Boa tarde**	Bo-a tard
Good evening/good night	**Boa noite**	Bo-a no-eet
Hello	**Olá**	Oh-la
How are you?	**Como está?**	Ko-moo esh-ta

Very well, thank you	**Muito bem obrigado**	Moo-ee-too bay^n o-bree-ga-doo
See you soon	**Até logo**	A-te lo-goo
Have a good journey	**Boa viagem**	Bo-a vee-a-zhay^n
Good luck/all the best	**Boa sorte**	Bo-a sort

POLITE PHRASES

Sorry/excuse me	**Desculpe**	Desh-kool-pe
That's all right	**Está bem**	Esh-ta bay^n
Not at all/don't mention it	**De nada**	De nah-da
With pleasure	**Com prazer**	Ko^n pra-zayr
Is everything all right?	**Está tudo bem?**	Esh-ta too-doo bay^n
Don't worry	**Não se preocupe**	Now^n se pray-o-koo-pe
It doesn't matter	**Não importa**	Now^n ee^n-por-ta
I beg your pardon?	**O quê/Como disse?**	Oo ke/ko-moo dee-se
Am I disturbing you?	**Incomodo?**	Ee^n-koo-mo-doo
I'm sorry to have troubled you	**Desculpe tê-lo incomodado**	Desh-kool-pe tay-loo ee^n-koo-moo-da-doo
Good/That's fine	**Bem/Está bem**	Bay^n/esh-ta bay^n

OPPOSITES

before/after	**antes/depois**	a^n-tesh/de-po-eesh
early/late	**cedo/tarde**	say-doo/tard

first/last	**primeiro/último**	pree-**may**-ee-roo/**ool**-tee-moo
now/later	**agora/mais tarde**	a-**go**-ra/**ma**-eesh tard
far/near	**longe/perto**	**lo**^{n}-zhe/**per**-too
here/there	**aqui/ali**	a-**kee**/a-**lee**
in/out	**entrada/saída**	e^{n}-**tra**-da/sa-**ee**-da
inside/outside	**dentro/fora**	**de**^{n}-troo/**fo**-ra
under/over	**debaixo/em cima**	de-**ba**-ee-shoo/ay^{n} **see**-ma
big, large/small	**grande/pequeno**	**gra**^{n}-de/pe-**kay**-noo
deep/shallow	**fundo/pouco fundo**	**foo**^{n}-doo/**po**-koo **foo**^{n}-doo
empty/full	**vazio/cheio**	va-**zee**-oo/**shayee**-oo
fat/lean	**gôrdo/magro**	**gor**-doo/**ma**-groo
heavy/light	**pesado/leve, ligeiro**	pe-**za**-doo/**le**-ve, lee-**zhayee**-roo
high/low	**alto/baixo**	**al**-too/**ba**-ee-shoo
long, tall/short	**comprido, alto/baixo**	ko^{n}-**pree**-doo, **al**-too/**bayee**-shoo
narrow/wide	**estreito/largo**	esh-**trayee**-too/**lar**-goo
thick/thin	**grosso/fino**	**gro**-soo/**fee**-noo
least/most	**menos/mais**	**me**^{n}-noosh/**ma**-eesh
many/few	**muitos/poucos**	**moo**-ee-toosh/**po**-koosh
more/less	**mais/menos**	**ma**-eesh/**may**^{n}-noosh
much/little	**muito/pouco**	**moo**-ee-too/**po**-koo
beautiful/ugly	**bonito, belo/feio**	boo-**nee**-too, **be**-loo/**fayee**-o

better/worse	**melhor/pior**	me-**llyor**/pee-**or**
cheap/expensive	**barato/caro**	ba-**ra**-too/**ka**-roo
clean/dirty	**limpo/sujo**	**lee**^{n}-poo/**soo**-zhoo
cold/hot, warm	**frio/quente, morno**	**free**-oo/**ke**^{n}-te, **mor**-noo
easy/difficult	**fácil/difícil**	**fa**-seel/dee-**fee**-seel
fresh/stale	**fresco/rançoso, estragado**	**fraysh**-koo/ra^{n}-**so**-zoo, esh-tra-**ga**-doo
good/bad	**bom/mau**	bo^{n}/**ma**-oo
new, young/old	**novo, jovem/velho**	**no**-voo, **zho**-vay^{n}/**ve**-llyoo
nice/nasty	**bonito, agradável, simpático/ desagradável, antipático**	boo-**nee**-too, a-gra-**da**-vel, see^{n}-**pa**-tee-koo/ de-za-gra-**da**-vel, a^{n}-tee-**pa**-tee-koo
right/wrong	**certo/errado**	**ser**-too/ay-**ra**-doo
open/closed, shut	**aberto/fechado, encerrado**	a-**ber**-too/fe-**sha**-doo, e^{n}-se-**ra**-doo
vacant/occupied	**livre/ocupado**	**lee**-vre/o-koo-**pa**-doo
quick/slow	**rápido/vagaroso, lento**	**ra**-pee-doo/va-ga-**ro**-zoo, **le**^{n}-too
quiet/noisy	**calado, silencioso/ barulhento, ruidoso**	ka-**la**-doo, see-le^{n}-see-**o**-zoo/ba-roo-**llye**^{n}-too, roo-ee-**do**-zoo
sharp/blunt	**agudo, afiado/boto, embotado**	a-**goo**-doo, a-fee-**a**-doo/ **bo**-too, e^{n}-boo-**ta**-doo

SIGNS & PUBLIC NOTICES[1]

Aberto	Open
Aberto das ... às ...	Open from ... to ...
Agua potável	Drinking water
Alugam-se quartos	Rooms to let
Ascensor/elevador	Lift/elevator
Banco	Bank
Caixa	Cash desk/cashier
Cautela/precaução	Caution
Cavalheiros/senhores	Gentlemen
Chamar/chamada	Knock/ring
Circule pela direita	Keep right
Correios	Post office
Direcção proibida	No entry

1. See also SIGNS TO LOOK FOR AT AIRPORTS AND STATIONS (p. 18) and ROAD SIGNS (p. 37).

Empurre	Push
Entrada	Entrance
Entrada gratuita	Admission free
É proibido fumar	No smoking
É proibida a entrada	No admission
Fechado	Closed
Guia	Guide
Há quartos	Vacancies/rooms to let
Hospital	Hospital
(Hotel) completo	No vacancies
Informação	Information
Intérprete	Interpreter
Lavabos	Lavatory
Livre	Vacant/free/unoccupied
Não ...	Do not ...
Não há lugares	House full (cinema etc.)
Não pisar a relva	Keep off the grass
Não tocar	Do not touch
Ocupado	Engaged/occupied
Para arrendar/alugar	To let/for hire
Para venda	For sale
Particular	Private
Pede-se para não ...	You are requested not to ...
Peões	Pedestrians
Perigo	Danger
Polícia	Police

Proibido ... sob multa de ...	Trespassers will be prosecuted
Puxe	Pull
Reservado	Reserved
Retretes	Lavatory
Saída	Exit
Saída de emergência	Emergency exit
Senhoras	Ladies
Senhores	Gentlemen
Venda (leilão)	Sale

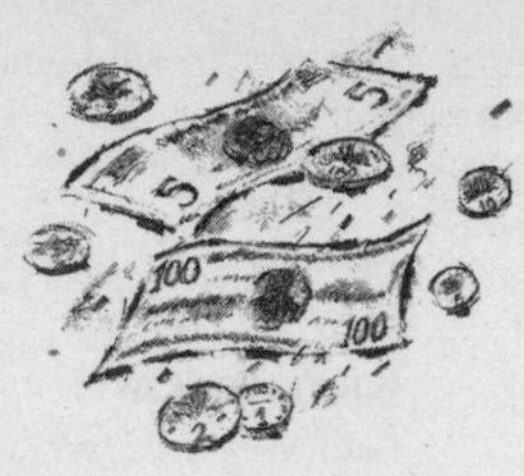

MONEY[1]

Is there a place to change money near here?	**Há alguma casa de câmbio perto de aqui?**	Ah al-**goo**-ma ka-za de **ka^{n}**-bee-oo **per**-too de a-**kee**
Do you cash travellers' cheques?	**Trocam cheques de viagem?**	**Tro**-kow^{n} sheksh de vee-**a**-zhayn
Where can I cash travellers' cheques?	**Onde posso trocar cheques de viagem?**	**O^{n}**-de **po**-soo troo-**kar** sheksh de vee-**a**-zhayn
Please cash this Eurocheque	**Por favor pague-me este Eurocheque**	Poor fa-**vor** **pa**-ge-me aysht ay-oo-ro-**shek**
Will you take a personal cheque?	**Aceita um cheque pessoal?**	A-**say**-ee-ta oo^{n} shek pe-soo-**al**

1. Portuguese banks are open from 9.30 a.m. to 12.00 p.m. and from 2.00 p.m. to 4.00 p.m., Monday to Friday. On Saturdays from 9.30 a.m. to 11.30 a.m. Exchange bureaux are open from 9.30 a.m. to 6.00 p.m., Monday to Friday and 9.30 a.m. to 1.00 p.m. on Saturdays.

Do you have any identification?	***Tem algum documento de identificação?**	Tay^{n} al-goom doo-koo-may^{n}-too de ee-day^{n}-tee-fee-ka-sow^{n}
Do you have a cheque card?	***Tem cartão bancário?**	Tay^{n} kar-tow^{n} ba^{n}-ka-ree-oo
Will you take a credit card?	**Aceita um cartão de crédito?**	A-say-ee-ta oo^{n} kar-tow^{n} de kre-dee-too
I want to change some English/South African/American money	**Quero trocar dinheiro inglês/sul-africano/americano**	Ke-roo troo-kar dee-nyay-ee-roo ee^{n}-glaysh/sool a-free-ka-noo/a-me-ree-ka-noo
How much do I get for a pound/dollar?	**Quanto pagam pela libra/dolar?**	Kwa^{n}-too pa-gow^{n} pay-la lee-bra/do-lar
What is the rate of exchange?	**Qual é o câmbio actual?**	Kwal eh oo ka^{n}-bee-oo a-too-al
Can you give me some small change?	**Dê-me algum dinheiro trocado, por favor**	Day-me al-goo^{n} dee-nyay-ee-roo troo-ka-doo poor fa-vor
Where do I sign?	**Onde é que assino?**	O^{n}-de eh ke a-see-noo
Sign here, please	***Assine aqui, por favor**	A-seen a-kee poor fa-vor
Go to the cashier	***Vá à caixa**	Va ah ka-ee-sha
I arranged for money to be transferred from England; has it arrived yet?	**Mandei transferir dinheiro da Inglaterra; já chegou?**	Ma^{n}-day tra^{n}zh-fe-reer dee-nyay-ee-roo da een-gla-te-ra; zha she-go
I want to open a bank account	**Quero abrir uma conta bancária**	Ke-roo a-breer oo-ma ko^{n}-ta ba^{n}-ka-ree-a

Please credit this to my account	**Por favor credite na minha conta**	Poor fa-vor kre-deet na mee-nya ko^n-ta
I'd like to get some cash with my credit card	**Gostaría de levantar dinheiro com o meu cartão de crédito**	Goosh-ta-ree-a de le-va^n-tar dee-nyay-ee-roo ko^n oo may-oo kar-tow^n de kre-dee-too
Current account	**Conta corrente**	Ko^n-ta koo-ray^{n}t
Deposit account	**Conta de depósito**	Ko^n-ta de de-po-zee-too
Statement	**Extracto de conta**	Esh-tra-too de ko^n-ta
Balance	**Saldo**	Sal-doo
Cheque book	**Livro de cheques**	Lee-vroo de she-ksh
Cheque card	**Cartão bancário**	Kar-tow^n ba^n-ka-ree-oo

CURRENCY

Portuguese currency is the **escudo**, and 100 **centavos** = 1 **escudo**. The escudo is represented by the symbol $ placed between the escudos and the centavos (e.g. 1$50 = one escudo, fifty centavos).

TRAVEL

ARRIVAL

PASSPORTS

English	Portuguese	Pronunciation
Passport control	***Contrôle de passaportes**	Ko^{n}-**trol** de pa-sa-**por**-tesh
Your passport, please	***O passaporte, por favor**	Oo pa-sa-**port** poor fa-**vor**
May I see your green card?	***Pode mostrar-me o certificado de seguro?**	**Po**-de moosh-**trar**-me oo ser-tee-fee-**ka**-doo de se-**goo**-roo
Are you together?	***Viajam juntos?**	Vee-**a**-zhow^{n} **zhoo**^{n}-toosh
I'm travelling alone	**Viajo só**	Vee-**a**-zhoo **so**

I'm travelling with my wife/a friend	**Viajo com a minha esposa/um amigo**	Vee-a-zhoo ko^n a mee-nya esh-po-za/oo^n a-mee-goo
I'm here on business/ on holiday	**Venho em negócios/ de férias**	Vay^n-nyoo ay^n ne-go-see-oosh/de fe-ree-ash
What is your address in Lisbon?	***Qual é a sua direcção em Lisboa?**	Kwal eh a soo-a dee-re-sow^n ay^n leezh-bo-a
How long are you staying here?	***Quanto tempo vai estar aqui?**	Kwa^n-too tay^n-poo vy esh-tar a-kee

CUSTOMS

Customs	***Alfândega**	Al-fa^n-de-ga
Goods/nothing to declare	***Artigos/nada a declarar**	Ar-tee-goosh/nah-da a de-kla-rar
Which is your luggage?	***Qual é a sua bagagem?**	Kwal eh a soo-a ba-ga-zhay^n
Do you have more luggage?	***Tem mais bagagem?**	Tay^n ma-eesh ba-ga-zhay^n
This is (all) my luggage	**Esta é (toda) a minha bagagem**	Esh-ta eh (toh-da) a mee-nya ba-ga-zhay^n
Have you anything to declare?	***Tem algo a declarar?**	Tay^n al-goo a de-kla-rar
I have only my personal things in it	**Tenho sómente as minhas coisas pessoais**	Tay^n-nyoo so-me^{n}t ash mee-nyash ko-ee-zash pe-soo-a-eesh
I have a carton of cigarettes and a bottle of wine/gin	**Tenho um pacote de maços de cigarro e uma garrafa de vinho/gin**	Tay^n-nyoo oo^n pa-kot de ma-soosh de see-ga-roo ee oo-ma ga-ra-fa de vee^n-nyoo/zhee^n

You will have to pay duty on this	***Tem que pagar direitos nisto**	Tay^n ke pa-**gar** dee-**ray**-ee-toosh **neesh**-too
Open your bag, please	***Abra a mala, por favor**	**A**-bra a **ma**-la poor fa-**vor**
Can I shut my case now?	**Posso fechar já a mala?**	**Po**-soo fe-**shar** zha a **ma**-la
May I go through?	**Já posso passar/posso ir-me embora?**	Zha **po**-soo pa-**sar**/**po**-soo **eer**-me ay^n-**bo**-ra

LUGGAGE

My luggage has not arrived	**A minha bagagem não chegou**	A **mee**-nya ba-**ga**-zhay^n now^n she-**go**
My luggage is damaged	**A minha bagagem está estragada**	A **mee**-nya ba-**ga**-zhay^n esh-**ta** esh-tra-**ga**-da
One suitcase is missing	**Falta uma das malas**	**Fal**-ta oo-ma dash **ma**-lash
Are there any luggage trollies?	**Há carrinhos de bagagem?**	Ah ka-**ree**-nyoosh de ba-**ga**-zhay^n
Where is the left luggage office?	**Onde é o balcão de depósito de bagagem?**	**O**^{n}-de eh oo bal-**kow**^{n} de de-**po**-zee-too dc ba-**ga**-zhay^n
Luggage lockers	***Caixas de bagagem**	**Ka**-ee-shash de ba-**ga**-zhay^n

MOVING ON

Porter!	**Porteiro!**	Poor-**tay**-ee-roo

Would you like to take these bags to a taxi/ the bus/coach?	**Pode levar esta bagagem para o taxi/autocarro/ camioneta?**	Po-de le-var esh-ta ba-ga-zhay^n pa-ra oo tak-see/ow-to-ka-roo/ ka-mee-o-nay-ta
What's the price for each piece of luggage?	**Qual é o preço por cada mala?**	Kwal eh oo pray-soo poor ka-da ma-la
I shall take this myself	**Eu levo esta**	Ay-oo le-voo esh-ta
That's not mine	**Essa não é minha**	E-sa now^n eh mee-nya
Would you call a taxi?	**Pode chamar-me um taxi?**	Po-de sha-mar-me oo^n tak-see
How much do I owe?	**Quanto lhe devo?**	Kwa^n-too llye day-voo
Is there a bus/train into the town?	**Há um autocarro/ comboio para a cidade?**	Ah oo^n ow-to-ka-roo/ ko^n-boy-oo pa-ra a see-dad
How can I get to ...?	**Como é que posso ir para ...?**	Ko-moo eh ke po-soo eer pa-ra

SIGNS TO LOOK FOR AT AIRPORTS AND STATIONS

Arrivals	**Chegadas**
Booking office	**Bilheteira**
Buses	**Autocarros**
Connections	**Correspondência**
Departures	**Partidas**
Gentlemen	**Cavalheiros/Senhores**
Information	**Informação**

Ladies	**Senhoras**
Left luggage	**Depósito de bagagem (consigna)**
Lost property	**Secção de objectos perdidos**
Luggage lockers	**Caixas de bagagem**
No smoking	**É proibido fumar**
Refreshments	**Bar/snack-bar**
Reservations	**Reservas**
Suburban lines	**Carreiras suburbanas**
Taxi rank	**Praça de taxis**
Tickets	**Bilhetes**

BUYING A TICKET[1]

Where is the travel agency?	**Onde é a agência de viagens?**	O^{n}-de eh a a-**zhay^{n}**-see-a de vee-a-**zhay^{n}sh**
Have you a timetable, please?	**Tem um horário, por favor?**	Tay^{n} oo^{n} o-ra-**ree**-oo poor fa-**vor**
How much is it first class to ...?	**Quanto custa um bilhete de primeira para ...?**	**Kwa^{n}**-too **koosh**-ta oo^{n} bee-**llyayt** de pree-**mayee**-ra **pa**-ra
A second class to ...	**Um bilhete de segunda para ...**	Oo^{n} bee-**llyayt** de se-**goo^{n}**-da **pa**-ra

1. You can buy a kilometre ticket for journeys of a minimum of 1,500 kilometres within Portugal. Application for such a ticket should be made to any principal Portuguese station at least a week before the journey commences.

First and second class travel are available on most trains, and on certain express trains a supplement is payable.

A return to ...	**Um bilhete de ida e volta a ...**	Oo^{n} bee-**llyayt** de **ee-d** **ee vol-ta** a
A single/one way	**Ida**	**Ee**-da
Is there a cheaper midweek/weekend fare?	**Há uma tarifa especial dias úteis/fim de semana?**	Ah **oo**-ma ta-**ree**-fa esh pe-see-**al dee**-ash **oo** tay-eesh/fee^{n} de se-**ma**-na
When are you coming back?	***Quando volta?**	**Kwan**-doo **vol**-ta
Is there a special rate for children?	**Há uma tarifa especial para crianças?**	Ah **oo**-ma ta-**ree**-fa esh pe-see-**al pa**-ra kree-**a^{n}**-sash
How old is he/she?	***Que idade tem ele/ela?**	Ke ee-**dad** tay^{n} **ay**-le/e-
A book of tickets, please[1]	**Uma caderneta de bilhetes**	**Oo**-ma ka-dair-**ne**-ta de bee-**llyay**-tesh
Can I use it on the bus/underground too?	**Posso usar no autocarro/no metropolitano?**	**Po**-soo oo-**zar** noo ow-to-**ka**-roo/noo me-troo-poo-lee-**ta**-noo
How long is this ticket valid?	**Por quanto tempo é válido este bilhete?**	Poor **kwa^{n}**-to **tay^{n}**-poo e **va**-lee-do aysht bee-**llyayt**
Is there a supplementary charge?	**Há que pagar algum suplemento?**	Ah ke pa-**gar** al-**goo^{n}** soo-ple-**may^{n}**-too

1. This is only available for underground and bus journeys.

BY TRAIN[1]

RESERVATIONS AND INQUIRIES

English	Portuguese	Pronunciation
Where's the railway station?	**Onde é a estação de caminho de ferro?**	O^{n}-de eh a esh-ta-sow^{n} de ka-mee^{n}-nyoo de fe-roo
Where is the ticket office?	**Onde é a bilheteira?**	O^{n}-de eh a bee-llye-tayee-ra
Two seats on the ... to ...	**Duas reservas para o comboio da ... para ...**	Doo-ash re-zer-vash pa-ra oo ko^{n}-boy-oo da ... pa-ra
I want	**Quero**	Ke-roo
a window seat	**um lugar com janela**	oo^{n} loo-gar ko^{n} zha-ne-la
an aisle seat	**um lugar de coxía**	oo^{n} loo-gar de koo-shee-a
a seat in a no-smoking compartment	**um lugar para não-fumadores**	oo^{n} loo-gar pa-ra now^{n}-foo-ma-do-resh
I want to reserve a sleeper	**Quero reservar uma cama**	Ke-roo re-zer-var oo-ma ka-ma
I want to register this luggage through to ...	**Quero despachar esta bagagem com destino a ...**	Ke-roo des-pa-shar esh-ta ba-ga-zhay^{n} ko^{n} desh-tee-no a

1. For help in understanding the answers to these and similar questions see TIME & DATES (p. 184), NUMBERS (p. 189), DIRECTIONS (p. 32).

When is the next train to ...?	**Quando é o proximo comboio para ...?**	Kwa^n-doo eh oo pro-see-moo ko^n-boy-oo pa-ra
Is it an express?[1]	**É rápido?**	Eh ra-pee-doo
Is there an earlier/later train?	**Há um comboio mais cedo/mais tarde?**	Ah oo^n ko^n-boy-oo ma-eesh say-doo/ma-eesh tard
Is there a restaurant car on the train?	**Há carruagem restaurante?**	Ah ka-roo-a-zhay^n resh-tow-ra^{n}t
I'd like to make a motorail reservation	**Quero fazer uma reserva na automotora**	Ke-roo fa-zayr oo-ma re-zer-va na ow-to-moo-to-ra
Where is the platform for ...?	**Onde é a plataforma para ...?**	O^n-de eh a pla-ta-for-ma pa-ra

CHANGING

Is there a through train to ...?	**Há comboio directo a ...?**	Ah ko^n-boy-oo dee-re-too a
Do I have to change?	**Tenho que fazer mudança?**	Tay^n-nyoo ke fa-zayr moo-da^n-sa
When is there a connection to ...?	**Quando se muda para ir a ...?**	Kwa^n-doo se moo-da pa-ra eer a
Change at ... and take the local train	***Mude em ... e tome o comboio local**	Moo-de ay^n ... ee to-me oo ko^n-boy-oo loo-kal

DEPARTURE

When does the train leave?	**A que horas parte o comboio?**	A ke o-rash par-te oo ko^n-boy-oo

1. Express trains are called **rápidos** and stopping-trains **combóios-correios.**

Which platform does the train to ... leave from?	**De que plataforma sai o comboio para ...?**	De ke pla-ta-**for**-ma sa-**ée** oo ko^{n}-**boy**-oo **pa**-ra
Is this the train for ...?	**É este o comboio para ...?**	Eh aysht oo ko^{n}-**boy**-oo **pa**-ra
There will be a delay of ...	***Haverá uma demora de ...**	A-ve-**ra** oo-ma de-**mo**-ra de

ARRIVAL

When does the train get to ...?	**A que horas chega o comboio a ...?**	A ke o-rash **shay**-ga oo ko^{n}-**boy**-oo a
Does the train stop at ...?	**O comboio pára em ...?**	Oo ko^{n}-**boy**-oo **pah**-ra ay^{n}
How long do we stop here?	**Quanto tempo paramos aqui?**	**Kwa^{n}**-too **tay^{n}**-poo pa-**ra**-mos a-**kee**
Is the train late?	**Está atrasado o comboio?**	Esh-**ta** a-tra-**za**-doo oo ko^{n}-**boy**-oo
When does the train from ... get in?	**A que horas chega o comboio que vem de ...?**	A ke o-rash **shay**-ga oo ko^{n}-**boy**-oo ke vay^{n} de
At which platform?	**Em que plataforma?**	Ay^{n} ke pla-ta-**for**-ma

ON THE TRAIN

We have reserved seats	**Temos lugares reservados**	**Tay**-moosh loo-**ga**-resh re-zer-**va**-doosh
Is this seat free?	**Está livre este lugar?**	Esh-**ta lee**-vre aysht loo-**gar**
This seat is taken	**Este lugar está ocupado**	Aysht loo-**gar** esh-**ta** o-koo-**pa**-doo

Is this a smoking/ non-smoking compartment?	**É este um compartimento para fumadores/ não fumadores?**	Eh aysht oo^{n} ko^{n}-par-tee-**may**^{n}-too **pa**-ra foo-ma-**do**-resh/now^{n} foo-ma-**do**-resh
Dining car	**Carruagem-restaurante**	Ka-roo-**a**-zhay^{n} resh-tow-**ra**^{n}t
Is the buffet car open?	**A carruagem-restaurante está aberta?**	A ka-roo-**a**-zhay^{n} resh-tow-**ra**^{n}t esh-**ta** a-**ber**-ta
Where is the sleeping car?	**Onde é a carruagem com beliches para dormir?**	O^{n}-de eh a ka-roo-**a**-zhay^{n} ko^{n} be-**lee**-shesh **pa**-ra door-**meer**
Which is my sleeper?	**Qual é a minha cama?**	Kwal eh a **mee**-nya **ka**-ma
The heating is too high/low	**O aquecimento está muito alto/muito baixo**	Oo a-ke-see-**may**^{n}-too esh-**ta** **moo**-ee-too **al**-too/**moo**-ee-too **ba**-ee-shoo
I can't open/close the window	**Não posso abrir/ fechar a janela**	Now^{n} **po**-soo a-**breer**/ fe-**shar** a zha-**ne**-la
What station is this?	**Que estação é esta?**	Ke esh-ta-**sow**^{n} eh **esh**-ta
How long do we stop here?	**Quanto tempo paramos aqui?**	**Kwa**^{n}-too **tay**^{n}-poo pa-**ra**-moosh a-**kee**

BY AIR

Where's the airline office?	**Onde são os escritórios da companhia de aviação?**	O^{n}-de sow^{n} oosh esh-kree-**to**-ree-oosh da ko^{n}-pa-**nyee**-a de a-vee-a-**sow**^{n}

d like to book two seats on the plane to …	**Quero marcar dois bilhetes de avião para …**	Ke-roo mar-**kar** do-eesh bee-**llyay**-tesh de a-vee-**ow^n** **pa**-ra
s there a flight to …?	**Há algum vôo para …?**	Ah al-**goo^n** vo-oo **pa**-ra
Vhat is the flight number?	**Qual é o número de vôo?**	Kwal eh oo **noo**-me-roo de vo-oo
Vhen does it leave/ arrive?	**A que horas parte/ chega o avião?**	A ke o-rash **par**-te/ **shay**-ga o a-vee-**ow^n**
Vhen's the next plane?	**A que horas é o próximo avião?**	A ke o-rash eh oo **pro**-see-moo a-vee-**ow^n**
s there a coach to the airport/to the town?	**Há autocarro para o aeroporto/para a cidade?**	Ah ow-to-**ka**-roo **pa**-ra oo a-e-ro-**port**-too/ **pa**-ra a see-**dad**
Vhen must I check in?	**A que horas me devo apresentar?**	A ke o-rash me **day**-voo a-pre-zay^n-**tar**
'lease cancel my reservation to …	**Quero anular a minha reserva para …**	**Ke**-roo a-noo-**lar** a **mee**-nya re-**zer**-va **pa**-ra
have an open ticket	**Eu tenho bilhete aberto**	**Ay**-oo **tay^n**-nyoo bee-**llyayt** a-**ber**-too
Can I change my ticket?	**Posso trocar o meu bilhete?**	**Po**-soo troo-**kar** oo **may**-oo bee-**llyayt**
Vill it cost more?	**Custará mais?**	Koosh-ta-**ra** **ma**-eesh
'd like to change my reservation to …	**Quero mudar a minha reserva para …**	**Ke**-roo moo-**dar** a **mee**-nya re-**zer**-va **pa**-ra

BY BOAT

English	Portuguese	Pronunciation
Is there a boat/(car) ferry from here to ...?	Há barco/ferry boat de aqui para ...?	Ah bar-koo/ferry boat d a-kee pa-ra
How long does the boat take?	Quanto tempo leva?	Kwa^n-too tay^n-poo le-va
How often does the boat leave?	De quanto em quanto tempo sai o barco?	De kwa^n-too ayn kwa^n-too tay^n-poo sy oo bar-koo
Does the boat call at ...?	O barco toca em ...?	Oo bar-koo to-ka ay^n
When does the next boat leave?	A que horas sai o próximo barco?	A ke o-rash sy oo pro-see-moo bar-koo
Can I book	Posso reservar	Po-soo re-zer-var
a single berth cabin?	um camarote individual?	oo^n ka-ma-rot ee^n-dee-vee-doo-al
a first class cabin?	um camarote de primeira?	oo^n ka-ma-rot de pree-mayee-ra
a second class cabin?	um camarote de segunda?	oo^n ka-ma-rot de se-goo^n-da
a luxury cabin?	um camarote de luxo?	oo^n ka-ma-rot de loo-shoo
How many berths are there in this cabin?	Quantas camas há neste camarote?	Kwa^n-tash ka-mash ah naysht ka-ma-rot
How do we get on to the deck?	Como é que vamos para o convés?	Ko-moo eh ke va-moosh pa-ra oo ko^n-vesh
When must we go on board?	A que horas há que estar a bordo?	A ke o-rash ah ke esh-tar a bor-doo

Vhen do we dock?	**A que horas atracamos?**	A ke o-rash a-tra-**ka**-moosh
Iow long do we stay in port?	**Quanto tempo ficamos no porto?**	**Kwa^{n}**-too **tay^{n}**-poo fee-**ka**-moosh noo **por**-too
Hovercraft	**Deslizador/ Hovercraft**	Dezh-lee-za-**dor**/o-ver-**kraft**
Hydrofoil	**Deslizador/Hydrofoil**	Dezh-lee-za-**dor**/ee-dro-fo-eel
Lifebelt	**Cinto de salvação**	**See^{n}**-too de sal-va-**sow^{n}**
Lifeboat	**Barco de salvação**	**Bar**-koo de sal-va-**sow^{n}**

BY UNDERGROUND

Where is the nearest underground station?	**Qual é a estação de metro mais perto?**	Kwal eh a esh-ta-**sow^{n}** de **me**-troo **ma**-eesh **per**-too
Which line goes to ...?	**Que linha vai para ...?**	Ke **lee**-nya vy **pa**-ra
Does this train go to ...?	**Este metro vai para ...?**	Aysht **me**-troo vy **pa**-ra
Where do I change for ...?	**Onde mudo para ...?**	**O^{n}**-de **moo**-doo **pa**-ra
What is the next station ...?	**Qual é a próxima estação?**	Kwal eh a **pro**-see-ma esh-ta-**sow^{n}**
What station is this?	**Que estação é esta?**	Ke esh-ta-**sow^{n}** eh **esh**-ta
Have you an underground map?	**Tem um mapa do metro?**	Tay^{n} oo^{n} **ma**-pa doo **me**-troo

BY BUS, TRAM OR COACH

Where's the bus station/coach station?	**Onde é a estação de autocarros/ camionetas?**	O^{n}-de eh a esh-ta-**sow**^{n} de ow-to-**ka**-roosh/ka-mee-oo-**nay**-tash
Bus stop	**Paragem de autocarros**	Pa-**ra**-zhay^{n} de ow-to-**ka**-roosh
Request stop	**Paragem facultativa**	Pa-**ra**-zhay^{n} fa-kool-ta-**tee**-va
Tram	**O eléctrico**	E-**le**-tree-koo
When does the coach leave?	**A que horas parte a camioneta?**	A ke **o**-rash **par**-te a ka-mee-o-**nay**-ta
When does the coach get to ...?	**A que horas chega a camioneta a ...?**	A ke **o**-rash **shay**-ga a ka-mee-o-**nay**-ta a
What stops does it make?	**Em que sítios pára?**	Ay^{n} ke **see**-tee-oosh **pah**-ra
How long is the journey?	**Quanto tempo é a viagem?**	**Kwa**^{n}-too **tay**^{n}-poo eh a vee-**a**-zhay^{n}
We want to take a coach tour round the sights	**Queremos visitar os sítios de interesse em autocarro turístico**	Ke-**ray**-moosh vee-see-**tar** oosh **see**-tee-oosh de ee^{n}-te-**re**-se ay^{n} ow-to-**ka**-roo too-**reesh**-tee-koo
Is there a sightseeing tour?	**Há uma viagem turística?**	Ah **oo**-ma vee-**a**-zhay^{n} too-**reesh**-tee-ka
What is the fare?	**Qual é a tarifa?**	Kwal eh a ta-**ree**-fa
Does the bus/coach stop at our hotel?	**A camioneta pára no nosso hotel?**	A ka-mee-o-**nay**-ta **pah**-ra noo **no**-soo o-**tel**

Is there an excursion to ... tomorrow?	**Há amanhã alguma excursão a ...?**	Ah a-may-**nya^{n}** al-**goo**-ma esh-koor-**sow^{n}** a
Does this bus go to	**Vai este autocarro para**	Vy aysht ow-to-**ka**-roo **pa**-ra
the town centre?	**o centro da cidade?**	oo **say^{n}**-troo da see-**dad**
the beach?	**a praia?**	a **pry**-a
the station?	**a estação?**	a esh-ta-**sow^{n}**
When's the next bus?	**A que horas é o próximo autocarro?**	A ke o-rash eh oo **pro**-see-moo ow-to-**ka**-roo
How often do the buses run?	**De quanto em quanto tempo há autocarros?**	De **kwa^{n}**-too ay^{n} **kwa^{n}**-too **tay^{n}**-poo ah ow-to-**ka**-roosh
Has the last bus gone?	**Já partiu o último autocarro?**	Zha par-**tee**-oo o **ool**-tee-moo ow-to-**ka**-roo
Does this bus go near ...?	**Este autocarro passa perto de ...?**	Aysht ow-to-**ka**-roo **pa**-sa **per**-too de
Where can I get a bus to ...?	**Onde posso tomar o autocarro para ...?**	**O^{n}**-de **po**-soo too-**mar** oo ow-to-**ka**-roo **pa**-ra
Is this the right stop for ...?	**Esta é a paragem para ...?**	**Esh**-ta eh a pah-ra-**zhay^{n}** **pa**-ra
Which bus goes to ...?	**Que autocarro vai a ...?**	Ke ow-to-**ka**-roo vy a
I want to go to ...	**Quero ir a ...**	**Ke**-roo eer a
Where do I get off?	**Onde tenho que apear-me/sair?**	**O^{n}**-de **tay^{n}**-nyoo ke a-pee-**ar**-me/sa-**eer**
I want to get off at ...	**Quero sair em ...**	**Ke**-roo sa-**eer** ay^{n}
The bus to ... stops over there	***O autocarro para ... pára alí**	Oo ow-to-**ka**-roo **pa**-ra ... **pah**-ra a-**lee**

Number ... goes to ...	***O número ... vai para ...**	Oo **noo**-me-roo ... vy **pa**-ra
You must take number ...	***Tem de tomar o número ...**	Tay^n de too-**mar** oo **noo**-me-roo
You get off at the next stop	***Saia na próxima paragem**	Sy-a na **pro**-see-ma pa-**ra**-zhay^n
The buses run every ten minutes/every hour	***Há autocarros de dez em dez minutos/de hora em hora**	Ah ow-to-**ka**-roosh de desh ay^n desh mee-**noo**-toosh/de **o**-ra ay^n **o**-ra

BY TAXI

Please call/get me a taxi	**É favor chamar-me/arranjar-me um taxi**	Eh fa-**vor** sha-**mar**-me/a-ran-**zhar**-me oo^n **tak**-see
Where can I find a taxi?	**Onde posso arranjar um taxi?**	**O**^{n}-de **po**-soo a-ran-**zhar** oo^n **tak**-see
Are you free?	**Está livre?**	Esh-**ta** **lee**-vre
Please take me to the hotel/to the station/to this address	**Ao hotel/à estação/a esta direcção por favor**	A-oo o-**tel**/ah esh-ta-**sow**^{n}/a **esh**-ta dee-re-**sow**^{n} poor fa-**vor**
Can you hurry, I'm late	**Pode ir mais depressa por favor, estou atrasado**	**Po**-de eer **ma**-eesh de-**pre**-sa poor fa-**vor** esh-**to** a-tra-**za**-doo
Please wait for me here	**Espere aqui por favor**	Esh-**pe**-re a-**kee** poor fa-**vor**
Stop here	**Pare aqui**	**Pa**-re a-**kee**
Is it far?	**É longe?**	Eh **lo**^{n}-zhe

Turn right/left at the next corner	**Vire à esquerda/ direita na próxima esquina**	Vee-re ah eesh-**kayr**-da/ dee-**ray**-ee-ta na **pro**-see-ma esh-**kee**-na
Straight on	**Em frente**	Ay^n fray^{n}t
How much do you charge by the hour/ for the day?	**Quanto leva por hora/por dia?**	**Kwa^n**-too **le**-va poor o-ra/poor **dee**-a
How much will you charge to take me to ...?	**Quanto me levaria para ir a ...?**	**Kwa^n**-too me le-va-**ree**-a **pa**-ra eer a
How much is it?	**Quanto é?**	**Kwa^n**-too eh
That's too much	**É demasiado/É muito caro**	Eh de-ma-zee-**a**-doo/eh **moo**-ee-too **ka**-roo

DIRECTIONS

Excuse me – could you tell me ...?	**Desculpe – pode dizer-me ...?**	Desh-**kool**-pe **po**-de dee-**zayr**-me
Where is ...?	**Onde é ...?**	**O^{n}**-de eh
How do I get to ...?	**Como se vai para ...?**	**Ko**-moo se vy **pa**-ra
How far is it to ...?	**A que distância fica ...?**	A ke deesh-**ta^{n}**-see-a **fee**-ka
How many kilometres?	**Quantos quilómetros?**	**Kwa^{n}**-toosh kee-**lo**-me-troosh
How do we get on to the motorway to ...?	**Como se vai para a auto-estrada de ...?**	**Ko**-moo se vy **pa**-ra a ow-to-esh-**tra**-da de
Which is the best road to ...?	**Qual é o melhor caminho para ...?**	Kwal eh oo me-**llyor** ka-**mee**-nyoo **pa**-ra
Is this the right road for ...?	**Este é o caminho certo para ...?**	**Aysht** eh oo ka-**mee**-nyoo **ser**-too **pa**-ra
Where does this road lead to?	**Para onde vai esta estrada?**	**Pa**-ra **o^{n}**-de vy **esh**-ta esh-**tra**-da
Is it a good road?	**É uma boa estrada?**	Eh **oo**-ma **bo**-a esh-**tra**-da

Is there a motorway?	**Há auto-estrada?**	Ah ow-to-esh-tra-da
Is there a toll?	**Há portagem?**	Ah poor-ta-zhay^n
Is the tunnel/pass open?	**O túnel/passagem está aberto/a?**	Oo too-nel/pa-sa-zhay^n esh-ta a-ber-too/a
Is the road to … clear?	**A estrada para … está livre?**	A esh-tra-da pa-ra … esh-ta lee-vre
How far is the next village/petrol station?	**A vila/a garagem mais perto é muito longe?**	A vee-la/a ga-ra-zhay^n ma-eesh per-too eh moo-ee-too lo^n-zhe
How long will it take	**Quanto tempo leva**	Kwa^n-too tay^n-poo le-va
by car?	**de carro?**	de ka-roo
by bicycle?	**de bicicleta?**	de bee-see-kle-ta
by foot?	**a pé?**	a pe
Where are we now?	**Onde estamos agora?**	O^n-de esh-ta-moosh a-go-ra
What is the name of this place?	**Qual é o nome deste lugar?**	Kwal eh oo no-me daysht loo-gar
Where is the super/mini-market?	**Onde é o super/mini mercado?**	O^n-de eh oo soo-per/mee-nee mer-ka-doo
Please show me on the map	**Indique-me no mapa, por favor**	Ee^n-deek-me noo ma-pa poor fa-vor
It's that way	***É por ali**	Eh poor a-lee
It isn't far	***Não é longe**	Now^n eh lo^n-zhe
Follow signs for …	***Siga os sinais para …**	See-ga oosh see-na-eesh pa-ra
Follow this road for 5 kilometres	***Siga uns cinco quilómetros nesta estrada**	See-ga oo^{n}sh see^n-koo kee-lo-me-troosh nesh-ta esh-tra-da
Keep straight on	***Siga em frente**	See-ga ay^n fray^{n}t

Turn right at the crossroads	***Volte à direita no cruzamento**	Vol-te ah dee-**ray**-ee-ta noo kroo-za-**may**^{n}-too
Take the second road on the left	***Tome a segunda estrada à esquerda**	To-me a se-**goo**^{n}-da esh-**tra**-da ah esh-**kayr**-da
Turn right at the traffic lights	***Volte à direita nos sinais luminosos**	Vol-te ah dee-**ray**-ee-ta noosh see-**na**-eesh loo-mee-**no**-zoosh
Turn left after the bridge	***Volte à esquerda depois da ponte**	Vol-te ah esh-**kayr**-da de-**po**-eesh da po^{n}t
The best road is the ...	***A melhor estrada é a ...**	A me-**llyor** esh-**tra**-da eh a
Take the ... and ask again	***Tome a ... e pergunte novamente**	To-me a ... ee per-**goo**^{n}-te no-va-**may**^{n}t
You are going the wrong way	***Vai pelo caminho errado**	Vy **pay**-loo ka-**mee**-nyoo ay-**ra**-doo
One-way system	**Sentido único**	Say^n-**tee**-doo **oo**-nee-koo
North	**Norte**	Nort
South	**Sul**	Sool
East	**Oriente/Leste**	O-ree-**ay**^{n}t/lesht
West	**Ocidente/Oeste**	O-see-**day**^{n}t/**oo**-esht

DRIVING

Have you a road map?	**Tem um mapa de estradas?**	Tay^n oo^n **ma**-pa de esh-**tra**-dash
Where is there a car park?	**Onde há um parque de estacionamento?**	**O**^{n}-de ah oo^n park de esh-ta-see-oo-na-**may**^{n}-too
Can I park here?	**Posso estacionar aqui?**	**Po**-soo esh-ta-see-oo-**nar** a-**kee**
How long can I park here?	**Por quanto tempo posso estacionar aqui?**	Poor **kwa**^{n}-too **tay**^{n}-poo **po**-soo esh-ta-see-oo-**nar** a-**kee**
Have you any change for the meter please?	**Tem algum troco para o parquímetro?**	Tay^n al-**goo**^{n} **tro**-koo **pa**-ra oo par-**kee**-me-troo
No parking	***Proibido o estacionamento**	Proo-ee-**bee**-doo oo esh-ta-see-oo-na-**may**^{n}-too
Is this your car?	***É este o seu carro?**	Eh aysht oo **se**-oo **ka**-roo

English	Portuguese	Pronunciation
May I see your licence, please?	***A sua carta de condução, por favor?**	A **soo**-a **kar**-ta de ko^{n}-doo-**sow^{n}** poor fa-**vor**
Where is the nearest petrol station?	**Onde é a estação de serviço mais próxima?**	**O^{n}**-de eh a esh-ta-**sow^{n}** de ser-**vee**-soo **ma**-eesh **pro**-see-ma
Speed limit	**Limite de velocidade**	Lee-**meet** de ve-loo-see-**dad**
Pedestrian precinct	**Precinto de peões**	Pre-**see^{n}**-too de pee-**oy^{n}sh**

CAR HIRE

English	Portuguese	Pronunciation
Where can I hire a car?	**Onde posso alugar um carro?**	**O^{n}**-de **po**-soo a-loo-**gar** oo^{n} **ka**-roo
I want to hire a car and a driver/self-drive car	**Quero alugar um carro com conductor/sem conductor**	**Ke**-roo a-loo-**gar** oo^{n} **ka**-roo ko^{n} ko^{n}-doo-**tor**/say^{n} ko^{n}-doo-**tor**
I want to hire an automatic	**Quero alugar um automático**	**Ke**-roo a-loo-**gar** oo^{n} ow-too-**ma**-tee-koo
Is there a weekend rate/a midweek rate?	**Há uma tarifa de fim de semana/de meio da semana?**	Ah **oo**-ma ta-**ree**-fa de fee^{n} de se-**ma**-na/de **may**-ee-oo da se-**ma**-na
How much is it to hire it by the day/week?	**Quanto custa o aluguer ao dia/à semana?**	**Kwa^{n}**-too **koosh**-ta oo a-loo-**ger** a-oo **dee**-a/ah se-**ma**-na

I need it for two days/a week	**Preciso por dois dias/uma semana**	Pre-**see**-zoo poor **do**-eesh **dee**-ash/**oo**-ma se-**ma**-na
Does that include mileage?	**Inclui a quilometragem?**	Ee^{n}-**kloo**-ee a kee-loo-me-**tra**-zhay^{n}
The charge per kilometre is ...	***A tarifa por quilómetro é ...**	A ta-**ree**-fa poor kee-**lo**-me-troo eh
Do you want full insurance?	***Quer um seguro para todos os riscos?**	Ker oo^{n} se-**goo**-roo **pa**-ra **toh**-doosh oosh **reesh**-koosh
May I see your driving licence?	***Posso ver a sua carta de condução?**	**Po**-soo vayr a **soo**-a **kar**-ta de ko^{n}-doo-**sow**^{n}
Can I return it to your office in ...?	**Posso devolver à vossa filial em ...?**	**Po**-soo de-vol-**vayr** ah vo-sa fee-lee-**al** ay^{n}
Do you want a deposit?	**Precisa de depósito?**	Pre-**see**-za de de-**po**-zee-to
I will pay by credit card	**Pago com cartão de crédito**	**Pa**-goo ko^{n} kar-**tow**^{n} de **kre**-dee-too
Could you show me	**Pode mostrar-me**	**Po**-de moosh-**trar**-me
the controls?	**o controle?**	oo ko^{n}-**trol**
the lights?	**as luzes?**	ash **loo**-zcsh
the gears?	**as mudanças?**	as moo-**da**^{n}-sash
the brakes?	**os travões?**	oosh tra-**voy**^{n}**sh**

ROAD SIGNS

Acenda os faróis da frente	Switch on headlights
Alfândega	Customs
Apenas para peões	Pedestrians only

Atenção	Attention
Caução	Caution
Circulação pela direita/esquerda	Keep right/left
Curvas (perigosas)	Winding roads/bends
Descida acentuada (íngreme)	Steep hill
Desvio	Diversion
Devagar	Slow
Direcção proibida	No entry
É proibido estacionar, estacionamento proibido	No parking
Estacionamento restricto	Restricted parking
Estrada cortada	Road blocked
Estrada estreita	Narrow road
Estrada fechada	Road closed
Facha de autocarro	Bus lane
Fim da zona de parquímetros	End of no parking zone
Guiar com cuidado	Drive with care
Inundação	Flooding
Luzes	Lights on
Parar	Stop
Passagem de nível	Level crossing
Pedras/rochedos caídos	Fallen rocks
Perigo	Danger
Piso irregular/perigoso	Surface uneven or dangerous
Saída para camionetas	Exit for lorries
Sem saída	No through road

Sentido único	One way street
Siga pela faixa	Get in lane
Sinais de trânsito	Traffic lights
Superfície escorregadía	Slippery surface
Trabalhos de estrada	Road works
Trânsito lento	Slow traffic
Trânsito livre	Through traffic
Trânsito vedado	Road closed
Ultrapassagem proibida	No overtaking
Use faróis máximos	Use headlights
Veículos longos	Long vehicles
Veículos pesados	Heavy vehicles
Velocidade limitada	Speed limit

AT THE GARAGE OR PETROL STATION

Fill it up, please	**Encha-o, por favor**	Ay^{n}-sha-oo poor fa-vor
... litres of	**... litros de**	... lee-trosh de
standard	**gasolina**	ga-zoo-lee-na
premium petrol	**quatro estrelas**	kwa-troo esh-tray-lash
diesel	**diesel**	dee-sel
... escudos worth of petrol, please	**... escudos de gasolina, por favor**	... esh-koo-doosh de ga-zoo-lee-na poor fa-vor
How much is a litre of petrol?	**Quanto custa um litro de gasolina?**	Kwa^{n}-too koosh-ta oo^{n} lee-troo de ga-zoo-lee-na

Please check the oil and water	**Reveja o óleo e a água, por favor**	Re-vay-zha oo o-lee-oo ee a a-gwa poor fa-vor
Could you check the brake/transmission fluid?	**Pode verificar o líquido dos travões/da transmissão?**	Po-de ve-ree-fee-kar oo lee-kee-doo dosh tra-voy^{n}sh/da tra^{n}zh-mee-sow^{n}
The oil needs changing	**O óleo necessita ser mudado**	Oo o-lee-oo ne-se-see-ta sayr moo-da-doo
Check the tyre pressure, please	**Verifique o ar, por favor**	Ve-ree-fee-ke oo ar poor fa-vor
Would you clean the windscreen, please?	**Pode limpar o pára-brisas, por favor?**	Po-de lee^{n}-par oo pa-ra-bree-zash poor fa-vor
Please wash the car	**Lave o carro, por favor**	La-ve oo ka-roo poor fa-vor
Can I leave the car here?	**Posso deixar o carro aqui?**	Po-soo day-ee-shar oo ka-roo a-kee
What time does the garage close?	**A que horas fecha a garagem?**	A ke o-rash fay-ee-sha a ga-ra-zhay^{n}
Where are the toilets?	**Onde são os lavabos/retretes?**	O^{n}-de sow^{n} oosh la-va-boosh/re-tre-tesh

REPAIRS

Can you give me a lift to a telephone?	**Pode dar-me uma boleia até um telefone?**	Po-de dar-me oo-ma boo-lay-ee-a a-te oo^{n} te-le-fon

Please tell the next garage to send help	**Por favor peça à garagem mais perto para mandar ajuda**	Poor fa-vor pe-sa ah ga-ra-zhay^{n} ma-eesh per-too pa-ra ma^{n}-dar a-zhoo-da
My car's broken down	**O meu carro está avariado**	Oo may-oo ka-roo esh-ta a-va-ree-a-do
Can I use your telephone?	**Posso usar o telefone?**	Po-soo oo-zar oo te-le-fon
Is there a ... agent here?	**Há aqui uma agência ...?**	Ah a-kee oo-ma a-zhay^{n}-see-a
Have you a breakdown service?	**Há serviço de reparações de emergência?**	Ah ser-vee-soo de re-pa-ra-soy^{n}sh de ee-mer-zhay^{n}-see-a
Is there a mechanic?	**Há um mecânico?**	Ah oo^{n} me-ka-nee-koo
Can you send someone to look at it/tow it away?	**Pode mandar alguém para o ver/rebocar?**	Po-de ma^{n}-dar al-gay^{n} pa-ra oo vayr/re-boo-kar
It is an automatic and cannot be towed	**É um automático e não pode ser rebocado**	Eh oo^{n} ow-too-ma-tee-koo ee now^{n} po-de sayr re-boo-ka-doo
Where are you?	***Onde estão?**	O^{n}-de esh-tow^{n}
Where is your car?	***Onde está o carro?**	O^{n}-de esh-ta oo ka-roo
I'm on the road from ... to ..., near kilometre post ...	**Estou na estrada de ... a ... ao quilómetro ...**	Esh-to na esh-tra-da de ... a ... a-oo kee-lo-me-troo
How long will you be?	**Quanto tempo demora?**	Kwa^{n}-too tay^{n}-poo de-mo-ra
I want the car serviced	**Quero uma revisão**	Ke-roo oo-ma re-vee-sow^{n}

The battery is flat, it needs charging	**A bateria está em baixo, precisa de ser carregada**	A ba-ta-**ree**-a esh-**ta** ay^n **ba-ee-shoo pre-see-za** de sayr ka-re-**ga**-da
The tyre is flat/punctured	**Esta câmara de ar está vazia/furada**	**Esh**-ta **ka**-ma-ra de ar esh-**ta** va-**zee**-a/foo-**ra**-da
The exhaust is broken	**O tubo de escape está partido**	Oo **too**-boo de esh-**ka**-pe esh-**ta** par-**tee**-doo
The windscreen wipers do not work	**Os limpa pára-brisas não funcionam**	Oosh **lee^n**-pa **pah**-ra-**bree**-zash now^n foo^n-see-**o**-now^n
The valve is leaking	**A válvula perde ar**	A **val**-voo-la **per**-de ar
The radiator is leaking	**O radiador perde água**	Oo ra-dee-a-**dor** **per**-de **a**-gwa
My car won't start	**O meu carro não arranca**	Oo **may**-oo **ka**-roo now^n a-**ra^n**-ka
It's not running properly	**Não anda bem**	Now^n **a^n**-da bay^n
The engine is overheating	**O motor está demasiado quente**	Oo moo-**tor** esh-**ta** de-ma-zee-**a**-doo kay^{n}t
The engine is firing badly	**O motor funciona mal**	Oo moo-**tor** foo^n-see-**o**-na mal
Can you change this faulty plug?	**Pode mudar-me esta vela defeituosa?**	**Po**-de moo-**dar**-me esh-ta **ve**-la de-fay-ee-too-**o**-za
There's a petrol/oil leak	**Perde gasolina/óleo**	**Per**-de ga-zoo-**lee**-na/**o**-lee-oo
There's a smell of petrol/rubber	**Cheira a gasolina/borracha**	**Shay**-ee-ra a ga-zoo-**lee**-na/boo-**ra**-sha
There's a rattle	**Há um ruido**	Ah oo^n roo-**ee**-doo

Something is wrong with	**Há algo que não está bem**	Ah al-goo ke now^{n} esh-ta bay^{n}
my car	**no meu carro**	noo may-oo ka-roo
the engine	**no motor**	noo moo-tor
the lights	**nas luzes**	nash loo-zesh
the clutch	**na embraiagem**	na ay^{n}-bri-a-zhay^{n}
the gearbox	**na caixa das velocidades**	na ka-ee-sha dash ve-loo-see-da-desh
the brakes	**nos travões**	noosh tra-voy^{n}sh
the steering	**na direcção**	na dee-re-sow^{n}
This doesn't work	**Isto não funciona**	Eesh-too now^{n} foo^{n}-see-o-na
The oil warning light is on	**Tem pouco óleo**	Tay^{n} po-koo o-lee-oo
The carburettor needs adjusting	**O carburador precisa de um ajuste**	Oo kar-boo-ra-dor pre-see-za de oo^{n} a-zhoosht
Can you repair it?	**Pode repará-lo?**	Po-de re-pa-ra-loo
How long will it take to repair?	**Quanto tempo necessita para repará-lo?**	Kwa^{n}-too tay^{n}-poo ne-se-see-ta pa-ra re-pa-ra-loo
What will it cost?	**Quanto custará?**	Kwa^{n}-too koosh-ta-ra
When will the car be ready?	**Quando estará pronto o carro?**	Kwa^{n}-doo esh-ta-ra pro^{n}-too oo ka-roo
I need it	**Preciso dele**	Pre-see-zoo day-le
as soon as possible	**o mais cedo possível**	oo ma-eesh say-doo poo-see-vel
in three hours	**dentro de três horas**	day^{n}-troo de traysh o-rash
in the morning	**pela manhã**	pay-la ma-nya^{n}
It will take two days	***Demorará dois dias**	De-moo-ra-ra do-eesh dee-ash

We can repair it temporarily	***Pode-se reparar provisóriamente**	Po-de-se re-pa-**rar** proo-vee-zo-ree-a-**may^{n}t**
We haven't the right spares	***Não temos as peças sobresselentes necessárias**	Now^n **tay**-moosh ash **pe**-sash soo-bre-se-**lay^n**-tesh ne-se-**sa**-ree-ash
We have to send for the spares	***Temos que pedir as peças sobresselentes**	Tay-moosh ke pe-**deer** ash **pe**-sash soo-bre-se-**lay^n**-tesh
You will need a new ...	***Vai precisar de um novo .../uma nova ...**	Vy pre-scc-**zar** de oo^n **no**-voo .../**oo**-ma **no**-va ...
Could I have an itemised bill, please?	**Pode dar uma factura, por favor?**	Po-de dar **oo**-ma fa-**too**-ra poor fa-**vor**

PARTS OF A CAR AND OTHER USEFUL WORDS

accelerate (to)	**acelerar**	a-se-le-**rar**
accelerator	**o acelerador**	a-se-le-ra-**dor**
airpump	**a bomba de ar**	**bo^n**-ba de ar
alternator	**o alternador**	al-ter-na-**dor**
anti-freeze	**o anti-congelante**	a^n-tee-con-zhe-**la^{n}t**
automatic transmission	**a transmissão automática**	tra^{n}zh-mee-**sow^n** ow-too-**ma**-tee-ka
axle	**o eixo**	ay-ee-**shoo**
battery	**a bateria**	ba-te-**ree**-a
bonnet	**a capota**	ka-**po**-ta

boot/trunk	**a mala**	ma-la
brake	**o travão**	tra-vow^n
brake lights	**as luzes dos travões**	loo-zesh doosh tra-voy^{n}sh
brake lining	**os compressores**	ko^n-pre-so-resh
brake pads	**os amortecedores**	a-moor-te-se-dorsh
breakdown	**a avaria**	a-va-ree-a
bulb	**a luz/lâmpada**	loosh/la^n-pa-da
bumper	**o pára-choques**	pah-ra-shoksh
carburettor	**o carburador**	kar-boo-ra-dor
choke	**o starter**	star-ter
clutch	**a embraiagem**	en-bri-a-zhay^n
cooling system	**o sistema de arrefecimento**	seesh-tay-ma de a-re-fe-see-may^n-too
crank-shaft	**a manivela**	ma-nee-ve-la
cylinder	**o cilindro**	see-lee^n-droo
differential gear	**o diferencial**	dee-fe-re^n-syal
dip stick	**o indicador de nível de óleo**	ee^n-dee-ka-dor de nee-vel de o-lee-oo
distributor	**o distribuidor**	deesh-tree-boo-ee-dor
door	**a porta**	por-ta
doorhandle	**o manípulo da porta**	ma-nee-poo-loo da por-ta
drive (to)	**conduzir**	ko^n-doo-zeer
drive shaft	**o veio de transmissão**	vay-oo de tra^{n}zh-mee-sow^n
driver	**o conductor**	ko^n-doo-tor

dynamo	o dínamo	dee-na-moo
engine	o motor	moo-tor
exhaust	o tubo de escape	too-boo de esh-ka-pe
fan	a ventoínha	vay^{n}-too-ee-nya
fanbelt	a correia da ventoínha	koo-ray-ee-a da vay^{n}-too-ee-nya
filter	o filtro	feel-troo
foglamp	o farol de nevoeiro	fa-rol de ne-voo-ay-ee-roo
fusebox	a caixa dos fusíveis	ka-ee-sha doosh foo-zee-vay-eesh
gasket	a junta de culatra	joon-ta de koo-la-tra
gear-box	a caixa de velocidades	ka-ee-sha de ve-loo-see-da-desh
gear-lever	a alavanca de velocidades	a-la-va^{n}-ka de ve-loo-see-da-desh
gears	as mudanças	moo-da^{n}-sash
grease (to)	lubrificar	loo-bree-fee-kar
handbrake	o travão de mão	tra-vow^{n} de mow^{n}
headlights	os faróis da frente	fa-roy-eesh da fray^{n}t
heater	o aquecedor	a-ke-se-dor
horn	a buzina	boo-zee-na
hose	a mangueira	man-gay-ee-ra
ignition key	a chave de ignição	shav de eeg-nee-sow^{n}
indicator	o pisca-pisca	peesh-ka-peesh-ka
jack	o macaco	ma-ka-koo
lights	os faróis	fa-roy-eesh

mirror	**o espelho**	esh-pay-llyoo
number plate	**a matrícula**	ma-tree-koo-la
nut	**a porca**	por-ka
oil	**o óleo**	o-lee-oo
parking lights	**as luzes de estacionamento**	loo-zesh de esh-ta-see-oo-na-may^n-too
petrol	**a gasolina**	ga-zoo-lee-na
petrol can	**a lata de gasolina**	la-ta de ga-zoo-lee-na
piston	**o piston**	pees-to^n
plug	**a vela**	ve-la
points	**os pontos/pontas**	po^n-toosh/po^n-tash
pump	**a bomba**	bo^n-ba
puncture	**o furo**	foo-roo
radiator	**o radiador**	ra-dee-a-dor
rear lights	**as luzes de trás**	loo-zesh de trash
reverse	**a marcha atrás**	mar-sha a-trash
reversing lights	**os indicadores de marcha atrás**	ee^n-dee-ka-do-resh de mar-sha a-trash
(sliding) roof	**o topo (corrediço)**	to-poo (ko-re-dee-soo)
screwdriver	**a chave de parafusos**	sha-ve de pa-ra-foo-zoosh
seat	**o assento**	a-se^n-too
shock absorber	**o amortecedor**	a-mor-te-se-dor
silencer	**o silenciador**	see-len-see-a-dor
spares	**os sobresselentes**	soo-bre-se-lay^n-tesh
spare wheel	**a roda sobresselente**	ro-da soo-bre-se-lay^{n}t
sparking plug	**a vela de ignição**	ve-la de eeg-nee-sow^n

speedometer	**o conta-quilómetros**	**ko^n**-ta kee-**lo**-me-troosh
spring	**a mola**	**mo**-la
stall (to)	**ir-se a baixo**	**eer**-se a **by**-shoo
starter	**o arranque**	a-**ra^{n}k**
starter motor	**o motor de arranque**	moo-**tor** de a-**ra^{n}k**
steering	**a direcção**	dee-re-**sow^n**
steering wheel	**o volante**	vo-**la^{n}t**
suspension	**a suspensão**	soos-pe^n-**sow^n**
tank	**o depósito**	de-po-zee-too
transmission	**a transmissão**	tra^{n}zh-mee-**sow^n**
tyre	**o pneu**	**pnay**-oo
valve	**a válvula**	**val**-voo-la
(distilled) water	**a água (distilada)**	**a**-gwa (dee-stee-**la**-da)
wheel	**a roda**	**ro**-da
back wheel	**a roda de trás**	**ro**-da de **trash**
front	**da frente**	da **fray^{n}t**
spare	**sobresselente**	soo-bre-se-**lay^{n}t**
window	**a janela**	zha-**ne**-la
windscreen	**o pára-brisas**	**pah**-ra-**bree**-zash
windscreen washers	**os lava pára-brisas**	**la**-va **pah**-ra **bree**-zash
windscreen wipers	**os limpa pára-brisas**	**lee^n**-pa **pah**-ra **bree**-zash

CYCLING

Where can I hire a bicycle?	**Onde posso alugar uma bicicleta?**	**O**^{n}-de **po**-soo a-loo-**gar** oo-ma bee-see-**kle**-ta
Do you have a bicycle with gears?	**Tem uma bicicleta com mudanças?**	Tay^{n} **oo**-ma bee-see-**kle**-ta ko^{n} moo-**da**^{n}-sash
The saddle is too high/too low	**A sela está muito alta/muito baixa**	A **se**-la esh-**ta** **moo**-ee-too **al**-ta/**moo**-ee-too **ba**-ee-sha
Where is the cycle shop?	**Onde é a loja de bicicletas?**	**O**^{n}-de eh a **lo**-zha de bee-see-**kle**-tash
Do you repair bicycles?	**Repara bicicletas?**	Re-**pa**-ra bee-see-**kle**-tash
The brake isn't working	**O travão não funciona**	Oo tra-**vow**^{n} now^{n} foo^{n}-see-**o**-na
Could you tighten/loosen the brake cable?	**Pode apertar/alargar o cabo do travão?**	**Po**-de a-per-**tar**/a-lar-**gar** oo **ka**-boo doo tra-**vow**^{n}

A spoke is broken	**Um dos raios está partido**	Oo^{n} doosh ra-ee-oosh esh-ta par-tee-doo
The tyre is punctured	**O pneu está furado**	Oo pnay-oo esh-ta foo-ra-doo
The gears need adjusting	**As mudanças precisam de ser ajustadas/afinadas**	Ash moo-da^{n}-sash pre-see-zow^{n} de sayr a-zhoosh-ta-dash
Could you straighten the wheel?	**Pode endireitar a roda?**	Po-de ay^{n}-dee-ray-ee-tar a ro-da
The handlebars are loose	**Os guiadores estão lassos**	Oosh gee-a-do-resh esh-tow^{n} la-soosh
Could you please lend me a spanner/a tyre lever?	**Pode emprestar uma chave inglesa (de fendas)/uma alavanca de pneus (um macaco)?**	Po-de ay^{n}-presh-tar oo-ma sha-ve ee^{n}-glay-za (de fay^{n}-dash)/oo-ma a-la-va^{n}-ka de pnay-oosh (oo^{n} ma-ka-koo)

PARTS OF A BICYCLE

axle	**o eixo**	ay-ee-shoo
bell	**a campaínha**	ka^{n}-pa-ee-nya
brake (front)	**o travão da frente**	tra-vow^{n} da fray^{n}t
brake (rear)	**o travão de trás**	tra-vow^{n} de trash
brake cable	**o cabo do travão**	ka-boo doo tra-vow^{n}
brake lever	**a alavanca do travão**	a-la-va^{n}-ka doo tra-vow^{n}
bulb	**a luz**	loosh
chain	**a correia**	koo-ray-ee-a
dynamo	**o dínamo**	dee-na-moo

frame	**o quadro**	**kwa**-droo
gear lever	**o cabo de mudanças**	**ka**-boo de moo-**da^{n}**-sash
gears	**as mudanças**	moo-**da^{n}**-sash
handlebars	**os guiadores**	gee-a-**do**-resh
inner tube	**o tubo interior**	**too**-boo ee^{n}-te-ree-**or**
light (front)	**a luz da frente**	loosh da fray^{n}t
light (rear)	**a luz de trás**	loosh de trash
mudguard	**o guarda-lamas**	**gwar**-da **la**-mash
pedal	**o pedal**	pe-**dal**
pump	**a bomba de ar**	**bo^{n}**-ba de ar
reflector	**o reflector**	re-**fle**-tor
rim	**o aro**	**a**-roo
saddle	**a sela**	**se**-la
saddlebag	**o saco da sela**	**sa**-koo da **se**-la
spoke	**o raio**	**ra**-ee-oo
tyre	**o pneu**	**pnay**-oo
valve	**a válvula**	**val**-voo-la
wheel	**a roda**	**ro**-da

HOTELS & GUEST HOUSES[1]

BOOKING A ROOM

Rooms to let/vacancies	***Alugam-se quartos/há quartos vagos**	A-loo-gow^{n}-se **kwar-**toosh/ah **kwar-**toosh **va-**goosh
No vacancies	***(Hotel) completo**	(O-**tel**) ko^{n}-**ple**-too
Have you a room for the night?	**Tem um quarto para esta noite?**	Tay^{n} oo^{n} **kwar**-too **pa**-ra **esh**-ta **no-eet**
Do you know another good hotel?	**Pode recomendar-me um outro bom hotel?**	**Po**-de re-koo-may^{n}-**dar**-me oo^{n} **o**-troo bo^{n} o-**tel**

1. In addition to privately owned hotels and pensions, Portugal also has state-owned country inns called **pousadas**. The maximum stay in a **pousada** is limited to five days. **Estalagens** are small hotels.

I've reserved a room; my name is ...	**Tenho um quarto reservado; o meu nome é ...**	Tay^{n}-nyoo oo^{n} **kwar**-too re-zer-**va**-doo; oo **may**-oo **no**-me eh
I want a single room with a shower	**Quero um quarto individual com duche**	**Ke**-roo oo^{n} **kwar**-too ee^{n}-dee-vee-doo-**al** ko^{n} doosh
We want a room with a double bed and a bathroom	**Queremos um quarto de casal e casa de banho**	Ke-**ray**-moosh oo^{n} **kwar**-too de ka-**zal** ee **ka**-za de **ba**-nyoo
Have you a room with twin beds?	**Tem um quarto com duas camas?**	Tay^{n} oo^{n} **kwar**-too ko^{n} **doo**-ash **ka**-mash
I want a room with a washbasin/a private toilet	**Quero um quarto com lavabo/com quarto de banho privativo**	**Ke**-roo oo^{n} **kwar**-too ko^{n} la-va-**boo**/ko^{n} **kwar**-too de **ba**-nyoo pree-va-**tee**-voo
Is there hot and cold water?	**Há água quente e fria?**	Ah **a**-gwa **kay^{n}t** ee **free**-a
I want a room for two or three days	**Quero um quarto para dois ou três dias**	**Ke**-roo oo^{n} **kwar**-too **pa**-ra **do**-eesh oh traysh **dee**-ash
for a week	**para uma semana**	**pa**-ra **oo**-ma se-**ma**-na
until Friday	**até sexta-feira**	a-**te** say-ccsh-ta-**fay**-ee-ra
What floor is the room on?	**Em que andar é o quarto?**	Ay^{n} ke a^{n}-**dar** eh oo **kwar**-too
Is there a lift/elevator?	**Há elevador?**	Ah ee-le-va-**dor**
Are there facilities for the disabled?	**Há facilidades para diminuídos físicos?**	Ah fa-see-lee-**da**-desh **pa**-ra dee-mee-noo-**ee**-dosh **fee**-see-koosh

Have you a room on the first floor?	**Tem um quarto no primeiro andar?**	Tay^n oo^n **kwar**-too noo pree-**may**-ee-roo a^n-**dar**
May I see the room?	**Posso ver o quarto?**	**Po**-soo vayr oo **kwar**-too
I'll take this room	**Fico com este quarto**	**Fee**-koo ko^n aysht **kwar**-too
I don't like this room	**Não gosto deste quarto**	Now^n **gosh**-too daysht **kwar**-too
Have you another one?	**Tem outro?**	Tay^n **o**-troo
I want a quiet room/a bigger room	**Quero um quarto sossegado/maior**	**Ke**-roo oo^n **kwar**-too soo-se-**ga**-do/may-**or**
There's too much noise	**Há muito barulho**	Ah **moo**-ee-too ba-**roo**-llyoo
I'd like a room with a balcony	**Desejaria um quarto com varanda**	De-ze-zha-**ree**-a oo^n **kwar**-too ko^n va-**ra^n**-da
Have you a room looking on to the street/the sea?	**Tem um quarto que dê para a rua/o mar?**	Tay^n oo^n **kwar**-too ke day **pa**-ra a **roo**-a/oo mar
Is there a telephone? a radio? a television?	**Há** **um telefone?** **um rádio?** **uma televisão?**	Ah oo^n te-le-**fon** oo^n **ra**-dee-oo **oo**-ma te-le-vee-**sow^n**
We've only twin-bedded rooms	***Temos só quartos de duas camas**	**Tay**-moosh so **kwar**-toosh de **doo**-ash **ka**-mash
This is the only room vacant	***Este é o único quarto vago**	Aysht eh oo **oo**-nee-koo **kwar**-too **va**-goo
We shall have another room tomorrow	***Teremos outro quarto amanhã**	Te-**ray**-moosh **o**-troo **kwar**-too a-ma-**nya^n**

The room is only available tonight	***O quarto só está vago por esta noite**	Oo **kwar**-too so esh-**ta** va-goo poor **esh**-ta **no-eet**
How much is the room per day?	**Quanto custa o quarto por noite?**	**Kwa^{n}**-too **koosh**-ta oo **kwar**-too poor **no**-eet
Have you nothing cheaper?	**Não tem nada mais barato?**	Now^{n} tay^{n} **na**-da **ma**-eesh ba-**ra**-too
What do we pay for the child/children?	**Quanto pagamos pela(s)/criança(s)?**	**Kwan**-too pa-**ga**-moosh **pe**-la(sh)/kree-a^{n}-sa(sh)
Could you put a cot/an extra bed in the room?	**Pode pôr uma cama de bebé/uma cama extra no quarto, por favor?**	**Po**-de por **oo**-ma **ka**-ma de be-**be**/**oo**-ma **ka**-ma **esh**-tra noo **kwar**-too poor fa-**vor**
Is the service included?	**O serviço está incluído?**	Oo ser-**vee**-soo esh-**ta** ee^{n}-kloo-**ee**-doo
Are meals included?	**As refeições estão incluídas?**	Ash re-fay-**soy^{n}sh** esh-**tow^{n}** een-kloo-**ee**-dash
How much is the room without meals?	**Quanto é o quarto sem refeições?**	**Kwan**-too eh oo **kwar**-too say^{n} re-fay-**soy^{n}sh**
How much is full board/half board?	**Quanto é a pensão completa/meia pensão?**	**Kwan**-too eh a pay^{n}-**sow^{n}** ko^{n}-**ple**-ta/**may**-ee-a pay^{n}-**sow^{n}**
Do you do bed and breakfast?	**Tem quarto com pequeno almoço?**	Tay^{n} **kwar**-too ko^{n} pe-**kay**-noo al-**mo**-soo
What is the weekly rate?	**Quanto é a tarifa semanal?**	**Kwan**-too eh a tar-**ee**-fa se-ma-**nal**
It's too expensive	**É muito caro**	Eh **moo**-ee-too **ka**-roo
Please fill in the registration form	***Pode preencher o registo?**	**Po**-de pre-ay^{n}-**shayr** oo re-**geesh**-to

Could I have your passport, please?	***Posso ver o passaporte?**	Po-soo vayr oo pa-sa-port

IN YOUR ROOM

Chambermaid	**Criada de quarto**	Kree-a-da de kwar-too
Room service	**Serviço de quarto**	Ser-vee-soo de kwar-too
I'd like breakfast in my room, please	**Quero o pequeno almoço no meu quarto**	Ke-roo oo pe-kay-noo al-mo-soo noo may-oo kwar-too
I'd like some ice cubes	**Gostava de ter ums cubos de gêlo**	Goosh-ta-va de tayr oo^{n}sh koo-boosh de zhay-loo
Please wake me at 8.30	**Chame-me às oito e meia, por favor**	Sha-me-me ash o-ee-too ee may-ee-a poor fa-vor
There's no ashtray in my room	**Não há cinzeiro no meu quarto**	Now^{n} ha see^{n}-zay-ee-roo no may-oo kwar-too
Can I have more hangers, please?	**Podem dar-me mais cabides, por favor**	Po-day^{n} dar-me ma-eesh ka-bee-desh poor fa-vor
Is there a point for an electric razor?	**Há tomada para máquina de barbear?**	Ah too-ma-da pa-ra ma-kee-na de bar-bee-ar
What's the voltage?[1]	**Qual é a voltagem?**	Kwal eh a vol-ta-zhay^{n}
Where is the bathroom?	**Onde é a casa de banho?**	O^{n}-de eh a ka-za de ba-nyoo

1. The most usual types of current in Portugal are 110 and 220 volts.

Where is the lavatory?	**Onde é a retrete?**	O^{n}-de eh a re-**tret**
Is there a shower?	**Há chuveiro?**	Ah shoo-**vay**-ee-roo
There are no towels in my room	**Não há toalhas no meu quarto**	Now^{n} ah too-**a**-llyash noo may-oo **kwar**-too
There's no soap	**Não há sabão**	Now^{n} ah sa-**bow^{n}**
There's no (hot) water	**Não há água (quente)**	Now^{n} ah **a**-gwa (kay^{n}t)
There's no plug in my washbasin	**Não há válvula no meu lavatório**	Now^{n} ah **val**-voo-la noo may-oo la-va-**to**-ree-oo
There's no toilet paper in the lavatory	**Não há papel higiénico na retrete**	Now^{n} ah pa-**pel** ee-zhee-e-nee-koo na re-**tret**
The washbasin is blocked	**O lavabo está entupido**	Oo la-va-boo esh-**ta** ay^{n}-too-**pee**-doo
The lavatory won't flush	**O autoclismo não funciona**	Oo ow-to-**kleezh**-moo now^{n} foo^{n}-see-**o**-na
The bidet leaks	**O bidé deita água**	Oo bee-**de** **day**-ee-ta **a**-gwa
The light doesn't work	**A luz não acende**	A loosh now^{n} a-**say^{n}**-de
The lamp is broken	**A lâmpada está partida**	A **la^{n}**-pa-da esh-**ta** par-**tee**-da
The blind is stuck	**O estor está emperrado**	Oo esh-**tor** esh-**ta** ay^{n}-pe-**ra**-do
The curtains won't close	**As cortinas não fecham**	Ash koor-**tee**-nash now^{n} **fay**-show^{n}
May I have another blanket/another pillow, please?	**Pode me arranjar outra manta/outra almofada?**	**Po**-de me a-ra^{n}-**zhar** o-tra **ma^{n}**-ta/o-tra al-moo-**fa**-da

The sheets on my bed haven't been changed	**Não mudaram os lençois da minha cama**	Now^{n} moo-da-row^{n} oosh lay^{n}-soy-eesh da mee-nya ka-ma
I can't open my window, please open it	**Não consigo abrir a janela, pode abrí-la por favor**	Now^{n} ko^{n}-see-goo a-breer a zha-ne-la po-de a-bree-la poor fa-vor
It's too hot/cold	**Está quente/frio demais**	Esh-ta ke^{n}t/free-oo de-mysh
Can the heating be turned up/down?	**Pode aumentar/ diminuir o aquecimento um pouco mais?**	Po-dc a oo-may^{n}-tar/ dee-mee-noo-eer oo a-ke-see-may^{n}-too oo^{n} po-koo ma-eesh
Can the heating be turned on/off?	**Pode abrir/fechar o aquecimento?**	Po-de a-breer/fe-shar oo a-ke-see-may^{n}-too
Is the room air-conditioned?	**O quarto tem ar condicionado?**	Oo kwar-too tay^{n} ar ko^{n}-dee-see-oo-na-doo
The air conditioning doesn't work	**O ar condicionado não funciona**	Oo ar ko^{n}-dee-see-oo-na-doo now^{n} foo^{n}-see-o-na
Come in	**Entre**	Ay^{n}-tre
Put it on the table, please	**Ponha em cima da mesa, por favor**	Po-nya ay^{n} see-ma da may-za poor fa-vor
How long will the laundry take?	**Quanto tempo demora a lavagem da roupa?**	Kwan-too tay^{n}-poo de-mo-ra a la-va-zhay^{n} da ro-pa
Have you a needle and thread?	**Tem uma agulha e linha?**	Tay^{n} oo-ma a-goo-llya ee lee^{n}-nya
I want these shoes cleaned	**Quero estes sapatos limpos**	Ke-roo aysh-tesh sa-pa-toosh lee^{n}-poosh

Could you get this dress/suit cleaned up a bit?	**Podem-me limpar um pouco este vestido/fato?**	**Po**-day^n-me lee^n-**par** oo^n po-koo aysht vesh-**tee**-doo/**fa**-too
I want this suit pressed	**Quero este fato passado**	**Ke**-roo aysht **fa**-too pa-**sa**-doo
When will it be ready?	**Quando estará pronto?**	**Kwan**-do esh-ta-**ra** **pro**^{n}-too
It will be ready tomorrow	***Estará pronto amanhã**	Esh-ta-**ra** **pro**^{n}-too a-ma-**nya**^{n}

OTHER SERVICES

Porter	**Porteiro**	Poor-**tay**-ee-roo
Hall porter	**Porteiro do hall**	Poor-**tay**-ee-roo doo **ol**
Page	**Pagem**	**Pa**-zhay^n
Manager	**Gerente**	Zhe-**ray**^{n}**t**
Telephonist	**Telefonista**	Te-le-foo-**neesh**-ta
The key to number ..., please	**A chave do número ..., por favor**	A **sha**-ve doo **noo**-me-roo ... poor fa-**vor**
Have you a map of the town/an amusement guide?	**Tem um mapa da cidade/guia de diversões?**	Tay^n oo^n **ma**-pa da see-**dad**/**gee**-a de dee-ver-**soy**^{n}**sh**
Can I leave this in your safe?	**Posso deixar isto no vosso cofre?**	**Po**-soo day-ee-**shar** **eesh**-too noo **vo**-soo **ko**-fre
Are there any letters for me?	**Há alguma carta para mim?**	Ah al-**goo**-ma **kar**-ta **pa**-ra mee^n
Are there any messages for me?	**Há alguma mensagem para mim?**	Ah al-**goo**-ma may^n-**sa**-zhay^n **pa**-ra mee^n

English	Portuguese	Pronunciation
Please post this	**Por favor ponha no correio**	Poor fa-**vor** **po**-nya noo koo-**ray**-ee-oo
Is there a telex?	**Tem algum telex?**	Tay^{n} al-**goo^{n}** te-**leks**
Can I dial direct to England/America?	**Posso ligar directo para a Inglaterra/ América?**	**Po**-soo lee-**gar** dee-**re**-too **pa**-ra a ee^{n}-gla-**te**-ra/a-**me**-ree-ka
If anyone phones, tell them I'll be back at 4.30	**Se alguém me telefonar digam que eu volto às quatro e meia**	Se al-**gay^{n}** me te-le-foo-**nar** **dee**-gow^{n} ke **ay**-oo **vol**-to ash **kwa**-troo ee **may**-ee-a
No one telephoned	***Ninguém telefonou**	Nee^{n}-**ge^{n}** te-le-fo-**no**
There's a lady/ gentleman to see you	***Há uma senhora/ um senhor perguntando por si**	Ah **oo**-ma se-**nyo**-ra/oo^{n} se-**nyor** per-goo^{n}-**ta^{n}**-doo poor see
Please ask her/him to come up	**Por favor, diga-lhe para subir**	Poor fa-**vor** **dee**-ga-llye **pa**-ra soo-**beer**
I'm coming down (at once)	**Desço imediatamente**	**Daysh**-soo ee-me-dee-a-ta-**may^{n}t**
Can I borrow a typewriter?	**Pode emprestar-me uma máquina de escrever?**	**Po**-de ay^{n}-presh-**tar**-me **oo**-ma **ma**-kee-na de esh-kre-**ver**
Have you any writing paper? envelopes? stamps?	**Tem papel de carta? envelopes? selos?**	Tay^{n} pa-**pel** de **kar**-ta ay^{n}-ve-**lo**-pesh **say**-loosh
Please send the chambermaid	**A empregada de quarto, por favor**	A ay^{n}-pre-**ga**-da de **kwar**-too poor fa-**vor**
I need a guide/ interpreter	**Necessito um guia/ um intérprete**	Ne-se-**see**-too oo^{n} **gee**-a/oo^{n} ee^{n}-**ter**-pre-te

Does the hotel have a baby-sitting service?	**O hotel tem quem cuide de crianças/ serviço de babysitter?**	Oo o-**tel** tay^n kay^n **koo**-ee-de de kree-**a**^{n}-sash/ ser-**vee**-soo de be-**be**-see-tair
Where are the toilets?	**Onde são os lavabos?**	**On**^{n}-de sow^n oosh la-**va**-boosh
Where is the cloakroom?	**Onde é o vestiário?**	**O**^{n}-de eh oo vesh-tee-**a**-ree-oo
Where is the dining room?	**Onde é a sala de jantar?**	**O**^{n}-de eh a **sa**-la de zha^n-**tar**
What time is breakfast?	**A que horas é o pequeno almoço?**	A ke **o**-rash eh oo pe-**kay**-noo al-**mo**-soo
lunch?	**o almoço?**	oo al-**mo**-soo
dinner?	**o jantar?**	oo zha^n-**tar**
Is there a garage?	**Tem aqui garagem?**	Tay^n a-**kee** ga-ra-zhay^n
Where can I park the car?	**Onde posso deixar/ estacionar o carro?**	**O**^{n}-de **po**-soo day-ee-**shar**/esh-ta-see-oo-**nar** oo **ka**-roo
Is the hotel open all night?	**O hotel está aberto toda a noite?**	Oo o-**tel** esh-**ta** a-**ber**-too **to**-da a **no**-eet
What time does it close?	**A que horas fecha?**	A ke **o**-rash **fay**-ee-sha

DEPARTURE

I'm leaving tomorrow	**Saio amanhã**	**Sa**-ee-oo a-ma-**nya**^{n}
Can you make up my bill?	**Pode tirar-me a conta?**	**Po**-de tee-**rar**-me a **ko**^{n}-ta
There is a mistake on the bill	**Há um engano na conta**	Ah oo^n ay^n-**ga**-noo na **ko**^{n}-ta

English	Portuguese	Pronunciation
Do you accept credit cards?	**Aceitam cartões de crédito?**	A-**say**-ee-tow^{n} kar-**toy**^{n}sh de **kre**-dee-too
I shall be coming back on ... can I book a room for that date?	**Regressarei no dia ... posso reservar um quarto para essa data?**	Re-gre-sa-**ray**-ee noo **dee**-a ... **po**-soo re-zer-**var** oo^{n} **kwar**-too **pa**-ra **e**-sa **da**-ta
Could you have my luggage brought down?	**Pode trazer a minha bagagem para baixo?**	Po-de tra-**zayr** a **mee**-nya ba-**ga**-zhay^{n} **pa**-ra ba-ee-shoo
Please store the luggage, we will be back at ...	**É favor guardar a bagagem, nós voltamos às ...**	Eh fa-**vor** gwar-**dar** a ba-**ga**-zhay^{n} nosh vol-**ta**-moosh ash ...
Please order a taxi for me at ... o'clock	**Chame-me um taxi para as ... horas, por favor**	**Sha**-me-me oo^{n} **tak**-see **pa**-ra ash ... **o**-rash poor fa-**vor**
Thank you for a pleasant stay	**Muito obrigado por tão agradável estadia**	**Moo**-ee-too o-bree-**ga**-doo poor tow^{n} a-gra-**da**-vel esh-ta-**dee**-a

CAMPING

English	Portuguese	Pronunciation
Is there a camp site nearby?	**Há um parque de campismo aqui perto?**	Ah oo^n park de ka^n-**peezh**-moo a-**kee** **per**-too
May we camp here? in your field? on the beach?	**Podemos acampar aqui? no seu terreno? na praia?**	Po-**day**-moosh a-ka^n-**par** a-**kee** noo **say**-oo te-**ray**-noo na **pry**-a
Where should we put our tent/caravan?	**Onde podemos pôr a nossa barraca/ caravana?**	**O**^{n}-de poo-**day**-moosh por a **no**-sa ba-**ra**-ka/ ka-ra-**va**-na
Can I park the car next to the tent?	**Posso estacionar junto da barraca?**	**Po**-soo esh-ta-see-oo-**nar** **zhoon**-too da ba-**ra**-ka
Can we hire a tent on the site?	**Podemos alugar uma barraca no parque de campismo?**	Poo-**day**-moosh a-loo-**gar** **oo**-ma ba-**ra**-ka noo park de ka^n-**peezh**-moo

Is there	**Há**	Ah
drinking water?	**água potável?**	a-gwa poo-**ta**-vel
electricity?	**electricidade?**	ee-le-tree-see-**dad**
showers?	**chuveiros?**	shoo-**vay**-ee-roosh
toilets?	**casas de banho?**	**ka**-zash de **ba**-nyo
a shop?	**alguma loja?**	al-**goo**-ma **lo**-zha
a swimming pool?	**uma piscina?**	**oo**-ma peesh-**see**-na
a playground?	**um recinto para brincar?**	oo^{n} re-**see^{n}**-too **pa**-ra bree^{n}-**kar**
a restaurant?	**um restaurante?**	oo^{n} resh-tow-**ra^{n}t**
a launderette?	**uma lavandaria?**	**oo**-ma la-va^{n}-da-**ree**-a
What does it cost	**Quanto custa**	**Kwan**-too **koosh**-ta
per night?	**por noite?**	poor **no**-eet
per week?	**por semana?**	poor se-**ma**-na
per person?	**por pessoa?**	poor pe-**so**-a
Can I buy ice?	**Posso comprar gêlo?**	**Po**-soo ko^{n}-**prar zhay**-loo
Where can I buy	**Onde posso comprar**	**O^{n}**-de **po**-soo ko^{n}-**prar**
oil?	**petróleo?**	pe-**tro**-lee-o
paraffin?	**parafina?**	pa-ra-**fee**-na
butane gas?	**gás butano?**	**gash** boo-**ta**-no
Where do I put rubbish?	**Onde posso deixar o lixo?**	**O^{n}**-de **po**-soo day-ee-**shar** oo **lee**-shoo
Where can I wash up/ wash clothes?	**Onde posso lavar a louça/lavar a roupa?**	**O^{n}**-de **po**-soo la-**var** a **lo**-sa/la-**var** a **ro**-pa
Is there somewhere to dry clothes/ equipment?	**Há onde secar a roupa/ equipamento?**	Ah **o^{n}**-de se-**kar** a **ro**-pa/ay-kee-pa-**may^{n}**-too
My camping gas has run out	**O meu gás acabou**	Oo **may**-oo **gash** a-ka-**bo**
The toilet is blocked	**A retrete está entupida**	A re-**tre**-te esh-**ta** ay^{n}-too-**pee**-da

The shower doesn't work/is flooded	**O chuveiro não funciona/está inundado**	Oo shoo-**vay**-ee-roo now^{n} foo^{n}-see-**o**-na/esh-**ta** ee-noo^{n}-**da**-doo
What is the voltage?	**Qual é a voltagem?**	Kwal eh a vol-**ta**-zhay^{n}
May we light a fire?	**Podemos fazer uma fogueira?**	Poo-**day**-moosh fa-**zair** **oo**-ma foo-**ge**-ra
Please prepare the bill, we are leaving	**Por favor prepare a conta; nós partimos hoje**	Poor fa-**vor** pre-**par** a **ko^{n}**-ta nosh par-**tee**-moosh **o**-zhe
How long do you want to stay?	***Quanto tempo vão ficar?**	**Kwan**-too **tay^{n}**-poo vow^{n} fee-**kar**
What is your car registration number?	***Qual é o número de matrícula do seu carro?**	Kwal eh oo **noo**-me-roo de ma-**tree**-koo-la doo **say**-oo **ka**-roo
I'm afraid the camp site is full	***Lamento mas o parque de campismo está cheio**	La-**may^{n}**-too mash oo park de ka^{n}-**peezh**-moo esh-**ta** **shay**-ee-oo
No camping	***É proibido acampar**	Eh proo-ee-**bee**-doo a-ka^{n}-**par**

YOUTH HOSTELLING

How long is the walk to the youth hostel?	**A que distância está o albergue da juventude?**	A ke deesh-**ta^n**-see-a esh-**ta** oo al-**berg** da zhoo-vay^n-**tood**
Is there a youth hostel here?	**Há aqui um albergue para jovens?**	Ah a-**kee** oo^n al-**berg** pa-ra **zho-vay^{n}sh**
Have you a room/bed for the night?	**Tem quarto/cama para esta noite?**	Tay^n **kwar**-too/**ka**-ma pa-ra **esh**-ta no-eet
How many days can we stay?	**Quantos dias podemos ficar?**	**Kwan**-toosh **dee**-ash poo-**day**-moosh fee-**kar**
Here is my membership card	**Aqui está o meu cartão de sócio/ membro**	A-**kee** esh-ta oo **may**-oo kar-**tow^n** de **so**-see-oo/**may^n**-broo
Do you serve meals?	**Servem refeições?**	**Ser**-vay^n re-fay-ee-**soy^{n}sh**
Can I use the kitchen?	**Posso usar a cozinha?**	**Po**-soo oo-**zar** a koo-**zee**-nya

s there somewhere cheap to eat nearby?	**Há algum sítio próximo onde se possa comer barato?**	Ah al-**goo**^{n} **see**-tee-oo **pro**-see-moo **o**^{n}-de se **po**-sa koo-**mayr** ba-**ra**-too
want to rent a sheet for my sleeping bag	**Quero alugar um lençol para o meu saco de dormir**	**Ke**-roo a-loo-**gar** oo^n lay^n-**sol** **pa**-ra oo **may**-oo **sa**-koo de door-**meer**

RENTING OR OWNING A PLACE

We have rented an apartment/villa	**Nós alugámos um apartamento/ chalet**	Nosh a-loo-**ga**-moosh oo a-part-ta-**may^{n}**-too/ sha-**le**
Here is our reservation	**Aqui está a nossa reserva**	A-**kee** esh-**ta** a **no**-sa re-**zer**-va
Please show us around	**Por favor mostrem-nos a casa/ apartamento**	Por fa-**vor** **mosh**-tray^{n}-noosh a **ka**-za/a-par-ta-**may^{n}**-too
Is the cost of	**O preço da**	Oo **pray**-soo da ee-le-
electricity	**electricidade**	tree-see-**dad**
the gas cylinder	**da botija/do cilindro de gás**	da boo-**tee**-zha/see-**lee^{n}**-droo de gash
the maid	**da criada**	da kree-**a**-da
included?	**está incluído?**	esh-**ta** ee^{n}-kloo-**ee**-doo

Where is the	**Onde está**	O^{n}-de esh-**ta**
electricity mains switch?	**o quadro da electricidade?**	oo **kwa**-droo da ee-le-tree-see-**dad**
water mains stopcock?	**a torneira-tampão?**	a toor-**nay**-ee-ra ta^{n}-**pow^{n}**
light switch?	**o interruptor da luz?**	oo ee^{n}-te-roop-**tor** da loosh
power-point?	**a derivação?**	a de-ree-va-**sow^{n}**
fuse box?	**o quadro de fusíveis?**	oo **kwa**-droo de foo-**zee**-vay-eesh
How does the heating/hot water work?	**Como é que o aquecimento/água quente funciona?**	**Ko**-moo eh ke oo a-ke-see-**may^{n}**-too/**a**-gwa kay^{n}t foo^{n}-see-**o**-na
Is there a spare gas cylinder?	**Há uma botija/um cilindro de gás de reserva?**	Ah **oo**-ma boo-**tee**-zha/oo^{n} see-**lee^{n}**-droo de gash de re-**zer**-va
Do gas cylinders get delivered?	**Fornecem-se cilindros/botijas de gás?**	Foor-**ne**-say^{n}-se see-**lee^{n}**-droosh/boo-**tee**-zhash de gash
Please show me how this works	**Por favor mostre-me como isto funciona**	Poor fa-**vor** **mosh**-tre-me **ko**-moo **eesh**-too foon-see-**o**-na
Which days does the maid come?	**Em que dias trabalha a criada?**	Ay^{n} ke **dee**-ash tra-**ba**-llya a kree-**a**-da
For how long?	**Por quanto tempo?**	Poor **kwan**-too **tay^{n}**-poo
Is there a fly screen?	**Têm uma rêde contra môscas/mosquitos?**	Tay^{n} **oo**-ma rayd **ko^{n}**-tra **mosh**-kash/moosh-**kee**-toosh
When is the rubbish collected?	**Quando é a recolha do lixo?**	**Kwan**-doo eh a re-**ko**-llya doo **lee**-shoo

Where can we buy logs for the fire?	**Onde podemos comprar lenha para o fogão de aquecimento?**	O^n-de poo-**day**-moosh ko^n-**prar lay**-nya **pa**-ra oo foo-**gow^n** de a-ke-see-**may^n**-too
Is there a barbecue?	**Há um churrasco?**	Ah oo^n shoo-**rash**-koo
Please give me another set of keys	**Por favor dê-me outro molho de chaves**	Poor fa-**vor day**-me o-troo **mo**-llyoo de **sha**-vesh
We have replaced ...	**Nós substituímos ...**	Nosh soobzh-tee-too-**ee**-moosh
Here is the bill	**Aqui está a conta**	A-**kee** esh-**ta** a **ko^n**-ta
Please return my deposit against breakages	**Por favor restitua-me o depósito contra danos**	Poor fa-**vor** res-tee-**too**-a-me oo de-**po**-zee-too **ko^n**-tra **da**-noosh

PROBLEMS

The drain/pipe/sink is blocked	**O esgôto/o cano/o lava-louça está entupido**	Oo eezh-**go**-too/oo **ka**-noo/la-va-**loh**-sa esh-**ta** ay^n-too-**pee**-doo
The toilet doesn't flush	**O autoclismo não funciona**	Oo ow-to-**kleezh**-moo now^n foo^n-see-**o**-na
There's no water	**Não há água**	Now^n ah **a**-gwa
We can't turn the water off/shower on	**Não podemos fechar a água/abrir o chuveiro**	Now^n poo-**day**-moosh fe-**shar** a **a**-gwa/a-**breer** oo shoo-**vay**-ee-roo
There is a leak/a broken window	**Há uma rotura/uma janela partida**	Ah **oo**-ma roo-**too**-ra/ **oo**-ma zha-**ne**-la par-**tee**-da

The shutters won't close	**As persianas não fecham**	Ash per-see-a-nash now^{n} fay-show^{n}
The window won't open	**A janela não abre**	A zha-ne-la now^{n} a-bre
The electricity has gone off	**Há uma falha de electricidade**	Ah oo-ma fa-llya de ee-le-tree-see-dad
The heating	**O aquecimento**	Oo a-ke-see-may^{n}-too
The cooker	**O fogão**	Oo foo-gow^{n}
The refrigerator	**O frigorífico**	Oo free-go-ree-fee-koo
The water heater doesn't work	**O aquecedor de água não funciona**	Oo a-ke-se-dor de a-gwa now^{n} foo^{n}-see-o-na
The lock is stuck	**A fechadura está encravada**	A fe-sha-doo-ra esh-ta ay^{n}-kra-va-da
This is broken	**Isto está partido**	Eesh-too esh-ta par-tee-doo
This needs repairing	**Isto precisa de conserto/reparação**	Eesh-too pre-see-za de ko^{n}-sayr-too/re-pa-ra-sow^{n}
The apartment/villa has been burgled	**O apartamento/vila foi roubado(a)/ arrombado(a)**	Oo a-par-ta-may^{n}-too/ vee-la fo-ee ro-ba-doo(a)/a-ro^{n}-ba-doo(a)

PARTS OF THE HOUSE

balcony	**a varanda**	va-ra^{n}-da
bathroom	**a casa de banho**	ka-za de ba-nyoo
bedroom	**o quarto de dormir**	kwar-too de door-meer
ceiling	**o tecto**	te-too

chimney	**a chaminé**	sha-mee-**ne**
corridor	**o corredor**	koo-re-**dor**
door	**a porta**	**por**-ta
fence	**a vedação**	ve-da-**sow**^{n}
fireplace	**o fogão de sala**	foo-**gow**^{n} de **sa**-la
floor	**o chão**	**show**^{n}
garage	**a garagem**	ga-**ra**-zhay^{n}
gate	**o portão**	poor-**tow**^{n}
hall	**a entrada**	ay^{n}-**tra**-da
kitchen	**a cozinha**	koo-**zee**-nya
living room	**a sala de estar**	**sa**-la de esh-**tar**
patio	**o pátio**	**pa**-tee-oo
roof	**o telhado**	te-**llya**-doo
shutters	**os estores/as persianas**	esh-**to**-resh/per-**see**-a-nash
stairs	**as escadas**	esh-**ka**-dash
terrace	**o terraço**	te-**ra**-soo
wall	**a parede**	pa-**red**
window	**a janela**	zha-**ne**-la

FURNITURE AND FITTINGS

armchair	**a cadeira de braços**	ka-**day**-ee-ra de **bra**-soosh
bath	**a banheira**	ba-**nyay**-ee-ra
bed	**a cama**	**ka**-ma

lanket	**o cobertor**	koo-ber-**tor**
olt (for door)	**o trinco (para porta)**	**tree^{n}**-koo (**pa**-ra **por**-ta)
room	**a vassoura**	va-**so**-ra
rush	**a escova**	esh-**ko**-va
ucket	**o balde**	**bal**-de
assette player	**o leitor de cassetes**	lay-ee-**tor** de ka-**se**-tesh
hair	**a cadeira**	ka-**day**-ee-ra
harcoal	**o fogareiro de carvão**	foo-ga-**ray**-ee-roo de kar-**vow^{n}**
lock	**o relógio**	re-**lo**-zhee-oo
ooker	**o fogão**	foo-**gow^{n}**
upboard	**o armário**	ar-**ma**-ree-oo
urtains	**as cortinas**	koor-**tee**-nash
ushions	**as almofadas**	al-moo-**fa**-dash
leckchair	**a cadeira de repouso**	ka-**day**-ee-ra de re-**po**-zoo
loorbell	**a campaínha da porta**	ka^{n}-pa-**ee**-nya da **por**-ta
loorknob	**o puxador da porta**	poo-sha-**dor** da **por**-ta
lustbin	**o caixote do lixo**	ka-ee-**shot** doo **lee**-shoo
luster	**o pano de pó**	**pa**-noo de po
lustpan	**a pá para o lixo**	pah **pa**-ra oo **lee**-shoo
hinge	**a dobradiça**	doo-bra-**dee**-sa
immersion heater	**o aquecedor de imersão**	a-ke-se-**dor** de ee-mer-**sow^{n}**
iron	**o ferro de passar/engomar**	**fe**-roo de pa-**sar**/ay^{n}-go-**mar**

lamp	**a lâmpada**	**la**^{n}-pa-da
lampshade	**o candieiro/o quebra luz**	kay^n-dee-**ay**-ee-roo/**ke**-bra loosh
light bulb	**a lâmpada eléctrica**	**la**^{n}-pa-da ee-**le**-tree-ka
lock	**a fechadura**	fe-sha-**doo**-ra
mattress	**o colchão**	kol-**show**^{n}
mirror	**o espelho**	esh-**pay**-llyoo
mop	**o esfregão**	esh-fre-**gow**^{n}
padlock	**o cadeado**	ka-dee-**a**-doo
pillow	**a almofada**	al-moo-**fa**-da
pipe	**o tubo/cano**	**too**-boo/**ka**-noo
plug (bath)	**o tampão**	tan-**pow**^{n}
plug (electric)	**a ficha (eléctrica)**	**fee**-sha (ee-**le**-tree-ka)
radio	**o rádio**	**ra**-dee-oo
refrigerator	**o frigorífico**	free-goo-**ree**-fee-koo
sheet	**o lençol**	layn-**sol**
shelf	**a prateleira**	pra-te-**lay**-ee-ra
shower	**o chuveiro**	shoo-**vay**-ee-roo
sink	**o lava-louça**	la-va-**loh**-sa
sofa	**o sofá**	soo-**fa**
sun-lounge	**a marquise**	mar-**keez**
table	**a mesa**	**may**-za
tap	**a torneira**	toor-**nay**-ee-ra
toilet	**a casa de banho**	**ka**-za de **ba**-nyoo
towel	**a toalha**	too-**a**-llya
vacuum cleaner	**o aspirador de pó**	ash-pee-ra-**dor** de po

washbasin	**a bacía**	ba-**see**-a
washing machine	**a máquina de lavar roupa**	ma-**kee**-na de la-**var ro**-pa
window catch	**o fecho da janela**	**fay**-shoo da zha-**ne**-la
window sill	**o peitoril**	pay-ee-too-**reel**

KITCHEN EQUIPMENT

bleach	**a lexívia**	le-**shee**-vee-a
bottle opener	**o abre garrafas**	a-bre ga-**rah**-fash
bowl	**a bacía**	ba-**see**-a
can opener	**o abre latas**	a-bre **la**-tash
candles	**as velas**	**ve**-lash
chopping board	**a tábua de cortar**	**ta**-boo-a de koor-**tar**
clothes line	**a corda de secar roupa**	**kor**-da de se-**kar ro**-pa
clothes pegs	**as molas (de secar ropa)**	**mo**-lash (de se-**kar ro**-pa)
coffee pot	**a cafeteira**	ka-fe-**tay**-ee-ra
colander	**o coador**	koo-a-**dor**
coolbox	**a caixa de refrêscos**	**ka**-ee-sha de re-**fraysh**-koosh
corkscrew	**o saca-rolhas**	**sa**-ka-**ro**-llyash
cup	**a taça**	**ta**-sa
detergent	**o detergente**	de-ter-**zhay^{n}t**
fork	**o garfo**	**gar**-foo
frying pan	**a frigideira**	free-zhee-**day**-ee-ra

glass	**o copo**	**ko-poo**
ice pack	**o pacote de gêlo**	**pa-kot** de **zhay-loo**
ice tray	**o tabuleiro de gêlo**	ta-boo-**lay**-ee-roo de **zhay**-loo
kettle	**a chaleira**	sha-**lay**-ee-ra
knife	**a faca**	**fa**-ka
matches	**os fósforos**	**fosh**-foo-roosh
pan	**a panela**	pa-**ne**-la
plate	**o prato**	**pra**-too
scissors	**a tesoura**	te-**zo**-ra
sieve	**a peneira**	pe-**nay**-ee-ra
spoon	**a colher**	koo-**llyer**
teatowel	**o pano de secar a louça**	**pa**-noo de se-**kar** a **loh**-sa
torch	**a tocha/lanterna eléctrica**	**to**-sha/la^{n}-**ter**-na ee-le-**tree**-ka
washing powder	**o pó de sabão**	po de sa-**bow**^{n}
washing-up liquid	**o detergente para lavar louça**	de-tair-**zhent pa**-ra la-**var loh**-sa

ODD JOBS[1]

bracket	**o suporte**	soo-**port**
hammer	**o martelo**	mar-**te**-loo

1. See also SHOPPING & SERVICES p. 107.

iron	**o ferro**	fe-roo
lacquer	**a laca**	la-ka
metal	**o metal**	me-tal
nails	**os pregos**	pre-goosh
paint	**a tinta**	tee^{n}-ta
paint brush	**o pincel de pintar**	pee^{n}-sel de pee^{n}-tar
plastic	**o plástico**	plash-tee-koo
pliers	**o alicate**	a-lee-kat
saw	**a serra**	se-ra
screwdriver	**a chave de parafusos**	sha-ve de pa-ra-foo-zoosh
screws	**os parafusos**	pa-ra-foo-zoosh
spanner	**a chave de fendas/ inglesa**	sha-ve de fay^{n}-dash/ee^{n}-glay-za
steel	**o aço**	a-soo
tile	**o azulejo**	a-zoo-lay-zhoo
wire	**o arame**	a-ra-me
wood	**a madeira**	ma-day-ee-ra

MEETING PEOPLE

How are you?	**Como está/estão?**	**Ko**-moo esh-**ta**/esh-**tow^{n}**
Fine thanks and you?	**Bem, obrigado/a, e você?**	Bay^{n} o-bree-**ga**-doo/a ee vo-**say**
What is your name?	**Como se chama?**	**Ko**-moo se **sha**-ma
May I introduce ...?	**Posso apresentar ...?**	**Po**-soo a-pre-say^{n}-**tar**
My name is ...	**O meu nome é ...**	Oo **may**-oo **no**-me eh
This is ...	**Este/a é ...**	**Aysht**/a eh
Have you met ...?	**Já foi apresentado a ...?**	Zha **fo**-ee a-pre-zay^{n}-**ta**-doo a
Glad to meet you	**Muito prazer em conhecê-lo/la**	**Moo**-ee-too pra-**zayr** ay^{n} koo-nye-**say**-loo/la
Am I disturbing you?	**Estou a perturbá-lo/la?**	Esh-**to** a per-toor-**ba**-loo/la
Go away	**Vá-se embora**	**Va**-se ay^{n}-**bo**-ra
Leave me alone	**Deixe-me só (em paz)**	**Dayeesh**-me so (ay^{n} pazh)

Sorry to have troubled you	**Desculpe ter incomodado**	Desh-**kool**-pe tayr ee^{n}-koo-moo-**da**-doo

MAKING FRIENDS

Do you live/are you staying here?	**Vive/está a viver aqui?**	**Vee**-ve/esh-**ta** a vee-**ver** a-**kee**
Do you travel a lot?	**Viaja muito?**	Vee-**a**-zha **moo-ee**-too
We've been here a week	**Já aqui estamos há uma semana**	**Zha** a-**kee** esh-**ta**-moosh ah **oo**-ma se-**ma**-na
Is this your first time here?	**É esta a primeira vez aqui?**	Eh **esh**-t a pree-**may**-ee-ra vayzh a-**kee**
Do you like it here?	**Gosta de aqui estar?**	**Gosh**-ta de a-**kee** esh-**tar**
Are you on your own?	**Está sozinho/a?**	Esh-**ta** so-**zee**-nyoo/a
I am with	**Estou com**	Esh-**to** ko^{n}
my husband/my wife	**o meu marido/a minha esposa**	oo **may**-oo ma-**ree**-doo/a **mee**-nya esh-**po**-za
my parents	**os meus pais**	oosh **may**-oosh **pa**-eesh
my family	**a minha família**	a **mee**-nya fa-**mee**-lee-a
a friend	**um amigo**	oo^{n} a-**mee**-goo
I am travelling alone	**Viajo sozinho/a**	Vee-**a**-zhoo so-**zee**-nyoo/a
Where do you come from?	**Donde vem?**	**Do^{n}**-de vay^{n}
I come from ...	**Venho de ...**	**Vay**-nyoo de
What do you do?	**Que faz você?**	Ke **fazh** vo-**say**

What are you studying?	**O que é que está a estudar?**	Oo ke eh ke esh-**ta** a esh-too-**dar**
I'm on holiday/a business trip	**Estou em viagem de férias/negócios**	Esh-**to** ay^n vee-**a**-zhay^n de **fe**-ree-ash/ne-**go**-see-oosh
Are you married/ single?	**É casado(a)/ solteiro(a)?**	Eh ka-**za**-doo(a)/sol-**tay**-ee-roo(a)
Do you have children?	**Tem filhos?**	Tay^n **fee**-llyoosh
Have you been to England/America?	**Já esteve na Inglaterra/ América?**	Zha esh-**tay**-ve na ee^n-gla-**te**-ra/a-**me**-ree-ka
I hope to see you again	**Espero vê-lo de novo**	Esh-**pe**-roo **vay**-loo de **no**-voo
Do you smoke?	**Fuma?**	**Foo**-ma
No, I don't, thanks	**Não, não fumo, obrigado/a**	Now^n now^n **foo**-moo o-bree-**ga**-doo/a
I have given it up	**Deixei de fumar**	Day-ee-**shay**-ee de foo-**mar**
Do you mind if I smoke?	**Importa-se que eu fume?**	Ee^n-**por**-ta-se ke **ay**-oo **foo**-me
Help yourself	**Sirva-se**	**Seer**-va-se
Can I get you a drink?	**Posso arranjar-lhe uma bebida?**	**Po**-soo a-ra^n-**zhar**-llye oo-ma be-**bee**-da
I'd like a ... please	**Gostaría de ... por favor**	Goosh-ta-**ree**-a de ... poor fa-**vor**

INVITATIONS

Would you like to have lunch tomorrow?	**Gostava de almoçar amanhã?**	Goosh-ta-va de al-moo-**sar** a-ma-**nya^{n}**
Can you come to dinner/for a drink?	**Pode vir jantar/ tomar uma bebida**	**Po**-de veer zha^{n}-**tar**/to-**mar** oo-ma be-**bee**-da
We are giving a party/ there is a party; would you like to come?	**Vamos dar uma festa; gostaría de vir?**	Va-moosh **dar oo**-ma **fesh**-ta; goosh-ta-**ree**-a de veer
May I bring a (girl) friend?	**Posso trazer um amigo (uma amiga)?**	**Po**-soo tra-**zayr** oo^{n} a-**mee**-goo (**oo**-ma a-**mee**-ga)
Thank you for the invitation	**Obrigado pelo convite**	O-bree-**ga**-doo **pay**-loo ko^{n}-**veet**
I'd love to come	**Gostaría muito de ir**	Goosh-ta-**ree**-a **moo**-ee-too de eer
I'm sorry, I can't come	**Desculpe, mas não posso**	Desh-**kool**-pe mash now^{n} **po**-soo
Are you doing anything tonight/tomorrow afternoon?	***Está ocupado esta noite/amanhã à tarde?**	Esh-**ta** o-koo-**pa**-doo **esh**-ta **no**-eet/a-ma-**nya** ah tard
Could we have coffee/a drink somewhere?	***Poderíamos tomar café/uma bebida em qualquer sítio?**	Poo-de-**ree**-a-moosh too-**mar** ka-**fe**/**oo**-ma be-**bee**-da ay^{n} **kwal-ker see**-tee-oo
Shall we go to the cinema/theatre/ beach?	***Vamos ao cinema/ teatro/à praia?**	**Va**-moosh **a**-oo see-**nay**-ma/tee-**a**-troo/ah **pry**-a

Would you like to go dancing?	***Quer ir dançar?**	Ker eer da^{n}-**sar**
Would you like to go for a drive?	***Quer ir dar uma volta de carro?**	Ker eer dar **oo**-ma **vol**-ta de **ka**-roo
Do you know a good disco/restaurant?	**Conhece uma discoteca boa/um restaurante bom?**	Koo-**nye**-se **oo**-ma deesh-koo-**teh**-ka boa/ oom resh-tow-**rant** bo^{n}
Where shall we meet?	**Onde nos poderemos encontrar?**	**O^{n}**-de nosh poo-de-**ray**-moosh ay^{n}-ko^{n}-**trar**
What time shall I/we come?	**A que horas devo/ devemos chegar?**	A ke **o**-rash **day**-voo/de-**vay**-moosh she-**gar**
I could pick you up at ...	**Eu podia ir buscá-lo ...**	**Ay**-oo poo-**dee**-a eer boosh-**ka**-lo ...
Could you meet me at ...?	**Podia encontrar-me em ...?**	Poo-**dee**-a ay^{n}-ko^{n}-**trar**-me ay^{n}
May I see you home?	**Posso levá-la a casa?**	**Po**-soo le-**va**-la a **ka**-za
Can I give you a lift home/to your hotel?	**Posso levá-la/levar-vos a casa/ao hotel?**	**Po**-soo le-**va**-la/le-**var**-voosh a **ka**-za/a-oo o-**tel**
May I see you again?	**Posso vê-la/lo outra vez?**	**Po**-soo **vay**-la/loo **o**-tra vaysh
Where do you live?	**Onde vive/mora?**	**O^{n}**-de **vee**-ve/**mo**-ra
What is your telephone number?	**Qual é o número do seu telefone?**	Kwal eh oo **noo**-me-roo doo **se**-oo te-le-**fon**
Thank you for the pleasant evening/ drink/ride	**Obrigado/a pela noite/bebida/pelo passeio agradável**	O-bree-**ga**-doo/a **pay**-la **no**-eet/be-**bee**-da/ **pay**-loo pa-**say**-ee-oo a-gra-**da**-vel
It was lovely	**Foi agradável**	**Fo**-ee a-gra-**da**-vel

It was nice talking to you	**Foi um prazer falar consigo**	**Fo-ee oo^n pra-zayr fa-lar ko^n-see-goo**
Hope to see you again soon	**Espero encontrá-lo/la outra vez em breve**	**Esh-pe-roo ay^n-ko^n-tra-loo/la o-tra vaysh ay^n bre-ve**
See you soon/later/tomorrow	**Até breve/até logo/até amanhã**	**A-te bre-ve/a-te lo-goo/a-te a-ma-nya^n**

GOING TO A RESTAURANT[1]

Can you suggest	**Pode recomendar-nos**	**Po**-de re-koo-may^n-**dar**-noosh
a good restaurant?	**um bom restaurante?**	oo^n bo^n resh-tow-**ra^{n}t**
a cheap restaurant?	**um restaurante económico?**	oo^n resh-tow-**ra^{n}t** ay-ko-**no**-mee-koo
a vegetarian restaurant?	**um restaurante vegetariano?**	oo^n resh-tow-**ra^{n}t** ve-zhe-ta-ree-**a**-noo
I'd like to book a table for four at 1 p.m.	**Queria reservar uma mesa para quatro, para a uma hora**	Ke-**ree**-a re-zer-**var** **oo**-ma **may**-za **pa**-ra **kwa**-troo **pa**-ra a **oo**-ma **o**-ra
I've reserved a table; my name is ...	**Tenho uma mesa reservada; o meu nome é ...**	**Tay^n**-nyoo **oo**-ma **may**-za re-zer-**va**-da oo **may**-oo **no**-me eh
We did not make a reservation	**Não fizemos reserva**	**Now^n** fee-**ze**-moosh re-**zer**-va

1. In Portugal lunch is usually served between 12.30 p.m. and 2.00 p.m. and dinner from 7.30 p.m. to 9.30 p.m.

Is there a table on the terrace? by the window in a corner?	**Tem uma mesa** **no terraço?** **perto da janela?** **a um canto?**	Tay^n **oo**-ma **may**-za noo te-**ra**-soo **per**-too da zha-**ne**-la a oo^n **ka**^{n}-too
Is there a table free on the terrace?	**Há uma mesa livre no terraço?**	Ah **oo**-ma **may**-za **lee**-vre noo te-**ra**-soo
Is there a non-smoking area?	**Há uma área para não-fumadores?**	Ah **oo**-ma a-ree-a **pa**-ra now^n foo-ma-**do**-resh
This way, please	***Por aqui, se faz favor**	Poor a-**kee** se fazh fa-**vor**
You will have to wait about ... minutes	***Terá que esperar ... minutos**	Te-**ra** ke esh-pe-**rar** ... mee-**noo**-toosh
We shall have a table free in half an hour	***Haverá uma mesa livre dentro de meia hora**	A-ve-**ra** **oo**-ma **may**-za **lee**-vre **day**^{n}-troo de **may**-ee-a **o**-ra
We don't serve lunch until 1 p.m.	***Não se servem almoços até à uma hora**	Now^n se **ser**-vay^n al-**mo**-soosh a-**te** ah **oo**-ma **o**-ra
We don't serve dinner until 8 p.m.	***Não se servem jantares até às oito horas**	Now^n se **ser**-vay^n zha^n-**ta**-resh a-**te** ash **oh**-ee-too **o**-rash
We stop serving at 2 o'clock	***Acabamos de servir às duas horas**	A-ka-**ba**-moosh de ser-**veer** ash **doo**-ash **o**-rash
Last orders at ...	***As últimas ordens são às ...**	Ash **ool**-tee-mash **or**-day^{n}sh sow^n ash
Sorry, the kitchen is closed	***Desculpe mas a cozinha fechou**	Desh-**kool**-pe mash a koo-**zee**-nya fe-**sho**
Where is the lavatory?	**Onde é a retrete?**	**O**^{n}-de eh a re-**tret**

It is downstairs	***É em baixo/É ao fundo das escadas**	Eh ay^{n} **ba-ee-shoo**/Eh a-oo **foo^{n}**-doo dash esh-**ka**-dash

ORDERING

Service and taxes (not) included	***Serviço e taxas (não) incluídos**	Ser-**vee**-soo ee **ta**-shash (now^{n}) ee^{n}-kloo-**ee**-doosh
Waiter/waitress (to call)	**Criado/criada**	Kree-**a**-do/kree-**a**-da
May I see the menu, please?	**O menu/a ementa, por favor**	Oo me-**noo**/a ee-**may^{n}**-ta poor fa-**vor**
May I see the wine list, please?	**A lista dos vinhos, por favor**	A **leesh**-ta doosh **vee**-nyoosh poor fa-**vor**
Is there a set menu?	**Há menu do dia/ menu turístico?**	Ah me-**noo** doo **dee**-a/ me-**noo** too-**reesh**-tee-koo
We are in a (great) hurry	**Temos (muita) pressa**	**Tay**-moosh (**moo**-ee-ta) **pre**-sa
Do you serve snacks?[1]	**Servem pratos combinados?**	Ser-**vay^{n}** **pra**-toosh ko^{n}-bee-**na**-doosh
I want something light	**Quero qualquer coisa leve**	**Ke**-roo **kwal**-ker ko-**ee**-za **le**-ve
Do you have children's helpings?	**Tem doses para crianças?**	Tay^{n} **do**-zesh **pa**-ra kree-**a^{n}**-sash

1. A **prato combinado** is a main dish served in bars and cafés. It consists of various types of meat, vegetables, fish, eggs, etc., in a number of different combinations.

English	Portuguese	Pronunciation
What is your dish of the day?	**Qual é o prato do dia?**	Kwal eh oo pra-too doo dee-a
What do you recommend?	**O que aconselha?**	Oo ke a-ko^n-say-llya
Can you tell me what this is?	**Pode dizer-me o que é isto?**	Po-de dee-zer-me oo ke eh eesh-too
What is the speciality of the restaurant?	**Qual é a especialidade da casa?**	Kwal eh a esh-pe-see-a-lee-dad da ka-za
What is the speciality of the region?	**Qual é o prato típico da região?**	Kwal eh oo pra-to tee-pee-koo da re-zhee-ow^n
Do you have any local dishes/vegetarian dishes?	**Tem alguns pratos regionais/pratos vegetarianos?**	Tay^n al-goo^{n}sh pra-toosh re-zhee-oo-na-eesh/pra-toosh ve-zhe-ta-ree-a-noosh
Would you like to try ...?	***Quer provar ...?**	Ker proo-var
There's no more ...	***Já não há ...**	Zha now^n ah
I'd like ...	**Quero ...**	Ke-roo
May I have peas instead of beans?	**Pode dar-me ervilhas em vez de feijão?**	Po-de dar-me eer-vee-llyash ay^n vaysh de fay-ee-zhow^n
Is it hot or cold?	**Este prato é quente ou frio?**	Aysht pra-too eh kay^{n}t oo free-oo
Without oil/sauce, please	**Sem azeite/môlho, por favor**	Say^n a-zay-eet/mo-llyoo poor fa-vor
Some more bread, please	**Mais pão, por favor**	Ma-eesh pow^n poor fa-vor
A little more ...	**Um pouco mais ...**	Oo^n po-koo ma-eesh

COMPLAINTS

Where are our drinks?	**Onde estão as nossas bebidas?**	O^n-de esh-**tow^n** ash **no**-sash be-**bee**-dash
Why is the food taking so long?	**Porque é que a comida demora tanto?**	**Poor**-ke eh ke a koo-**mee**-da de-**mo**-ra **ta^n**-too
This isn't what I ordered, I want ...	**Isto não é o que pedi, eu quero ...**	**Eesh**-too now^n eh oo ke pe-**dee ay**-oo **ke**-roo
This isn't fresh	**Isto não está fresco**	**Eesh**-too now^n esh-**ta fraysh**-koo
This is	**Está**	Esh-**ta**
stale	**passado**	pa-**sa**-doo
tough	**duro**	**doo**-roo
undercooked	**pouco cozido**	**po**-koo koo-**zee**-doo
too cold	**muito frio**	**moo**-ee-too **free**-oo
salty	**salgado**	sal-**ga**-doo
This plate/knife/spoon/glass is not clean	**Este prato/faca/colher/copo não está limpo**	Aysht **pra**-too/**fa**-ka/koo-**llyer**/**ko**-poo now^n esh-**ta lee^n**-poo
I'd like to see the headwaiter	**Gostava de ver o chefe dos empregados**	Goosh-**ta**-va de vayr oo **she**-fe doosh e^n-pre-**ga**-doosh

PAYING

The bill, please	**A conta, por favor**	A **ko^n**-ta poor fa-**vor**
Is service included?	**Está serviço incluído?**	Esh-**ta** ser-**vee**-soo een-kloo-**ee**-doo

Please check the bill – I don't think it's correct	**Reveja a conta, por favor, penso que não está certa**	Re-vay-zha a ko^n-ta poor fa-vor pe^n-soo ke now^n esh-ta ser-ta
What is this amount for?	**Para que é esta quantia?**	Pa-ra ke eh esh-ta kwa^n-tee-a
I didn't have soup	**Não comi sopa**	Now^n koo-mee so-pa
I had chicken, not lamb	**Comi galinha, não carneiro**	Koo-mee ga-lee-nya now^n kar-nay-ee-roo
May we have separate bills?	**Pode dar-nos a conta em separado?**	Po-de dar-noosh a ko^n-ta ay^n se-pa-ra-doo
Do you take travellers' cheques/a credit card?	**Aceita cheques de viagem/cartão de crédito?**	A-say-ee-ta she-ksh de vee-a-zhay^n/kar-tow^n de kre-dee-too
Keep the change	**Guarde o troco**	Goo-ar-de oo tro-koo
It was very good	**Estava muito bom**	Esh-ta-va moo-ee-too bo^n
We enjoyed it, thank you	**Gostei muito, obrigado**	Goosh-tay-ee moo-ee-too o-bree-ga-doo

BREAKFAST AND TEA

Breakfast	**Pequeno almoço**	Pe-kay-noo al-mo-soo
A large white coffee/a black coffee, please	**Um café com leite duplo/um café, por favor**	Oo^n ka-fe ko^n lay-eet doo-ploo/oo^n ka-fe poor fa-vor
I would like decaffeinated coffee	**Quero café sem cafeína**	Ke-roo ka-fe se^n ka-fe-ee-na
I would like tea with milk/lemon	**Quero chá com leite/limão**	Ke-roo sha ko^n lay-eet/lee-mow^n

I would like a herb tea	**Quero chá de ervas**	**Ke**-roo sha de **er**-vash
Drinking chocolate	**(Bebida) chocolate**	(Be-**bee**-da) sho-ko-**lat**
May we have some sugar, please?	**Pode dar-nos açúcar?**	**Po**-de **dar**-noosh a-**soo**-kar
Do you have artificial sweeteners?	**Tem açúcar artificial?**	Tay^{n} a-**soo**-kar ar-tee-fee-see-**al**
Hot/cold milk	**Leite quente/frio**	**Lay**-eet kay^{n}t/**free**-oo
Bread and butter	**Pão com manteiga**	Pow^{n} ko^{n} ma^{n}-**tay**-ee-ga
Toast	**Torradas**	Too-**ra**-dash
More butter, please	**Mais manteiga, por favor**	**Ma**-eesh ma^{n}-**tay**-ee-ga poor fa-**vor**
Have you some jam?	**Tem alguma compota?**	Tay^{n} al-**goo**-ma ko^{n}-**po**-ta
What fruit juices have you?	**Que sumos de fruta tem?**	Ke **soo**-moosh de **froo**-ta tay^{n}
Orange/grapefruit/tomato juice	**Sumo de laranja/toranja/tomate**	**Soo**-moo de la-**ra**^{n}-zha/too-**ra**^{n}-zha/too-**mat**
Yoghurt	**Yogurte**	Ee-o-**goort**
Fried/poached/scrambled eggs	**Ovos estrelados/escalfados/mexidos**	**O**-voosh esh-tre-**la**-doosh/esh-kal-**fa**-doosh/me-**shee**-doosh
Hard/soft boiled eggs	**Ovos cozidos duros/moles**	**O**-voosh koo-**zee**-doosh **doo**-roosh/**mo**-lesh
Ham and eggs	**Ovos com presunto**	**O**-voosh ko^{n} pre-**zoo**^{n}-too
Cereal	**Cereal**	Se-ree-**al**
Fresh fruit	**Fruta fresca**	**Froo**-ta **fraysh**-ka
Help yourself at the buffet	**Sirva-se na mesa do buffet**	**Seer**-va-se na **may**-za doo boo-**fay**

SNACKS AND PICNICS

Can I have a ... sandwich, please?	Posso comprar/ tirar/comer uma sandes ... por favor	Po-soo ko^{n}-prar/tee-rar/koo-mayr oo-ma sa^{n}-desh ... poor fa-vor
Toasted sandwich	A tosta	Tosh-ta
What are those things over there?	O que são aquelas coisas?	Oo ke sow^{n} a-ke-lash ko-ee-zash
What are they made of?	De que são feitas?	De ke sow fayee-tash
What is in them?	O que têm dentro?	Oo ke tay^{n}-ay^{n} day^{n}-troo
I'll have one of these, please	Quero um destes, por favor	Ke-roo oo^{n} daysh-tesh poor fa-vor
It's to take away	É para levar	Eh pa-ra le-var
biscuits	os biscoitos/as bolachas	beesh-ko-ee-toosh/boo-la-shash
bread	o pão	pow^{n}
butter	a manteiga	ma^{n}-tayee-ga
cheese	o queijo	kay-ee-zhoo
chips	as batatas fritas	ba-ta-tash free-tash
chocolate bar	a barra de chocolate	ba-ra de shoo-koo-lat
cold cuts	as carnes frias	kar-nesh free-ash
egg	o ovo	o-voo
ham	o fiambre	fee-a^{n}-bre
ice cream	o gêlado	zhe-la-do
pancake	o crépe	krep
pastries	os folhados	foo-llya-doosh
pickles	as conservas (em vinagre)	ko^{n}-ser-vash (ay^{n} vee-na-gre)

roll	**o papo sêco**	pa-poo say-koo
salad	**a salada**	sa-la-da
sausage	**a salsicha**	sal-see-sha
soup	**a sôpa**	so-pa
tomato	**o tomate**	to-mat

DRINKS[1]

What will you have to drink?	***O que desejam beber?**	Oo ke de-zay-zhow^n be-bayr
A bottle of the house wine, please	**Uma garrafa de vinho da casa**	Oo-ma ga-ra-fa de vee-nyoo da ka-za
Do you serve wine by the glass?	**Servem vinho a copo?**	Ser-vay^n vee-nyoo a ko-poo
Do you serve cocktails?	**Serve coqueteis?**	Ser-ve kok-tay-eesh
I'd like	**Gostava de**	Goosh-ta-va de tayr
a long drink with ice	**um refresco grande com gêlo**	oo^n re-fraysh-koo gra^n-de ko^n zhay-loo
apple juice	**um sumo de maçã**	oo^n soo-moo de ma-sa^n
orange juice	**um sumo de laranja**	oo^n soo-moo de la-ra^n-zha
a fruit juice	**um sumo de frutas**	oo^n soo-moo de froo-tash
a milk shake	**um batido de leite**	oo^n ba-tee-doo de lay-eet
an iced coffee	**um café gelado**	oo^n ka-fe zhe-la-doo
hot chocolate	**um chocolate quente**	oo^n shoo-koo-lat kay^{n}t
iced tea	**um chá gelado**	oo^n sha zhe-la-doo

1. For the names of beverages see p. 104.

Carafe/glass	**Jarra/copo**	Zhar-ra/ko-poo
Bottle/half bottle	**Garrafa/meia-garrafa**	Ga-ra-fa/may-ee-a ga-ra-fa
Three glasses of beer, please	**Três cervejas, por favor**	Traysh ser-**vay**-zhash poor fa-**vor**
Do you have draught beer?	**Tem cerveja de barril?**	Tay^n ser-**vay**-zha de ba-**reel**
Two more beers	**Mais duas cervejas**	Ma-eesh **doo**-ash ser-**vay**-zhash
Large/small beer	**Grande/pequena cerveja**	**Gra**^{n}-de/pe-**kay**-na ser-**vay**-zha
Soft drinks	**Refrigerantes/ refrescos**	Re-free-zhe-**ra**^{n}-tesh/re-**fraysh**-koosh
Neat/straight up	**Simples/sem água**	**See**^{n}-plesh/se^n **a**-gwa
On the rocks	**Com gêlo**	Ko^n **zhay**-loo
With water (mineral)	**Com água (mineral)**	Ko^n **a**-gwa (mee-ne-**ral**)
With soda water	**Com soda**	Ko^n **so**-da
Mineral water (with/ without gas)	**Água mineral (com/ sem gás)**	A-gwa mee-ne-**ral** (ko^n/ se^n gash)
Cheers!	**À saúde!**	Ah sa-oo-de
I'd like a glass of water, please	**Um copo de água, por favor**	Oo^n **ko**-poo de **a**-gwa poor fa-**vor**
The same again, please	**O mesmo novamente, por favor**	Oo **mayzh**-moo **no**-va-may^{n}t poor favor
Three black coffees and one with milk	**Três cafés e um café com leite**	Traysh ka-**fesh** ee oo^n ka-**fay** ko^n **lay**-eet
China tea	**Chá da China**	Sha da **shee**-na
Indian tea	**Chá da Índia**	Sha da **ee**^{n}-dee-a

May we have an ashtray?	**Pode dar-nos um cinzeiro?**	**Po-de dar-noosh oo^{n} see^{n}-zay-ee-roo**

RESTAURANT VOCABULARY

ashtray	**o cinzeiro**	**seen-zay-ee-roo**
bill	**a conta**	**ko^{n}-ta**
cigar	**o charuto**	**sha-roo-too**
cigarettes	**os cigarros**	**see-gar-roosh**
cloakroom	**o vestiário**	**vesh-tee-a-ree-oo**
course/dish	**o prato**	**pra-too**
cup	**a chávena**	**sha-ve-na**
fork	**o garfo**	**gar-foo**
glass	**o copo**	**ko-poo**
hungry (to be)	**ter fome**	**ter fom**
jug of water	**a jarra de água**	**zhar-ra de a-gwa**
knife	**a faca**	**fa-ka**
matches	**os fósforos**	**fosh-foo-roosh**
menu	**o menu/a lista/a ementa**	**me-noo/leesh-ta/ee-me^{n}-ta**
mustard	**a mostarda**	**moosh-tar-da**
napkin	**o guardanapo**	**guard-a-na-poo**
oil	**o óleo**	**o-lee-oo**
olive oil	**o azeite**	**a-zayt**
pepper	**a pimenta**	**pee-me^{n}-ta**
plate	**o prato**	**pra-too**

salt	**o sal**	sal
sauce	**o molho**	**mo**-llyoo
saucer	**o pires**	**pee**-resh
service	**o serviço**	ser-**vee**-soo
spoon	**a colher**	koo-**llyer**
table	**a mesa**	**may**-za
tablecloth	**a toalha de mesa**	too-**a**-llya de **may**-za
terrace	**o terraço**	te-**ra**-soo
thirsty (to be)	**ter sede**	ter sayd
tip	**a taxa de serviço/ gorjeta**	**ta**-sha de ser-**vee**-soo/ goor-**zhe**-ta
toothpick	**o palito**	pa-**lee**-too
vegetarian	**o vegetariano**	ve-ge-ta-ree-**a**-noo
vinegar	**o vinagre**	vee-**na**-gre
waiter	**o empregado de mesa**	e^{n}-pre-**ga**-doo de **may**-za
waiter/waitress *to call*	**criado/criada**	kree-**a**-doo/da
waitress	**a empregada de mesa**	e^{n}-pre-**ga**-da de **may**-za
water	**a água**	**a**-gwa
wine list	**a lista de vinhos**	**lleesh**-ta de **vee**-nyoosh

THE MENU

SOPAS

açorda	garlic and bread
caldo	consommé
caldo de galinha	chicken consommé
caldo verde	green cabbage
sopa de cebola	onion
sopa de galinha	chicken
sopa de mariscos	shellfish
sopa de massa	noodle
sopa de peixe	fish
sopa de rabo de boi	oxtail
sopa de tomate	tomato
sopa de verduras/legumes	vegetable

HORS D'ŒUVRES

alcachofras artichokes
anchovas anchovies
arenques herring
azeitonas olives
biqueirões fresh anchovies
caracóis snails
espargos asparagus
fiambre (fumado) (smoked) ham
gambas prawns
melão melon
omeleta (de espargos) (asparagus) omelette
ostras oysters
ovos eggs
percceves goose barnacles
salada salad
sardinhas sardines

PEIXE

ameijoas clams
atum tunny
bacalhau dried salt cod
bacalhau à Gomes de Sá dried cod with potatoes, onions and garlic

bacalhau cozido com batatas/ grão	stewed cod (unspiced) with potatoes/chick peas
besugo	sea bream
bolinhos de bacalhau	cod fish cakes
caldeirada de peixe	fish stew
caranguejo (de mar)	crab
caranguejo (de rio)	crayfish
cherne	bass
choco/calamar	squid
chocos com tinta	squid cooked in their own ink
enguias	eels
gambas	prawns
garoupa	grouper
goraz	bream
lagosta	lobster
lampreia	lamprey
linguado	sole
mexilhão	mussels
peixe espada	swordfish
peixe frito	fried fish
pescada	hake
polvo	octopus
raia	skate
robalo	turbot
salmão	salmon
salmonete	red mullet

sardinhas	sardines
sardinhas assadas	grilled sardines
sardinhas de escabeche	pickled sardines

CARNE

almôndegas	meatballs/rissoles in a spicy sauce
borrego	mutton
carne assada (de vaca)	roast beef
carneiro	lamb
carneiro assado	roast lamb
chouriço	sausage made from spiced, cured pork
costeleta	chop
enchidos	sausages
escalope	escalope
feijoada	beans and meat
fígado	liver
filetes de carne	fillet of beef
guisado de vitela	braised veal
leitão	suckling pig
língua	tongue
linguiça	spiced sausage
lombo	loin
mioleira	brains
morcela	spiced blood sausage

pé de porco	pig's trotters
presunto	raw cured ham
rabo de vaca (boi)	oxtail
rins	kidneys
salpicão	smoked, spiced pork sausage
salsicha	sausage
toucinho	bacon
vaca	beef
vitela	veal
vitela assada	roast veal
vitela estufada	veal stew

AVES E CAÇA

cabrito	kid
coelho	rabbit
faisão	pheasant
frango	chicken
frango de piri-piri	chicken with a seasoning made from dried red chillies and olive oil
galinha	hen/boiling fowl
galinhola	woodcock
galo	cock
ganso	goose
javali	boar
lebre	hare

pato	duck
pato bravo	wild duck
perdiz	partridge
peru	turkey
pombo	pigeon

ARROZ

arroz de bacalhau	rice with salt cod
arroz de caril	curry and rice
arroz de galinha	rice with chicken
arroz de peixe	rice with fish

LEGUMES E VERDURAS

aipo	celery
alcachofra	artichoke
alface	lettuce
alho	garlic
azeitonas	olives
batatas	potatoes
batatas assadas	roast potatoes
batatas cozidas	boiled potatoes
batatas fritas	fried potatoes/chips
beringela	aubergine/eggplant
beterraba	beetroot

cebola	onion
cenoura	carrot
cogumelos	mushrooms
couve	cabbage
couves de Bruxelas	Brussels sprouts
couve-flor	cauliflower
ervilhas	peas
espargos	asparagus
espinafres	spinach
favas	broad beans
feijão	beans
nabo	turnip
pepino	cucumber
pimento	pepper
rábanos	radishes
salada	salad
salsa	parsley
tomate	tomato

SOBREMESA

compota	preserved fruit
doce de ovos	candied egg yolks
filhós	fritters
gelado	ice-cream
merengue	meringue

pastel/bolo	cake
pudim flan	crème caramel
tarta de fruta	fruit tart
torrão	nougat

FRUTAS FRESCAS E SECAS

alperce	apricot
amêndoa	almond
amendoim	peanut
ananás	pineapple
avelã	hazel-nut
banana	banana
cereja	cherry
figo	fig
laranja	orange
limão	lemon
maçã	apple
melancia	water melon
melão	melon
morango	strawberry
noz	walnut
papaia	papaya
passa	raisin
pera	pear
pêssego	peach
tâmara	date

toranja	grapefruit
uva	grape

BEBIDAS

água	water
água gasosa de soda	soda water
água mineral	mineral water
água termal	thermal water
batido de leite	milk shake
bebidas alcoólicas	alcoholic drinks
brande/aguardente	brandy
cacau	cocoa
café	coffee (black)
café com leite	white coffee
cerveja	beer
branca	light
em lata	in a can
engarrafada	bottled
preta	dark
tirada (de barril)	draught
chá	tea
de ervas	herb
de hortelã pimenta	mint
de tília	camomile
da China	China
da Índia	Indian
de limão	lemon
gelado com limão	iced tea with lemon

champanhe	champagne
chocolate quente	hot chocolate
cidra	cider
conhaque	cognac
laranjada	orangeade
leite (quente)	(hot) milk
licor	liqueur
limonada	lemonade, lemon-squash
sumos	juices
sumo de toranja	grapefruit juice
sumo de laranja	orange juice
sumo de maçã	apple juice
sumo de tomate	tomato juice
sumo de uva	grape juice
vinho	wine
branco	white
da Madeira	Madeira
doce	sweet
do Porto	Port
espumante	sparkling
rosé	rosé
seco	dry
tinto	red
verde	light wine, made from not fully matured grapes

WAYS OF COOKING

cozido no forno	baked
grelhado na braza	barbecued
cozido	boiled
guizado	braised
frito	fried
grelhado	grilled
marinade/em vinhas de alho	marinated
carne	meat
mal passada	rare
média	medium
bem passada	well-done
escalfado	poached
em puré/creme	pureed/creamed
cru	raw
assado	roast
fumado	smoked
cozido a vapor	steamed
estufado	stewed
recheado	stuffed
quente/frio	hot/cold
com manteiga/óleo	with butter/oil

SHOPPING[1] & SERVICES

WHERE TO GO

Which is the best ...?	**Qual é o melhor ...?**	Kwal eh oo me-**llyor**
Where is the nearest ...?	**Onde é o mais próximo ...?**	O^n-de eh oo **ma**-eesh **pro**-see-moo
Can you recommend a ...?	**Pode recomendar ...?**	**Po**-de re-koo-may^n-**dar**
Where are the best department stores?	**Onde são os melhores armazéns?**	O^n-de sow^n oosh me-**llyo**-resh ar-ma-**zhay^{n}sh**
Where is the market/ supermarket?	**Onde é o mercado/ supermercado?**	O^n-de eh oo mer-**ka**-doo/soo-per-mer-**ka**-doo

1. Shops are open from 9.00 or 9.30 a.m. to 1.00 p.m. and from 3.00 p.m. to 7.00 or 8.00 p.m., Monday to Friday. On Saturdays hours are variable.

Is there a market every day?	**Há mercado todos os dias?**	Ah mer-**ka**-doo to-doosh oosh **dee**-ash
Where can I buy ...?	**Onde posso comprar ...?**	O^{n}-de **po**-soo ko^{n}-**prar**
When are the shops open?	**Quando abrem as lojas?**	**Kwa^{n}**-doo a-bray^{n} ash lo-zhash

SHOPS AND SERVICES

antique shop	**a loja de antiguidades**	**lo**-zha de a^{n}-tee-gwee-**da**-desh
baker	**a padaria**	pa-da-**ree**-a
bank	**o banco**	**ba^{n}**-koo
barber (see p. 124)	**a barbearia**	bar-bee-a-**ree**-a
bookshop	**a livraria**	lee-vra-**ree**-a
builder	**o constructor**	ko^{n}sh-troo-**tor**
butcher (see p. 99)	**o talho**	**ta**-llyoo
cake shop	**a pastelaria**	pash-te-la-**ree**-a
camera shop	**a loja de artigos fotográficos**	**lo**-zha de ar-**tee**-goosh foo-too-**gra**-fee-koosh
camping equipment	**o equipamento de campismo**	ay-kee-pa-**may^{n}**-too de ka^{n}-**peezh**-moo
carpenter	**o carpinteiro**	kar-pee^{n}-**tay**-ee-roo
chemist (see p. 117)	**a farmácia**	far-**ma**-see-a
confectioner	**a confeitaria**	kon-fay-ee-ta-**ree**-a
dairy	**a leitaria**	lay-ee-ta-**ree**-a
decorator/painter	**o decorador**	de-koo-ra-**dor**

dentist	**o dentista**	day^{n}-**teesh**-ta
department store (see p. 111)	**o armazém**	ar-ma-**zay**^{n}
doctor	**o médico**	me-**dee**-koo
dry cleaner (see p. 127)	**a limpeza a sêco**	lee^{n}-**pey**-za a **say**-koo
electrical appliances	**os electrodomésticos**	ee-le-tro-do-**mes**-tee-koosh
electrician	**o electricista**	ee-le-tree-**seesh**-ta
fishmonger (see p. 97)	**a peixaria**	pey-ee-sha-**ree**-a
florist	**a florista**	floo-**reesh**-ta
gardener	**o jardineiro**	zhar-dee-**nay**-ee-roo
greengrocer (see pp. 101, 103)	**a loja de hortaliça**	lo-zha de or-ta-**lee**-sa
grocer (see pp. 122)	**a mercearia**	mer-see-a-**ree**-a
hairdresser (see p. 124)	**o cabeleireiro (women's)**	ka-be-lay-ee-**ray**-ee-roo
hardware shop (see p. 126)	**a loja de ferragens**	lo-zha de fe-**ra**-zhay^{n}sh
hypermarket	**o hiper-mercado**	ee-per-mer-**ka**-doo
ironmonger	**o ferreiro**	fe-**ray**-ee-roo
jeweller	**a joalharia**	zho-a-**llyay**-ree-a
launderette/laundry (see p. 127)	**a lavandaria**	la-va^{n}-da-**ree**-a
market	**o mercado**	mer-**ka**-doo
mini-market	**o mini-mercado**	**mee**-nee-mer-**ka**-doo
notary	**o notário**	no-**ta**-ree-oo

odd job man	**o homem de reparações**	o-me^n de re-pa-ra-**soy^{n}sh**
optician	**o oculista**	o-koo-**leesh**-ta
painter	**o pintor**	pee^n-**tor**
pastry shop	**a pastelaria/ confeitaria**	pash-te-la-**ree**-a/ko^n-fay-ee-ta-**ree**-a
photographer	**o fotógrafo**	foo-**to**-gra-foo
plasterer	**o estocador**	esh-to-ka-**dor**
plumber	**o canalizador**	ka-na-lee-za-**dor**
police	**a polícia**	po-**lee**-see-a
post office	**o correio**	koo-**ray**-ee-oo
shoemaker	**o sapateiro**	sa-pa-**tay**-ee-roo
shoe shop (see p. 119)	**a sapataria**	sa-pa-ta-**ree**-a
sports shop	**a loja de artigos desportivos**	lo-zha de ar-**tee**-goosh desh-poor-**tee**-voosh
stationer (see p. 129)	**a papelaria**	pa-pe-la-**ree**-a
supermarket	**o supermercado**	soo-per-mer-**ka**-doo
sweet shop	**a loja de dôces**	lo-zha de **do**-sesh
tobacconist (see p. 134)	**a tabacaria**	ta-ba-ka-**ree**-a
toy shop	**a loja de brinquedos**	lo-zha de bree^n-**kay**-doosh
travel agent	**a agência de viagens**	a-**zhay^n**-see-a de vee-a-**zhay^{n}sh**
wine merchant	**o comerciante/ negociante de vinhos**	koo-mer-see-**a^{n}t**/ne-goo-see-**an^{n}t** de **vee**-nyoosh

IN THE SHOP

Self-service	***Auto-serviço**	Ow-to-sair-vee-soo
Sale (clearance)	***Saldo**	Sal-doo
Cash desk	***Caixa**	Ka-ee-sha
Shop assistant	**O empregado**	Oo ay^n-pre-ga-do
Manager	**O gerente/o responsável**	Oo zhe-ray^{n}t/oo resh-po^n-sa-vel
Can I help you?	***Que deseja?**	Ke de-zay-zha
I want to buy ...	**Quero comprar ...**	Ke-roo ko^n-prar
Do you sell ...?	**Vende ...?**	Vay^n-de
I'm just looking round	**Estou sómente a escolher**	Esh-to so-me^{n}t a esh-koo-llyayr
I don't want to buy anything now	**De momento não estou interessado em nada**	De moo-may^n-too now^n esh-to ee^n-te-re-sa-doo ay^n nah-da
Could you show me ...?	**Pode mostrar-me ...?**	Po-de moosh-trar-me
I don't like this	**Não gosto disto**	Now^n gosh-too deesh-too
I'll have this	**Eu compro isto**	Ay-oo ko^n-proo eesh-too
We do not have that	***Nós não temos isso**	Nosh now^n tay-moosh ee-soo
You'll find them in the ... department	***Encontrará isso na secção de ...**	Ay^n-ko^n-tra-ra ee-soo na sek-sow^n de
We've sold out but we'll have more tomorrow	***Não temos por agora mas amanhã já teremos**	Now^n tay-moosh poor a-go-ra mash a-ma-nya^n zha te-ray-moosh

Anything else?	***Mais alguma coisa?**	Ma-eesh al-goo-ma ko-ee-za
That will be all	**É tudo**	Eh too-doo
Shall we send it, or will you take it with you?	***Prefere que lhe enviemos ou leva já consigo?**	Pre-fe-re ke llye ay^{n}-vee-ay^{n}-moosh oh le-va zha ko^{n}-see-goo
I will take it with me	**Vou levá-lo comigo**	Vo le-va-loo koo-mee-goo
Please send them to ...	**Por favor, envie para ...**	Poor fa-vor ay^{n}-vee-e pa-ra

CHOOSING

I want something in leather/green	**Quero algo em cabedal/verde**	Ke-roo al-goo ay^{n} ka-be-dal/vayrd
I need it to match this	**Preciso que dê com isto**	Pre-see-zoo ke day ko^{n} eesh-too
I like the colour but not the style	**Gosto da cor mas não do feitio**	Gosh-to da kor mash now^{n} do fay-ee-tee-oo
I want a darker/lighter shade	**Quero um tom mais escuro/leve**	Ke-roo oo^{n} to^{n} ma-eesh esh-koo-roo/le-ve
I need something warmer/thinner	**Quero algo mais quente/leve**	Ke-roo al-goo ma-eesh kay^{n}t/le-ve
Do you have one in another colour/size?	**Tem outro noutra cor/tamanho?**	Tay^{n} o-troo no-tra kor/ta-ma-nyoo
Have you anything better/cheaper?	**Tem algo melhor/mais barato?**	Tay^{n} al-goo me-llyor/ma-eesh ba-ra-too
How much is this?	**Quanto custa isto?**	Kwa^{n}-too koosh-ta eesh-too

English	Portuguese	Pronunciation
That is too much for me	**Isto é muito/demasiado para mim**	Eesh-too eh moo-ee-too/de-ma-zee-a-doo pa-ra mee^n
For how long is it guaranteed?	**Quanto tempo tem de garantia?**	Kwa^n-too tay^n-poo tay^n de ga-ran-tee-a
What size is this?	**Que medida é esta?**	Ke me-dee-da eh esh-ta
Have you a larger/smaller one?	**Tem um maior/mais pequeno?**	Tay^n oo^n ma-ee-or/ma-eesh pe-kay-noo
I want size ...[1]	**Quero o número ...**	Ke-roo oo noo-me-roo
The English/American size is ...	**A medida inglesa/americana é ...**	A me-dee-da ee^n-glay-za/a-me-ree-ka-na eh
My collar size is ...	**A minha medida de colarinho é ...**	A mee-nya me-dee-da de koo-la-ree-nyoo eh
My waist measurement is ...	**A minha medida de cintura é ...**	A mee-nya me-dee-da de see^n-too-ra eh
My chest measurement is ...	**A minha medida de peito é ...**	A mee-nya me-dee-da de pay-ee-too eh
Can I try it on?	**Posso provar?**	Po-soo proo-var
It's too short/long/tight/loose	**É muito curto/comprido/apertado/largo**	Eh moo-ee-to koor-too/ko^n-pree-doo/a-per-ta-doo/lar-goo
Is there a mirror?	**Tem um espelho?**	Tay^n oo^n esh-pay-llyoo
Is it colourfast?	**Desbota?**	Desh-bo-ta
Is it machine washable?	**Pode-se lavar na máquina?**	Po-de-se la-var na ma-kee-na
Will it shrink?	**Pode encolher?**	Po-de ay^n-koo-llyayr
Is it handmade?	**É feito à mão?**	Eh fay-ee-too ah mow^n

1. See p. 121 for continental sizes.

MATERIALS

cotton	**o algodão**	al-goo-**dow^{n}**
lace	**a renda**	**re^{n}**-da
leather	**o cabedal**	ka-be-**dal**
linen	**o linho**	**lee^{n}**-nyoo
plastic	**o plástico**	**plash**-tee-koo
silk	**a seda**	**say**-da
suede	**a camurça**	ka-**moor**-sa
synthetic	**o sintético**	see^{n}-**te**-tee-koo
wool	**a lã**	la^{n}

COLOURS

beige	**bege**	**bey**-zhe
black	**preto**	**pray**-too
blue	**azul**	a-**zool**
brown	**castanho**	kash-**ta**-nyoo
gold	**dourado**	doh-**ra**-doo
green	**verde**	vayrd
grey	**cinzento**	see^{n}-**ze^{n}**-too
mauve	**violeta**	vee-o-**le**-ta
orange	**laranja**	la-**ra^{n}**-zha
pink	**rosa**	**ro**-za
purple	**roxo**	**ro**-shoo

red	**vermelho/encarnado**	ver-may-llyoo/e^{n}-kar-na-doo
silver	**prateado**	pra-te-a-doo
white	**branco**	bra^{n}-koo
yellow	**amarelo**	a-ma-re-loo

COMPLAINTS

I want to see the manager	**Quero falar com o gerente**	Ke-roo fa-lar ko^{n} oo zhe-ray^{n}t
I bought this yesterday	**Comprei isto ontem**	Ko^{n}-pray-ee eesh-too o^{n}-tay^{n}
It doesn't work/fit	**Não funciona/cabe**	Now^{n} foo^{n}-see-o-na/ka-be
This is	**Está**	Esh-ta
dirty	**sujo**	soo-zhoo
stained	**manchado**	ma^{n}-sha-doo
torn	**roto**	ro-too
broken	**partido**	par-tee-doo
cracked	**rachado**	ra-sha-doo
bad	**em más condições**	ay^{n} mash ko^{n}-dee-soy^{n}sh
I want to return this	**Quero devolver isto**	Ke-roo de-vol-vayr eesh-too
Will you change it, please?	**Podem trocá-lo, por favor?**	Po-day^{n} troo-ka-loo poor fa-vor
Will you refund my money?	**Podem devolver-me o dinheiro?**	Po-day^{n} de-vol-vayr-me oo dee-nyay-ee-roo
Here is the receipt	**Aqui está o recibo**	A-kee esh-ta oo re-see-boo

PAYING

How much does that come to?	**Qual é o total da conta?**	Kwal eh oo too-tal da ko^{n}-ta
That will be ...	***O total é ...**	Oo too-tal eh
That's ... escudos, please	***São ... escudos**	Sow^{n} ... esh-koo-doosh
They are ... escudos each	***São ... escudos cada**	Sow^{n} ... esh-koo-doosh ka-da
Will you take English/American/South African currency?	**Aceitam dinheiro inglês/americano/sul-africano?**	A-say-ee-tow^{n} dee-nyay-ee-roo ee^{n}-glaysh/a-me-ree-ka-noo/sool-a-free-ka-noo
Do you take travellers' cheques?	**Aceitam cheques de viagem?**	A-say-ee-tow^{n} she-ksh de vee-a-zhay^{n}
Do I have to pay VAT?	**Tenho que pagar IVA?**	Tay^{n}-nyoo ke pa-gar ee-va
Please pay the cashier	***Pague na caixa, por favor**	Pa-ge na ka-ee-sha poor fa-vor
May I have a receipt, please	**Passe-me um recibo, por favor**	Pa-se-me oo^{n} re-see-boo poor fa-vor
You've given me the wrong change	**O troco não está certo**	Oo tro-koo now^{n} esh-ta ser-too

CHEMIST[1]

English	Portuguese	Pronunciation
Can you prepare this prescription for me, please?	**Pode aviar-me esta receita, por favor?**	Po-de a-vee-**ar**-me **esh**-ta re-**say**-ee-ta poor fa-**vor**
Have you a small first-aid kit?	**Tem um estojo de primeiros socorros?**	Tay^{n} oo^{n} esh-**to**-zho de pree-**may**-ee-roosh soo-**ko**-roosh
A bottle of aspirin, please	**Um tubo de aspirinas, por favor**	Oo^{n} **too**-boo de ash-pee-**ree**-nash poor fa-**vor**
I want	**Quero**	**Ke**-roo
a mosquito repellant	**algo contra os mosquitos**	**al**-goo **ko**^{n}-tra oosh moosh-**kee**-toosh
an antiseptic cream	**creme antiséptico**	krem a^{n}-tee-**se**-tee-koo
a disinfectant	**desinfectante**	de-see^{n}-fe-**tant**
a mouthwash	**antiséptico para a boca**	a^{n}-tee-**se**-tee-koo **pa**-ra a **bo**-ka
some nose drops	**pingos para o nariz**	**pee**^{n}-goosh **pa**-ra oo na-**reesh**
throat lozenges	**pastilhas para a garganta**	pash-**tee**-**llyash** **pa**-ra a gar-**ga**^{n}-ta
I need something for a hangover/travel sickness	**Preciso de algo para indisposição/enjôo**	Pre-**see**-zoo de **al**-goo **pa**-ra ee^{n}-deesh-poo-zee-**sow**^{n}/ay^{n}-**zho**-oo

1. See also AT THE DOCTOR'S (p. 168).

Can you give me something for constipation?	**Pode dar-me algum remédio para prisão de ventre?**	Po-de **dar**-me al-**goo**^{n} re-**me**-dee-oo **pa**-ra pree-**sow**^{n} de **vay**^{n}-tre
diarrhoea?	**soltura/diarreia?**	sol-**too**-ra/dee-a-**ray**-ee-a
indigestion?	**indigestão?**	ee^n-dee-ges-**tow**^{n}
Do you sell contraceptives?	**Vende contraceptivos?**	**Vay**^{n}-de ko^n-tra-se-**tee**-voosh
cotton wool?	**algodão em rama?**	al-goo-**dow**^{n} ay^n **ra**-ma
sanitary towels?	**pensos higiénicos?**	pe^n-soosh ee-zhee-e-**nee**-kosh
tampons?	**tampões?**	ta^n-**poy**^{n}**sh**
I need a doctor	**Preciso dum médico**	Pre-**see**-zoo de oo^n **me**-dee-koo

TOILET ARTICLES

A packet of razor blades, please	**Um pacote de lâminas de barbear, por favor**	Oo^n pa-**kot** de **la**-mee-nash de bar-bee-**ar** poor fa-**vor**
How much is this after-shave lotion?	**Quanto custa esta loção de barba?**	**Kwa**^{n}-too **koosh**-ta **esh**-ta loo-**sow**^{n} de **bar**-ba
A tube of toothpaste	**Um tubo de pasta para os dentes**	Oo^n **too**-boo de **pash**-ta **pa**-ra oosh **day**^{n}-tesh
A box of paper handkerchiefs	**Uma caixa de lenços de papel**	Oo-ma **ka**-ee-sha de **lay**^{n}-soosh de pa-**pel**
Toilet paper	**Papel higiénico**	Pa-**pel** ee-zhee-e-**nee**-koo

English	Portuguese	Pronunciation
I want some eau-de-cologne/perfume[1]	**Quero um frasco de água de colónia/perfume**	Oo^{n} **frash**-koo de a-gwa de koo-lo-nee-a/per-foom
May I try it?	**Posso experimentar?**	Po-soo esh-pe-ree-may^{n}-**tar**
A shampoo for dry/greasy hair	**Um shampô para cabelo seco/oleoso**	Oo^{n} **sha**^{n}-po **pa**-ra ka-**bay**-loo **say**-koo/o-lee-**o**-zoo
I'd like some	**Queria**	Ke-**ree**-a
cleansing cream/lotion	**creme de limpeza/loção**	krem de lee^{n}-**pay**-za/loo-**sow**^{n}
hair conditioner	**fixador de cabelo**	feek-sa-**dor** de ka-**bay**-loo
hand cream	**creme para as mãos**	krem **pa**-ra ash mow^{n}sh
lipsalve	**creme para os lábios**	krem **pa**-ra oosh la-bee-oosh
moisturizer	**creme hidratante**	krem ee-dra-**ta**^{n}t

CLOTHES AND SHOES[2]

English	Portuguese	Pronunciation
I want a hat/sunhat	**Quero um chapéu/chapéu de sol**	**Ke**-roo oo^{n} sha-**pe**-oo/sha-**pe**-oo de sol
I'd like a pair of cotton gloves/leather gloves	**Desejava um par de luvas de algodão/de pele**	De-ze-**zha**-va oo^{n} par de **loo**-vash de al-goo-**dow**^{n}/de pel
Where are beach clothes?	**Onde está a roupa de praia?**	O^{n}-de esh-**tah** a **ro**-pa de **pray**-a

1. In Portugal you can buy loose perfume or eau-de-cologne if you take your own bottle. This is called **perfume hágua de colónia avulso.**
2. For sizes see p. 121.

Where can I find socks/stockings?	**Onde posso comprar meias/peúgas?**	O^n-de **po**-soo ko^n-**prar may**-ee-ash/pee-**oo**-gash
I am looking for	**Estou à procura**	Esh-**to** ah pro-**koo**-ra
a blouse	**duma blusa**	**doo**-ma **bloo**-za
a bra	**dum soutien**	doo^n soo-tee-**a**^{n}
a dress	**dum vestido**	doo^n vesh-**tee**-doo
a sweater	**dum pulover**	doo^n pool-**o**-ver
I need a coat/raincoat	**Preciso dum casaco/gabardine**	Pre-**see**-zo de oo^n ka-**za**-koo/ga-**bar**-deen
I want a short-/long-sleeved shirt, collar size ...	**Quero uma camisa de manga curta/ comprida, medida de colarinho ...**	**Ke**-roo **oo**-ma ka-**mee**-za de **ma**^{n}-ga **koor**-ta/ ko^n-**pree**-da me-**dee**-da de koo-la-**ree**-nyoo
Do you sell	**Vende**	**Vay**^{n}-de
buttons?	**botões?**	boo-**toy**^{n}**sh**
elastics?	**elástico?**	ee-**lash**-tee-koo
zips?	**fechos éclair?**	fe-shoosh **ay-klair**
I need a pair of	**Quero um par de**	**Ke**-roo oo^n par de
walking shoes	**sapatos confortáveis**	sa-**pa**-toosh ko^n-foor-**ta**-vay-eesh
sandals	**sandálias**	sa^n-**da**-lee-ash
black shoes with flat heels	**sapatos pretos de tacão raso**	sa-**pa**-toosh **pray**-toosh de ta-**kow**^{n} **ra**-zoo
These heels are too high/too low	**Este tacão é demasiado alto/ baixo**	Aysht ta-**kow**^{n} eh de-ma-zee-a-doo **al**-too/ **ba**-ee-shoo
This doesn't fit	**Isto não me serve**	**Eesh**-too now^n me **ser**-ve
I don't know the size	**Não sei a medida portuguesa**	Now^n **say**-ee a me-**dee**-da poor-too-**gay**-za
Can you measure me?	**Pode tirar-me as medidas?**	**Po**-de tee-**rar**-me ash me-**dee**-dash

t's for a 3-year-old	**É para uma criança de três anos**	Eh pa-ra oo-ma kree-a^{n}-sa de traysh a-noosh

CLOTHING SIZES[1]

VOMEN'S DRESSES, ETC.

merican	8	10	12	14	16	18
ritish	10	12	14	16	18	20
ontinental	30	32	34	36	38	40

MEN'S SUITS

ritish and American	36	38	40	42	44	46
ontinental	46	48	50	52	54	56

WAIST, CHEST/BUST AND HIPS

nches	28	30	32	34	36	38	40
entimetres	71	76	81	87	92	97	102
nches	42	44	46	48	50	52	54
entimetres	107	112	117	122	127	132	137

MEN'S SHIRTS

British and American	14	14½	15	15½	16	16½	17
Continental	36	37	38	39	41	42	43

. This table is only intended as a rough guide since sizes vary from manufacturer to nanufacturer.

STOCKINGS

British and American	8	8½	9	9½	10	10½	11
Continental	0	1	2	3	4	5	6

SOCKS

British and American	9½	10	10½	11	11½
Continental	38–39	39–40	40–41	41–42	42–43

SHOES

British	1	2	3	4	5	6	7	8	9	10	11	12
American	2½	3½	4½	5½	6½	7½	8½	9½	10½	11½	12½	13½
Continental	33	34–5	36	37	38	39–40	41	42	43	44	45	46

FOOD[1]

Give me a kilo/half a kilo of ..., please	**Um quilo (kilo)/meio quilo de ..., por favor**	Ooⁿ kee-loo/may-ee-oo kee-loo de ... poor fa-vor
100 grammes of sweets/chocolates	**Cem gramas de rebuçados/bombons, por favor**	Sayⁿ gra-mash de re-boo-sa-doosh/boⁿ-boⁿsh poor fa-vor
A bottle/litre of milk/wine/beer	**Uma garrafa/um litro de leite/vinho/cerveja**	Oo-ma ga-ra-fa/ooⁿ lee-troo de lay-eet/vee-nyoo

1. See also the various MENU sections (pp. 96-105) and WEIGHTS AND MEASURES (p. 192).

Is there anything back on the bottle?	**Devolvem algum dinheiro pela garrafa?**	De-vol-vay^n al-goo^n dee-nyay-ee-roo pay-la ga-ra-fa
I want a jar/can/packet of ...	**Quero um boião/uma lata/um pacote de ...**	Ke-roo oo^n bo-ee-ow^n/oo-ma la-ta/oo^n pa-kot de
... slices of ham please	**... fatias de fiambre por favor**	... fa-tee-ash de fee-a^n-bre poor fa-vor
Is it fresh or frozen?	**É fresco ou congelado?**	Eh fraysh-koo oh ko^n-zhe-la-doo
Do you sell frozen foods?	**Vende alimentos congelados?**	Vay^n-de a-lee-may^n-toosh ko^n-zhe-la-doosh
These pears are very hard/soft	**Estas peras estão muito duras/maduras**	Esh-tash pay-rash esh-tow^n moo-ee-too doo-rash/ma-doo-rash
Is it fresh?	**É fresco?**	Eh fraysh-koo
Are they ripe?	**Estão maduros?**	Esh-tow^n ma-doo-roosh
This is bad	**Isto não está bom**	Eesh-too now^n esh-ta bo^n
A loaf of bread, please[1]	**Um pão, por favor**	Oo^n pow^n poor fa-vor
How much a kilo/a bottle?	**Quanto custa um quilo/uma garrafa?**	Kwa^n-too koosh-ta oo^n kee-loo/oo-ma ga-ra-fa
Will you mince it?	**Pode picar a carne?**	Po-de pee-kar a karn
Will you bone it?	**Pode tirar os ossos?**	Po-de tee-rar oosh o-soosh
Will you clean the fish?	**Pode limpar o peixe?**	Po-de lee^n-par oo pay-ee-she

1. Portuguese bread: **um pão de quilo (meio quilo)** – a loaf weighing 1 kilo (½ kilo); **pãezinhos** – rolls; **um pão de forma** – English loaf; **pão de centeio** – rye bread; **broa** – maize bread.

Leave/take off the head	**Deixe/tire a cabeça**	Day-ee-she/tee-re a ka-bay-sa
Please fillet the fish	**Corte o peixe em fatías**	Kor-te oo pay-ee-she ay^n fa-tee-ash
Is there any shellfish?	**Tem alguns mariscos?**	Tay^n al-goo^{n}sh ma-reesh-koosh
Shall I help myself?	**Posso servir-me?**	Po-soo ser-veer-me

HAIRDRESSER AND BARBER

May I make an appointment for this morning/tomorrow afternoon?	**Posso marcar hora para esta manhã/para amanhã à tarde?**	Po-soo mar-kar o-ra pa-ra esh-ta ma-nya^n/pa-ra a-ma-nya^n ah tard
What time?	**A que horas?**	A ke o-rash
I want my hair cut/trimmed	**Quero o meu cabelo cortado/aparado**	Ke-roo oo may-oo ka-bay-loo koor-ta-doo/a-pa-ra-doo
No shorter	**Não quero mais curto**	Now^n ke-roo ma-eesh koor-too
Not too short at the sides	**Não demasiado curto dos lados**	Now^n de-ma-zee-a-doo koor-too doosh la-doosh
I'll have it shorter at the back/on top	**Mais curto atrás/em cima**	Ma-eesh koor-too a-trash hay^n see-ma
I want a shampoo	**Quero que me lavem a cabeça**	Ke-roo ke me la-vay^n a ka-bay-sa
Please use conditioner	**Por favor use o creme amaciador**	Poor fa-vor oo-se oo krem a-ma-see-a-dor

I want my hair washed and set	**Quero que me lavem o cabelo e façam uma mise**	Ke-roo ke me la-vay^{n} oo ka-bay-loo ee fa-sow^{n} oo-ma mee-ze
I want a blow dry	**Quero um 'brushing'**	Ke-roo oo^{n} bra-shee^{n}g
I want a colour rinse	**Quero uma pintura (ransagem)**	Ke-roo oo-ma pee^{n}-too-ra (ra^{n}-sa-zhay^{n})
I'd like to see a colour chart	**Gostava de ver o catálogo das cores**	Goosh-ta-va de vayr oo ka-ta-loo-goo dash ko-resh
I want a darker/lighter shade	**Quero um tom mais escuro/mais claro**	Ke-roo oo^{n} to^{n} ma-eesh esh-koo-roo/ma-eesh kla-roo
I want my hair tinted/ permed	**Quero fazer uma pintura/uma permanente**	Ke-roo fa-zayr oo-ma pee^{n}-too-ra/oo-ma per-ma-nay^{n}t
The water is too cold	**A água está demasiado fria**	A a-gwa esh-ta de-ma-zee-a-doo free-a
The dryer is too hot	**O secador está demasiado quente**	Oo se-ka-dor esh-ta de-ma-zee-a-doo kay^{n}t
Thank you, I like it very much	**Obrigado, está muito bem**	O-bree-ga-doo esh-ta moo-ee-too bay^{n}
I want a shave/ manicure	**Quero fazer a barba/manicura**	Ke-roo fa-zayr a bar-ba/ma-nee-koo-ra
Please trim my beard/ my moustache	**Pode aparar-me a barba/o bigode?**	Po-de a-pa-rar-me a bar-ba/oo bee-god
That's fine	**Está bem**	Esh-ta bay^{n}

HARDWARE[1]

Where is the camping equipment?	**Onde está o equipamento de campismo?**	O^n-de esh-ta oo ay-kee-pa-may^n-too de ka^n-peezh-moo
Do you have a battery for this?	**Tem uma bateria para isto?**	Tay^n oo-ma ba-te-ree-a pa-ra eesh-too
Where can I get butane gas/paraffin?	**Onde posso obter gás butano/ parafina?**	O^n-de po-soo ob-tayr gash boo-ta-noo/pa-ra-fee-na
I need a	**Preciso dum**	Pre-see-zoo doo^n
bottle-opener	**abre-garrafas**	a-bre-ga-ra-fash
tin-opener	**abre-latas**	a-bre-la-tash
corkscrew	**saca-rôlhas**	sa-ka-ro-llyash
I'd like some candles/ matches	**Preciso de velas/ fósforos**	Pre-see-zoo de ve-lash/ fosh-foo-roosh
I want a	**Preciso**	Pre-see-zoo
flashlight	**duma lanterna**	doo-ma la^n-ter-na
(pen) knife	**dum canivete**	doo^n ka-nee-vet
pair of scissors	**duma tesoura**	doo-ma te-zo-ra
Do you sell string/ rope?	**Vende cordel/corda?**	Vay^n-de koor-del/kor-da
Where can I find washing-up liquid/ scouring powder?	**Onde posso encontrar líquido para lavar louça/ pó de arear?**	On^n-de po-soo ay^n-ko^n-trar lee-ke-doo pa-ra la-var loh-sa/po de a-ree-ar
Do you have dishcloths/a brush?	**Tem panos de cozinha/escôva?**	Tay^n pa-noosh de koo-zee-nya/esh-ko-va

1. See also CAMPING (p. 63) and RENTING OR OWNING A PLACE (p. 68).

I need a bucket/frying pan	**Preciso dum balde/ frigideira**	Pre-**see**-zoo doo^n **bal**-de/free-zhee-**day**-ee-ra
I want to buy a barbecue	**Quero comprar uma grelha/churrasco**	**Ke**-roo ko^n-**prar oo**-ma **gre**-llya/shoo-**rash**-koo
Do you sell charcoal?	**Vende carvão?**	**Vay^n**-de kar-**vow^n**
adaptor	**o adaptador**	a-dap-ta-**dor**
basket	**o cesto**	**saysh**-too
duster	**o espanador/pano do pó**	esh-pa-na-**dor/pa**-noo doo po
electrical flex	**o fio eléctrico**	**fee**-oo ee-**le**-tree-koo
extension lead	**o fio de extensão/ derivador**	**fee**-oo de esh-tay^n-**sow^n**/ de-ree-va-**dor**
fuse	**o fusível**	foo-**zee**-vel
fuse wire	**o fio de fusível**	**fee**-oo de foo-**zee**-vel
insulating tape	**o fio isolador**	**fee**-oo ee-zoo-la-**dor**
lightbulb	**a lâmpada eléctrica**	**la^n**-pa-da ee-**le**-tree-ka
penknife	**o canivete**	ka-nee-**vet**
plug (bath)	**o tampão**	ta^n-**pow^n**
plug (electrical)	**a tomada/ficha eléctrica**	too-**ma**-da/**fee**-sha ee-**le**-tree-ka

LAUNDRY AND DRY CLEANING

Where is the nearest launderette?	**Onde é a lavandaria mais próxima?**	**O^n**-de eh a la-va^n-da-**ree**-a **ma**-eesh **pro**-see-ma
I want to have this washed/cleaned	**Quero isto lavado/ limpo**	**Ke**-roo **eesh**-too la-**va**-doo/**lee^n**-poo

Can you get this stain out?	**Pode tirar esta nódoa?**	Po-de tee-rar esh-ta no-doo-a
It is	**É**	Eh
coffee	**café**	ka-fe
wine	**vinho**	vee-nyoo
grease	**gordura**	goor-doo-ra
These stains won't come out	***Estas nódoas não saiem**	Esh-tash no-doo-ash now^n sy-e^n
It only needs to be pressed	**Só falta passar**	So fal-ta pa-sar
This is torn; can you mend it?	**Isto está roto; podem cosê-lo?**	Eesh-too esh-ta ro-too; po-day^n koo-zay-loo
There's a button missing	**Falta um botão**	Fal-ta oo^n boo-tow^n
Will you sew on another one, please?	**Podem pôr-me outro, por favor?**	Po-day^n por-me o-troo poor fa-vor
When will it be ready?	**Quando estará pronto?**	Kwa^n-doo esh-ta-ra pro^n-too
I need them by this evening/tomorrow	**Necessito para esta noite/para amanhã**	Ne-se-see-too pa-ra esh-ta no-eet/pa-ra a-ma-nya^n
Call back at 5 o'clock	***Volte às cinco horas**	Vol-te ash see^n-koo o-rash
We can't do it before Thursday	***Não podemos fazê-lo antes de quinta-feira**	Now^n poo-day-moosh fa-zay-loo a^n-tesh de kee^n-ta-fay-ee-ra
It will take three days	***Estará pronto dentro de três dias**	Esh-ta-ra pro^n-too day^n-troo de traysh dee-ash
This isn't mine	**Isto não é meu**	Eesh-too now^n eh may-oo

I've lost my ticket	**Perdi o talão**	Per-dee oo ta-**low**^{n}

HOUSEHOLD LAUNDRY

bath towel	**a toalha de banho**	too-**a**-llya de **ba**-nyoo
blanket	**o cobertor**	koo-ber-**tor**
napkin	**o guardanapo**	gwar-da-**na**-poo
pillow case	**a fronha**	**fro**-nya
sheet	**o lençol**	lay^{n}-**sol**
table cloth	**a toalha de mesa**	too-**a**-llya de **may**-za
tea towel	**o pano de secar a louça**	**pa**-noo de se-**kar** a **loh**-sa

NEWSPAPERS, BOOKS AND WRITING MATERIALS

Do you sell English/American/South African newspapers?	**Vendem jornais ingleses/americanos/sul africanos?**	**Vay**^{n}-day^{n} zhoor-**na**-eesh ee^{n}-**glay**-zesh/a-me-ree-**ka**-noosh/sool a-free-**ka**-noosh
Can you get ... newspaper/magazine for me?	**Podem arranjar-me o jornal .../a revista ...?**	**Po**-day^{n} a-ra^{n}-**zhar**-me oo zhoor-**nal** a re-**veesh**-ta
I want a map of the city/a road map	**Quero um mapa da cidade/um mapa da estrada**	**Ke**-roo oo^{n} **ma**-pa da see-**dad**/oo^{n} **ma**-pa da esh-**tra**-da
Is there an entertainment/amusements guide?	**Tem um guia dos espectáculos/divertimentos?**	Tay^{n} oo^{n} **gee**-a doosh esh-pe-ta-**koo**-loosh/dee-ver-tee-**may**^{n}t-oosh

Do you have any English books?	**Tem livros ingleses?**	Tay^n **lee**-vroosh ee^n-**glay**-zesh
Have you any books by ...?	**Tem algum livro de ...?**	Tay^n al-**goo^n** **lee**-vroo de
I want some	**Quero**	**Ke**-roo
colour postcards	**postais coloridos**	**poosh-ta-eesh koo-loo-ree-doosh**
black and white postcards	**postais a preto e branco**	**poosh-ta-eesh** a **pray**-too ee **bra^n**-koo
plain postcards	**postais de correio**	**poosh-ta-eesh** de koo-**ray-ee-oo**
Do you sell souvenirs/toys?	**Vende lembranças/ brinquedos?**	**Vay^n**-de lay^n-**bra^n**-sash/ bree^n-**kay**-doosh
calculator	**calculador**	kal-koo-la-**dor**
card	**cartão**	kar-**tow^n**
dictionary	**dicionário**	dee-see-oo-**na**-ree-oo
drawing paper	**papel de desenho**	pa-**pel** de de-**say**-nyoo
felt-tip pen	**caneta de ponta de feltro**	ka-**nay**-ta de **po^n**-ta de **fel**-troo
guide book	**guia**	**gee**-a
notebook	**caderno de notas**	ka-**der**-noo de **no**-tash
paperclip	**agrafo**	a-**gra**-foo
pen	**caneta**	ka-**nay**-ta
pen cartridge	**cápsula de caneta**	**kap**-soo-la de ka-**nay**-ta
pencil sharpener	**aparador de lápis**	a-pa-ra-**dor** de **la**-peesh
rubber	**borracha de apagar**	boo-**ra**-sha de a-pa-**gar**
sellotape	**fita adesiva**	**fee**-ta a-de-**zee**-va

OPTICIAN

I have broken my glasses; can you repair them?	**Parti os óculos; pode rcpará-los?**	Par-**tee** oosh **o**-koo-loosh; **po**-de re-pa-**ra**-loosh
Can you give me a new pair of glasses with the same prescription?	**Pode arranjar-me um novo par de óculos coma mesma receita?**	**Po**-de ar-ra^n-**zhar**-me oo^n **no**-voo par de **o**-koo-loosh ko^n a **mezh**-ma re-**say**-ee-ta
I have difficulty in reading	**Tenho dificuldade em ler**	**Te**^{n}-nyoo dee-fee-kool-**dad** ay^n ler
Please test my eyes	**Por favor faça-me um exame à vista**	Por fa-**vor** **fa**-sa-me oo^n ee-**za**-me ah **veesh**-ta
I have lost one of my contact lenses	**Perdi uma das lentes de contacto**	Per-**dee** **oo**-ma dash **le**^{n}-tesh de ko^n-**tak**-too
I should like to have contact lenses	**Queria lentes de contacto**	Ke-**ree**-a **le**^{n}-tesh de ko^n-**tak**-too
I am short-sighted	**Sou míope**	Soo **mee**-oop
I am long-sighted	**Não vejo bem ao longe**	Now^n **ve**-zhoo bay^n **a-oo** **lon**-zhe

PHOTOGRAPHY

I want to buy a camera	**Quero comprar uma máquina**	**Ke**-roo ko^n-**prar** **oo**-ma **ma**-kee-na
Have you a film/ cartridge for this camera?	**Tem um rolo/carga para esta máquina?**	Tay^n oo^n **ro**-lo/**kar**-ga **pa**-ra **esh**-ta **ma**-kee-na

A 100/400/1000 ASA film please	**Um filme ASA 100/ 400/1000 por favor**	Oo^n feelm a-sa say^n/ kwa-troo-se^n-toosh/ meel poor fa-vor
What is the fastest film you have?	**Qual é o filme mais rápido que tem?**	Kwal eh oo feelm ma-eesh ra-pee-doo ke tay^n
Film for slides/prints	**Filme para slides/ fotos**	Feelm pa-ra sly-desh/ fo-toosh
Give me a 35 mm. colour film with 24/36 exposures	**Um rolo de cor de trinta e cinco milímetros e de vinte e quatro/ trinta e seis fotos**	Oo^n ro-loo de kor de tree^n-ta ee see^n-koo mee-lee-me-troosh ee de vee^{n}t ee kwa-troo/ tree^n-ta ee saysh fo-toosh
Would you fit the film in the camera for me, please?	**Podia fazer o favor de meter o rolo na máquina?**	Poo-dee-a fa-zayr oo fa-vor de me-tayr oo ro-loo na ma-kee-na
Does the price include processing?	**A revelação está incluída no preço?**	A re-ve-la-sow^n esh-ta ee^n-kloo-ee-da noo pray-soo
I'd like this film developed and printed	**Quero revelação e cópias deste rolo**	Ke-roo re-ve-la-sow^n ee ko-pee-ash daysht ro-loo
Can I have ... prints/ enlargements of this negative?	**Posso obter ... fotos/ampliações deste negativo?**	Po-soo ob-tayr fo-toosh/a^n-plee-a-soy^{n}sh daysht ne-ga-tee-voo
When will it be ready?	**Quando estará pronto?**	Kwa^n-doo esh-ta-ra pro^n-too
Will it be done tomorrow?	**Estará pronto amanhã?**	Esh-ta-ra pro^n-too a-ma-nya^n
Will it be ready by ...?	**Pode estar pronto para ...?**	Po-de esh-tar pro^n-too pa-ra

My camera's not working, can you check it/mend it?	**A minha máquina não funciona, podem vê-la/ consertá-la?**	A mee-nya ma-kee-na now^{n} foo^{n}-see-o-na po-day^{n} vay-la/ko^{n}-ser-ta-la
The film is jammed	**O rolo não passa**	Oo ro-loo now^{n} pa-sa
There is something wrong with the	**Está qualquer coisa avariada com este**	Esh-ta kwal-ker ko-ee-za a-va-ree-a-da ko^{n} aysht
flash	**'flash'**	flash
film winder	**carreto**	ka-re-too
light meter	**medidor de luz**	me-dee-dor de loozh
shutter	**shutter**	sha-tar
battery	**bateria**	ba-te-ree-a
cine film	**filme de cinema**	feelm de see-nay-ma
filter	**filtro**	feel-troo
lens	**lente**	lay^{n}t
lens cap	**capa das lentes**	ka-pa dash lay^{n}-tesh
video camera	**camara de vídeo**	ka-ma-ra de vee-dee-oo

RECORDS AND CASSETTES

Do you have any records/cassettes of local music?	**Tem alguns discos/ cassetes de música local?**	Tay^{n} al-goo^{n}sh deesh-koosh/ka-se-tesh de moo-zee-ka loo-kal
Are there any new records by ...?	**Tem alguns discos novos por ...?**	Tay^{n} al-goo^{n}sh deesh-koosh no-voosh poor
Do you sell compact discs?	**Vende discos compactos?**	Vay^{n}-de deesh-koosh ko^{n}-pak-toosh
Do you sell video cassettes?	**Vende video cassetes?**	Vay^{n}-de vee-dee-oo ka-se-tesh

TOBACCONIST[1]

English	Portuguese	Pronunciation
Do you stock English/American/South African cigarettes?	**Tem cigarros ingleses/americanos/sul africanos?**	Tay^n see-**ga**-roosh ee^n-**glay**-zesh/a-me-ree-**ka**-noosh/sool a-free-**ka**-noosh
Virginia/dark tobacco	**Tabaco amarelo/negro (preto)**	Ta-**ba**-koo a-ma-**re**-loo/**nay**-groo (**pray**-too)
I want some filter-tip cigarettes	**Um maço de cigarros com filtro**	Oo^n **ma**-soo de see-**ga**-roosh ko^n **feel**-troo
cigarettes without filter	**cigarros sem filtro**	see-**ga**-roosh se^n **feel**-troo
menthol cigarettes	**cigarros mentolados**	see-**ga**-roosh may^n-too-**la**-doosh
A box of matches, please	**Uma caixa de fósforos, por favor**	**Oo**-ma **ka**-ee-sha de **fosh**-foo-roosh poor fa-**vor**
Do you have cigarette papers/pipe cleaners?	**Tem papel para cigarros/limpadores de cachimbo?**	Tay^n pa-**pel** **pa**-ra see-**ga**-roosh/lee^n-pa-**do**-resh de ka-**shee**^{n}-boosh
I want to buy a lighter	**Quero comprar um isqueiro**	**Ke**-roo ko^n-**prar** oo^n eesh-**kay**-ee-roo
Do you sell lighter fuel?	**Tem gasolina para o isqueiro?**	Tay^n ga-zoo-**lee**-na **pa**-ra oo eesh-**kay**-ee-roo

1. Tobacconists often sell postage stamps.

I want a gas refill for this lighter	**Quero uma recarga de gás para este isqueiro**	**Ke**-roo oo-ma re-**kar**-ga de gash pa-ra aysht eesh-**kay**-ee-roo

REPAIRS

This is broken; could somebody mend it?	**Isto está partido; há alguém que possa arranjar?**	**Eesh**-too esh-**ta** par-**tee**-doo ah al-**ge^n** ke **po**-sa a-ra^n-**zhar**
Could you do it while I wait?	**Pode arranjar enquanto eu espero?**	**Po**-de a-ra^n-**zhar** ay^n-**kwa^n**-too **ay**-oo esh-**pe**-roo
When should I come back for it?	**Quando posso voltar para vir buscá-lo/a?**	**Kwa^n**-doo **po**-soo vol-**tar** **pa**-ra veer boosh-**ka**-loo/la
I want these shoes soled (in leather)	**Quero meias-solas nestes sapatos (em cabedal)**	**Ke**-roo **may**-ee-ash-**so**-lash **naysh**-tesh sa-**pa**-toosh (ay^n ka-be-**dal**)
I want these shoes heeled (with rubber)	**Quero tacões nestes sapatos (em borracha)**	**Ke**-roo ta-**koy^{n}sh** **naysh**-tesh sa-**pa**-toosh (ay^n boo-**ra**-sha)
Can you repair this watch?	**Pode reparar-me este relógio?**	**Po**-de re-pa-**rar**-me aysht re-**lozh**-ee-oo
I have broken the	**Parti**	**Par**-tee
glass	**o vidro**	oo **vee**-droo
strap	**a correia**	a koo-**ray**-ee-a
spring	**a corda**	a **kor**-da
I have broken my glasses/the arm	**Parti os óculos/a haste**	**Par**-tee oosh **o**-koo-loosh/a **ash**-te

How much would a new one cost?	**Quanto custaria um novo?**	Kwa^n-too koosh-ta-ree-a oo^n no-voo
The stone/charm/ screw has come loose	**A pedra/amuleto/ parafuso está solto (solta)**	A pe-dra/a-moo-lay-too/pa-ra-foo-zoo esh-ta sol-too (sol-ta)
The fastener/clip/ chain is broken	**O fecho/mola/ colar/cadeia está partido (partida)**	Oo fay-shoo/mo-la/koo-lar/ka-day-ee-a esh-ta par-tee-doo (par-tee-da)
How much will it cost?	**Quanto custa?**	Kwa^n-too koosh-ta
It can't be repaired	***Não tem arranjo/ conserto**	Now^n tay^n a-ra^n-zhoo/ ko^n-sayr-too
You need a new one	***Necessita um novo/uma nova**	Ne-se-see-ta oo^n no-voo/oo-ma no-va

POST OFFICE

Where's the main post office?	**Onde é a estação principal dos correios?**	O^{n}-de eh a esh-ta-sow^{n} pree^{n}-see-pal doosh koo-ray-ee-oosh
Where's the nearest post office?	**Onde é a estação de correios mais próxima?**	O^{n}-de eh a esh-ta-swo^{n} de koo-ray-ee-oosh ma-eesh pro-see-ma
What time does the post office open/close?	**A que horas abrem/fecham os correios?**	A ke o-rash a-bray^{n}/fay-ee-show^{n} oosh koo-ray-ee-oosh
Where's the post box?	**Onde há um marco de correio?**	O^{n}-de ah oo^{n} mar-koo de koo-ray-ee-oo
Which counter do I go to for	**Qual é o balcão para**	Kwal eh oo bal-kow^{n} pa-ra
stamps?	**selos?**	say-loosh
telegrams?	**telegramas?**	te-le-gra-mash
money orders?	**vales de correio?**	va-lesh de koo-ray-ee-oo

LETTERS AND TELEGRAMS[1]

How much is a postcard to England?	**Que franquia levam os postais para Inglaterra?**	Ke fra^{n}-kee-a le-vow^{n} oosh poosh-ta-eesh pa-ra ee^{n}-gla-te-ra
What's the airmail rate for letters to the U.S.A.?	**Que franquia levam as cartas por avião para os Estados Unidos da América?**	Ke fra^{n}-kee-a le-vow^{n} ash kar-tash poor a-vee-ow^{n} pa-ra oosh esh-ta-doosh oo-nee-doosh da a-me-ree-ka
How much is it to send a letter surface mail?[2]	**Que franquia levam as cartas por correio ordinário?**	Ke fra^{n}-kee-a le-vow^{n} ash kar-tash poor koo-ray-ee-oo or-dee-na-ree-oo
It's inland	**É para Portugal**	Eh pa-ra por-too-gal
Give me three 10$00 and five 20$00 stamps, please	**Dê-me três selos de dez escudos e cinco de vinte escudos, por favor**	Day-me traysh say-loosh de desh es-koo-doosh ee see^{n}-koo de vee^{n}t esh-koo-doosh poor fa-vor
I want to send this letter express	**Quero mandar esta carta expresso**	Ke-roo ma^{n}-dar esh-ta kar-ta esh-pre-soo
I want to register this letter	**Quero registar esta carta**	Ke-roo re-zheesh-tar esh-ta kar-ta
I want to send a parcel	**Quero mandar uma encomenda postal**	Ke-roo ma^{n}-dar oo-ma ay^{n}-koo-may^{n}-da poosh-tal

1. You can buy stamps from a tobacconist's as well as from a post office.
2. All letters within the EEC go air mail.

Where is the poste restante section?	**Onde é a secção de posta restante?**	O^{n}-de eh a **sek-sow^{n}** de **posh**-ta resh-**ta^{n}t**
Are there any letters for me?	**Há alguma carta para mim?**	Ah al-**goo**-ma **kar**-ta **pa**-ra mee^{n}
What is your name?	***Qual é o seu nome?**	Kwal eh oo **say**-oo **no**-me
Have you any means of identification?	***Tem algum documento de identificação?**	Tay^{n} al-**goo^{n}** doo-koo-**may^{n}**-too de ee-day^{n}-tee-fee-ka-**sow^{n}**
Can I send a telex?	**Posso mandar um telex?**	**Po**-soo ma^{n}-**dar** oo^{n} te-**leks**
I want to send a (reply paid) telegram	**Quero mandar um telegrama (com resposta paga)**	**Ke**-roo ma^{n}-**dar** oo^{n} te-le-**gra**-ma (ko^{n} resh-**posh**-ta **pa**-ga)
How much does it cost per word?	**Quanto custa por palavra?**	**Kwa^{n}**-too **koosh**-ta poor pa-**la**-vra

TELEPHONING[1]

Where's the nearest phone box?	**Onde é a cabine telefónica mais próxima?**	O^{n}-de eh a ka-**been** te-le-fo-**nee**-ka **ma**-eesh **pro**-see-ma
May I use your phone?	**Posso usar o telefone?**	**Po**-soo oo-**zar** oo te-le-**fon**
Do you have a telephone directory for ...?	**Tem uma lista telefónica de ...?**	Tay^{n} **oo**-ma **leesh**-ta te-le-fo-**nee**-ka de

1. Telephone boxes are rare, but you can telephone from most cafés and bars which are equipped with time meters. Pay phones occasionally operate on special tokens (**fichas**) rather than on coins.

Please give me a token	Uma ficha, por favor	Oo-ma fee-sha poor fa-vor
Please get me Lisbon ...	Quero uma chamada para o ... de Lisboa	Ke-roo oo-ma sha-ma-da pa-ra oo ... de leezh-bo-a
What do I dial to get the international operator?[1]	Qual é o número do operador internacional?	Kwal eh oo noo-me-roo do o-pe-ra-dor ee^{n}-ter-na-see-oo-nal
I want to telephone to England	Quero telefonar para Inglaterra	Ke-roo te-le-foo-nar pa-ra ee^{n}-gla-te-ra
What is the code for ...?	Qual é o código para ...?	Kwal eh oo ko-dee-goo pa-ra
I want to place a personal (person-to-person) call	Quero fazer uma chamada pessoal para ...	Ke-roo fa-zayr oo-ma sha-ma-da pe-soo-al pa-ra
Could you give me the cost (time and charges) afterwards?	Pode dar-me o custo depois?	Po-de dar-me oo koosh-too de-po-eesh
I was cut off, can you reconnect me?	Fui cortado, pode voltar a ligar-me?	Foo-ee koor-ta-doo po-de vol-tar a lee-gar-me
I want extension ...	Quero a extensão ...	Ke-roo a esh-tay^{n}-sow^{n}
May I speak to Senhor Alves?	Posso falar com o senhor Alves, por favor?	Po-soo fa-lar ko^{n} oo se-nyor al-vesh poor fa-vor
Who's speaking?	Quem fala?	Kay^{n} fa-la
Hold the line	*Não desligue	Now^{n} dezh-lee-ge
Put the receiver down	*Desligue	Dezh-lee-ge

1. International or trunk calls can be made at post offices at considerably cheaper rates than most hotels.

He's not here	*Não está aqui	Now^n esh-ta a-kee
He's at ...	*Está ...	Esh-ta
When will he be back?	A que horas volta?/ Quando voltará?	A ke o-rash vol-ta/ kwa^n-doo vol-ta-ra
Will you take a message?	Faz o favor de dizer-lhe ...?	Fazh oo fa-vor de dee-zayr-llye
Tell him that ... phoned	Diga-lhe que ... telefonou	Dee-ga-llye ke ... te-le-foo-no
I'll ring again later	Telefonarei mais tarde	Te-le-fo-na-ray ma-eesh tard
Please ask him to phone me	Por favor diga-lhe que me telefone	Poor fa-vor dee-ga-llye ke me te-le-fon
What's your number?	*Qual é o seu número?	Kwal eh oo say-oo noo-me-roo
My number is ...	O meu número é ...	Oo may-oo noo-me-roo eh
I can't hear you well	Não o oiço bem	Now^n oo o-ee-soo bay^n
The line is engaged	*Está impedido	Esh-ta ee^n-pe-dee-doo
There's no reply	*Não respondem	Now^n res-po^n-day^n
You have the wrong number	*Enganou-se no número	Ay^n-ga-no-se noo noo-me-roo
The number is out of order	*O número está avariado	Oo noo-me-roo esh-ta a-va-ree-a-doo
Telephone box	Cabine telefónica	Ka-been te-le-fo-nee-ka
Telephone directory	Lista telefónica	Leesh-ta te-le-fo-nee-ka
Telephone number	Número de telefone	Noo-me-roo de te-le-fon
Telephone operator	Telefonista	Te-le-foo-neesh-ta

SIGHTSEEING[1]

Where is the tourist office?	**Onde é o centro de turismo?**	O^{n}-de eh oo **say**^{n}-troo de too-**reezh**-moo
What should we see here?	**O que é que há para ver aqui?**	Oo ke eh ke a **pa**-ra ver a-**kee**
Is there a map/plan of the places to visit?	**Há um mapa/planta dos locais/lugares de interêsse?**	Ah oo^{n} **ma**-pa/**pla**^{n}-ta doosh loo-**ka**-eesh/ loo-**ga**-resh de ee^{n}-te-**ray**-se
I want a guide book	**Quero um livro-guia**	**Ke**-roo oo^{n} **lee**-vroo **gee**-a
Is there a good sightseeing tour?	**Há alguma boa excursão turistícoa?**	Ah al-**goo**-ma **bo**-a esh-koor-sow^{n} too-**reesh**-tee-ka
Does the coach stop at ... hotel?	**O autocarro pára no ... hotel?**	Oo ow-to-**ka**-roo **pah**-ra noo ... o-**tel**

1. See also TRAVEL (p. 15) and DIRECTIONS (p. 32).

Is there an excursion to ...?	**Há uma excursão para ...?**	Ah oo-ma esh-koor-sow^{n} pa-ra
How long does the tour take?	**Quanto tempo leva a excursão?**	Kwa^{n}-too tay^{n}-poo le-va a esh-koor-sow^{n}
Are there guided tours of the museum?	**Há uma visita com guia ao museu?**	Ah oo-ma vee-zee-ta ko^{n} gee-a a-oo moo-zay-oo
Does he speak English?	**Ele fala inglês?**	Ay-le fa-la ee^{n}-glaysh
We don't need a guide	**Nós não precisamos de guia**	Nosh now^{n} pre-see-za-moosh de gee-a
I would prefer to go round alone; is that all right?	**Eu preferia visitar/ir sozinho; é possível?**	Ay-oo pre-fe-ree-a vee-zee-tar/eer so-zee-nyoo; eh poo-see-vel
How much does the tour cost?	**Quanto custa a excursão?**	Kwa^{n}-too koosh-ta a esh-koor-sow^{n}
Are all admission fees included?	**Estão incluídas todas as entradas?**	Esh-tow^{n} ee^{n}-kloo-ee-dash to-dash as ay^{n}-tra-dash
Does it include lunch?	**Está incluído o almoço?**	Esh-ta ee^{n}-kloo-ee-doo oo al-mo-soo

MUSEUMS AND ART GALLERIES

When does the muscum open/close?	**Quando abre/fecha o museu?**	Kwa^{n}-doo a-bre/fay-sha oo moo-zay-oo
Is it open every day?	**Está aberto todos os dias?**	Esh-ta a-ber-too to-doosh oosh dee-ash
The gallery is closed on Mondays	***A galeria está fechada às segundas-feiras**	A ga-le-ree-a esh-ta fe-sha-da ash se-goo^{n}-dash-fay-ee-rash

How much does it cost?	**Quanto custa?**	Kwa^n-too koosh-ta
Are there reductions for	**Há descontos para**	Ah desh-ko^n-toosh pa-ra
children?	**crianças?**	kree-a^n-sash
students?	**estudantes?**	esh-too-da^n-tesh
the elderly?	**pensionistas?**	pay^n-see-oo-neesh-tash
Are admission fees lower on any special day?	**Há bilhetes mais baratos em dias especiais?**	Ah bee-llyay-tesh ma-eesh ba-ra-toosh ay^n dee-ash esh-pe-see-a-eesh
Admission free	***Entrada gratuita**	Ay^n-tra-da gra-too-ee-ta
Have you got a ticket?	***Tem bilhete?**	Tay^n bee-llyayt
Where do I buy a ticket?	**Onde posso comprar bilhete?**	On-de po-soo ko^n-prar bee-llyayt
Please leave your bag in the cloakroom	***Por favor deixe o saco no bengaleiro**	Poor fa-vor day-eesh oo sa-koo noo bay^n-ga-lay-ee-roo
It's over there	***É ali**	Eh a-lee
Where is the ... collection/exhibition?	**Onde é a exposição?**	O^n-de eh a esh-poo-zee-sow^n
Can I take photographs?	**Posso tirar fotografias?**	Po-soo tee-rar foo-too-gra-fee-ash
Can I use a tripod?	**Posso usar um tripé?**	Po-soo oo-zar oo^n tree-pe
Photographs are not allowed	***Não são permitidas fotografias**	Now^n sow^n per-mee-tee-dash foo-too-gra-fee-ash
I want to buy a catalogue	**Quero comprar um catálogo**	Ke-roo ko^n-prar oo^n ka-ta-loo-goo

Will you make photocopies?	**Vai tirar fotocópias?**	Vy tee-rar fo-to-ko-pee-ash
Could you make me a transparency of this painting?	**Pode fazer-me uma transparência deste quadro?**	Po-de fa-zayr-me oo-ma tra^{n}zh-pa-ray^{n}-see-a daysht kwa-droo
How long will it take?	**Quanto tempo demora?**	Kwa^{n}-too tay^{n}-poo de-mo-ra

HISTORICAL SIGHTS

We want to visit ... can we get there by car?	**Nós queremos visitar ... podemos ir lá de carro?**	Nosh ke-ray-moosh vee-zee-tar ... poo-day-moosh eer lah de ka-roo
Is there far to walk?	**Quanto tempo demora a andar?**	Kwa^{n}-too tay^{n}-poo de-mo-ra a a^{n}-dar
Is it an easy walk?	**É fácil ir a pé?**	Eh fa-seel eer a pe
Is there access for wheelchairs?	**Há acesso para uma cadeira de rodas?**	Ah a-se-soo pa-ra oo-ma ka-day-ee-ra de ro-dash
Is it far to the aqueduct? castle? fort? fountain? gate? ruins? walls?	**É longe** **o aqueduto?** **o castelo?** **o forte?** **a fonte?** **o portão?** **as ruínas?** **os muros/as paredes?**	Eh lon-zhe oo a-ke-doo-too oo kash-te-loo oo fort a fo^{n}t oo poor-tow^{n} as roo-ee-nash os moo-roosh/as pa-ray-desh
When was it built?	**Quando foi construído?**	Kwa^{n}-doo fo-ee ko^{n}sh-troo-ee-doo

Who built it?	**Quem construiu?**	Ke^n ko^{n}sh-troo-**yoo**
Where is the old part of the city?	**Onde é a parte velha da cidade?**	O^n-de eh a part **ve**-llya da see-**dad**
What is this building?	**O que é este edifício?**	Oo ke eh aysht ee-dee-**fee**-see-oo
Where is	**Onde é**	O^n-de eh
the ... house?	**a casa ...?**	a **ka**-za
the ... church?	**a igreja ...?**	a ee-**gray**-zha
the ... cemetery?	**o cemitério ...?**	oo se-mee-**te**-ree-oo

GARDENS, PARKS AND ZOOS

Where is the botanical garden/zoo?	**Onde é o jardim botânico/ zoológico?**	O^n-de eh oo zhar-**dee^n** boo-**ta**-nee-koo/zoo-oo-**lozh**-ee-koo
How do I get to the park?	**Como posso ir ao parque?**	**Ko**-moo **po**-soo eer **a-oo** park
Can we walk there?	**Pode-se ir a pé?**	**Po**-de-se eer a **pe**
Can we drive through the park?	**Pode-se guiar através do parque?**	**Po**-de-se gee-**ar** a-tra-**vesh** doo **park**
Are the gardens open to the public?	**Os jardins estão abertos ao público?**	Oosh zhar-**dee^{n}sh** esh-**tow^n** a-**ber**-toosh **a-oo poo**-blee-koo
What time does the garden close?	**A que horas fecham?**	A ke **o**-rash fay-ee-**show^n**
Is there a plan of the gardens?	**Há uma planta do jardim?**	Ah **oo**-ma **pla^n**-ta do zhar-**dee^n**
Who designed the gardens?	**Quem criou os jardins?**	**Kay^n** kree-**oh** oosh zhar-**dee^{n}sh**

Where is the tropical plant house/lake?	**Onde é a estufa de plantas tropicais/o lago?**	O^n-de eh a esh-**too**-fa de **pla^n**-tash troo-pee-**ka**-eesh/oo **la**-goo

EXPLORING

I'd like to walk round the old town	**Gostava de dar uma volta pela cidade velha**	Goosh-**ta**-va de dar **oo**-ma **vol**-ta **pay**-la see-**dad ve**-llya
Is there a good street plan showing the buildings?	**Há uma boa planta das ruas indicando os edifícios?**	Ah **oo**-ma **bo**-a **pla^n**-ta dash **roo**-ash ee^n-dee-**ka^n**-doo oosh ee-dee-**fee**-see-oosh
We want to visit	**Queremos visitar**	Ke-**ray**-moosh vee-zee-**tar**
the cathedral	**a catedral**	a ka-te-**dral**
the fortress	**a fortaleza**	a foor-ta-**lay**-za
the library	**a biblioteca**	a bee-blee-oo-**te**-ka
the monastery	**o mosteiro**	oo moosh-**tay**-ee-roo
the palace	**o palácio**	oo pa-**la**-see-oo
the ruins	**as ruínas**	ash roo-**ee**-nash
May we walk around the walls?	**Podemos andar à volta das muralhas?**	Po-**day**-moosh a^n-**dar** ah **vol**-ta dash moo-**ra**-llyash
May we go up the tower?	**Podemos subir à torre?**	Poo-**day**-moosh soo-**beer** ah **to**-re
Where is the antiques market/flea market?	**Onde é a feira (mercado) de antiguidades/feira da ladra?**	O^n-de eh a **fay**-ee-ra (mer-**ka**-doo) de a^n-tee-gwee-**da**-desh/**fay**-ee-ra da **la**-dra

GOING TO CHURCH

Is there a Catholic church?	**Há uma igreja Católica?**	Ah **oo**-ma ee-**gray**-zha ka-**to**-lee-ka
Protestant church?	**igreja Protestante?**	ee-**gray**-zha proo-tesh-**ta^{n}t**
mosque?	**mesquita?**	mesh-**kee**-ta
synagogue?	**sinagoga?**	see-na-**go**-ga
What time is mass/the service?	**Qual é a hora da missa/do ofício religioso?**	Kwal eh a **o**-ra da **mee**-sa/doo of-**ee**-syo re-lee-zhee-**o**-so
I'd like to look round the church	**Gostava de dar uma volta pela igreja**	Goosh-**ta**-va de dar **oo**-ma **vol**-ta **pay**-la ee-**gray**-zha
When was the church built?	**Quando foi construída a igreja?**	**Kwa^n**-doo **fo**-ee ko^{n}sh-troo-**ee**-da a ee-**gray**-zha
Should women cover their heads?	**As mulheres cobrem a cabeça?**	Ash moo-**llye**-resh **ko**-bray^n a ka-**bay**-sa

ENTERTAINMENT

Is there an entertainment guide?	**Há um guia de diversões?**	Ah oo^{n} **gee**-a de dee-ver-**soy^{n}sh**
What's on at the theatre/cinema[1]?	**O que vai no teatro/ cinema?**	Oo ke vy noo tee-**a**-troo/ see-**nay**-ma
Is there a concert?	**Há algum concerto?**	Ah al-**goo^{n}** kon-**sayr**-too
Can you recommend a good	**Pode recomendar um bom**	**Po**-de re-koo-may^{n}-**dar** oo^{n} bo^{n}
ballet?	**ballet?**	ba-**lay**
film?	**filme?**	feelm
musical?	**(uma boa) revista musical?**	(oo-ma **bo**-a) re-**veesh**-ta moo-zee-**kal**
Who is	**Quem**	Kay^{n}
directing?	**dirige?**	dee-**ree**-zhe
conducting?	**conduz?**	ko^{n}-**doozh**
singing?	**canta?**	**ka^{n}**-ta

1. Cinemas usually have two or three separate performances a day. Many English and American films are shown both in cinemas and on TV channels.

I want two seats for tonight	**Quero dois lugares para esta noite**	**Ke**-roo **do-eesh** loo-**ga**-resh **pa**-ra **esh**-ta **no**-eet
Is the matinée sold out?	**A matiné está esgotada?**	A ma-tee-**ne** esh-**ta** ezh-goo-**ta**-da
I'd like seats	**Queria bilhetes**	Ke-**ree**-a bee-**llyay**-tesh
in the stalls	**na plateia**	na pla-**tay**-ee-a
in the circle	**no balcão**	noo bal-**kow**^{n}
in the gallery	**na galeria/geral**	na ga-le-**ree**-a/zhe-**ral**
The cheapest seats please	**Os bilhetes mais baratos**	Oosh bee-**llyay**-tesh **ma-eesh** ba-**ra**-toosh
I want to book seats for Thursday	**Quero reservar lugares para quinta-feira**	**Ke**-roo re-zer-**var** loo-**ga**-resh **pa**-ra **kee**^{n}-ta-**fay**-ee-ra
We're sold out (for this performance)	***Estamos com lotação esgotada (para esta sessão)**	Esh-**ta**-moosh ko^{n} loo-ta-**sow**^{n} ezh-goo-**ta**-da (**pa**-ra **esh**-ta se-**sow**^{n})
Are they good seats?	**São bons lugares?**	Sow^{n} bo^{n}sh loo-**ga**-resh
Where are these seats?	**Onde são estes lugares?**	**O**^{n}-de sow^{n} **aysh**-tesh loo-**ga**-resh
What time does the performance start?	**A que horas começa a sessão?**	A ke **o**-rash koo-**me**-sa a se-**sow**^{n}
What time does it end?	**A que horas termina?**	A ke **o**-rash ter-**mee**-na
Where is the cloakroom?	**Onde é o vestiário?**	**O**^{n}-de eh oo vesh-tee-**a**-ree-oo
This is your seat	***Este é o seu lugar**	Aysht eh oo **say**-oo loo-**gar**
A programme, please	**Um programa, por favor**	Oo^{n} proo-**gra**-ma poor fa-**vor**

Which is the best nightclub?	**Qual é a melhor boîte?**	Kwal eh a me-**llyor** bwat
What time is the floorshow?	**A que horas é o espectáculo?**	A ke **o**-rash eh oo esh-pe-**ta**-koo-loo
Would you like to dance?	**Quer dançar?**	Ker da^{n}-**sar**
Is there a jazz club here?	**Há aqui algum clube de jazz?**	Ah a-**kee** al-**goo**^{n} kloob de zhaz
Where can we go dancing?	**Onde podemos ir para dançar?**	**O**^{n}-de po-**de**-moosh eer **pa**-ra da^{n}-**sar**
Where is the best disco?	**Onde é o melhor disco?**	**O**^{n}-de eh oo me-**llyor** **deesh**-koo

SPORTS & GAMES

English	Portuguese	Pronunciation
Where is the nearest tennis court/golf course?	**Onde é o campo de tenis/campo de golfe mais perto?**	O^n-de eh oo **ka^n**-poo de te-**neesh**/**ka^n**-poo de golf **ma-eesh per**-too
What is the charge per	**Quanto levam por**	**Kwa^n**-too le-**vow^n** poor
game?	**jogo?**	**zho**-goo
hour?	**hora?**	**o**-ra
day?	**dia?**	**dee**-a
Is it a club?	**É um clube?**	Eh oo^n kloob
Do I need temporary membership?	**Preciso de ser sócio temporário?**	Pre-**see**-zoo de sayr **so**-see-oo tay^n-poo-**ra**-ree-oo
Where can we go swimming/fishing?	**Onde podemos ir nadar/pescar?**	**O^n**-de poo-**day**-moosh eer na-**dar**/pesh-**kar**
Can I hire	**Posso alugar**	**Po**-soo a-loo-**gar**
a racket?	**uma raquete?**	**oo**-ma ra-**ket**
clubs?	**clubes de golf?**	**kloo**-besh de golf
fishing tackle?	**apetrechos de pesca?**	a-pe-**tray**-ee-shoosh de **pesh**-ka

Do I need a permit?	**É preciso autorização/passe?**	Eh pre-see-zoo ow-too-ree-za-sow^{n}/pa-se
Where do I get a permit?	**Onde obtenho um passe?**	O^{n}-de ob-tay^{n}-nyoo oo^{n} pa-se
Can we swim in the river?	**Podemos nadar no rio?**	Poo-day-moosh na-dar noo ree-oo
Is there an open air/indoor swimming pool?	**Há uma piscina ao ar livre/coberta?**	Ah oo-ma peesh-see-na a-oo ar lee-vre/koo-ber-ta
Is it heated?	**É aquecida?**	Eh a-ke-see-da
Is there a skating rink?	**Há um ringue de patinagem?**	Ah oo^{n} ree^{n}g de pa-tee-na-zhay^{n}
Can I hire roller skates?	**Posso alugar patins?**	Po-soo a-loo-gar pa-tee^{n}sh
We want to go to a football match/a tennis tournament	**Queremos ir a um desafío de futebol/a um torneio de ténis**	Ke-ray-moosh eer a oo^{n} de-za-fee-oo de foot-bol/a oo^{n} toor-nay-ee-oo de te-neesh
Can you get us tickets?	**Pode arranjar bilhetes?**	Po-de a-ra^{n}-zhar bee-llyay-tesh
Are there seats in the grandstand?	**Ha lugares na bancada?**	Ah loo-ga-resh na ba^{n}-ka-da
How much are the cheapest seats?	**Quanto custam os bilhetes mais baratos?**	Kwa^{n}-too koosh-tow^{n} oosh bee-llyay-tesh ma-eesh ba-ra-toosh
Are they in the sun or the shade?	**São ao sol ou à sombra?**	Sow^{n} a-oo sol oh ah so^{n}-bra
Who is playing?	**Quem joga?**	Kay^{n} zho-ga
When does it start?	**A que horas começa?**	A ke o-rash koo-me-sa

Who is winning?	**Quem está a ganhar?**	Kay^{n} esh-ta a ga-nyar
What is the score?	**Qual é o resultado?**	Kwal eh oo re-sool-ta-doo
I'd like to ride	**Gostaria de andar a cavalo**	Goosh-ta-ree-a de a^{n}-dar a ka-va-loo
Is there a riding stable nearby?	**Há uma cavalariça?**	Ah oo-ma ka-va-la-ree-sa
Do you give lessons?	**Dá lições?**	Da lee-soy^{n}sh
I am an inexperienced rider/a good rider	**Sou um cavaleiro inexperiente/um bom cavaleiro**	So oo^{n} ka-va-lay-ee-roo ee-nesh-pe-ree-ay^{n}t/ oo^{n} bo^{n} ka-va-lay-ee-roo
I'd like to try waterskiing	**Gostaria de experimentar esqui aquático**	Goosh-ta-ree-a de esh-pe-ree-may^{n}-tar shkee a-kwa-tee-koo
I haven't waterskied before	**Nunca fiz esqui aquático**	Noo^{n}-ka feesh shkee a-kwa-tee-koo
Can I rent/borrow a wetsuit?	**Posso alugar/pedir emprestado um fato impermeável?**	Po-soo a-loo-gar/pe-deer e^{n}-pres-ta-doo oo^{n} fa-too ee^{n}-per-mee-a-vel
Should I wear a life jacket?	**Devo usar cinto de salvação?**	De-voo oo-zar see^{n}-too de sal-va-sow^{n}
Can I hire a rowing boat? motor boat? surf board?	**Posso alugar um barco a remo? um barco a motor? uma placa de surf?**	Po-soo a-loo-gar oo^{n} bar-koo a ray-moo oo^{n} bar-koo a moo-tor oo-ma pla-ka de sarf
Is there a map of the river?	**Há um mapa do rio?**	Ah oo^{n} ma-pa doo ree-oo
Are there many locks to pass?	**Há muitas comportas a passar?**	Ah moo-ee-tash ko^{n}-por-tash a pa-sar

Can I get fuel here?	**Posso obter combustível aqui?**	**Po**-soo ob-**tayr** ko^{n}-boosh-**tee**-vel a-**kee**
Would you like to go hunting?	***Quer ir a uma caçada?**	Ker eer a **oo**-ma ka-**sa**-da
Do you play cards?	**Sabe jogar às cartas?**	Sab zho-**gar** ash **kar**-tash
Would you like a game of chess?	**Quer jogar xadrez?**	Ker zho-**gar** sha-**draysh**
I'll give you a game of checkers if you like	**Posso jogar damas se quizer**	**Po**-soo zho-**gar** **da**-mash se kee-**zayr**

THE BULLFIGHT[1]

The bull	**O touro**	Oo **to**-roo
The bullfight	**A corrida de touros**	A koo-**ree**-da de **to**-roosh
The bull-ring	**A praça de touros**	A **pra**-sa de **to**-roosh
Tickets	**Bilhetes**	Bee-**llyay**-tesh
in the sun (*cheaper*)	**de sol**	de sol
in the shade (*more expensive*)	**de sombra**	de **so^{n}**-bra
Ringside (*best*) seats	**Barreiras**	Ba-**ray**-ee-rash
Second-best seats	**Contra-barreiras**	**Ko^{n}**-tra-ba-**ray**-ee-rash
A box	**Um camarote**	Oo^{n} ka-ma-**rot**
The balcony	**A varanda**	A va-**ra^{n}**-da
The bullfighter	**O toureiro**	Oo to-**ray**-ee-roo

1. **A novilhada** is a corrida with young bulls and inexperienced bullfighters (**novilheiros**).
In Portuguese bullfighting the bull is never killed.

Who's fighting?	**Quem toureia?**	Ke^{n} to-ray-ee-a
Horsemen with lances who weaken the bull	**Os picadores**	Oosh pee-ka-dor-esh
The men who place the darts in the bull's shoulder muscles	**Os bandarilheiros**	Oosh ba^{n}-da-ree-llyay-ee-roosh
The darts	**As bandarilhas**	Ash ba^{n}-da-ree-llyash
Red and yellow cloak used at the beginning of the **corrida**	**A capa/o capote**	A ka-pa/oo ka-pot
Small cape used for dangerous passes	**A muleta**	A moo-le-ta

ON THE BEACH[1]

Which is the best beach?	**Qual é a melhor praia?**	Kwal eh a me-**llyor** **pry**-a
Is there a quiet beach near here?	**Há por aqui alguma praia sossegada?**	Ah poor a-**kee** al-**goo**-ma **pry**-a soo-se-**ga**-da
Is it far to walk?	**Pode-se ir a pé?**	**Po**-de-se eer a pe
Is there a bus to the beach?	**Há autocarro para a praia?**	Ah ow-to-**ka**-roo **pa**-ra a **pry**-a
Is the beach sand/ pebbles/rocks?	**A praia é de areia ou de pedras?**	A **pry**-a eh de a-**ray**-a o de **pe**-drash
Is it safe for swimming?	**Pode-se nadar sem perigo?**	**Po**-de-se na-**dar** se^{n} pe-**ree**-goo
Is there a lifeguard?	**Há um guarda salva-vidas?**	Ah oo^{n} **gwar**-da **sal**-va-**vee**-dash
Is it safe for small children?	**Não tem perigo para crianças?**	Now^{n} tay^{n} pe-**ree**-goo **pa**-ra kree-**a^{n}**-sash

1. See also SPORTS AND GAMES (p. 152).

Does it get very rough?	**Fica muito agitado?**	Fee-ka moo-ee-too a-zhee-ta-doo
Bathing prohibited	***Proibido tomar banho**	Proo-ee-bee-doo too-mar ba-nyoo
It's dangerous	***É perigoso**	Eh pe-ree-go-zoo
What time is high/low tide?	**A que horas é a maré alta/baixa?**	A ke o-rash eh a ma-re al-ta/ba-ee-sha
Is the tide rising/falling?	**A maré está a subir/a baixar?**	A ma-re esh-ta a soo-beerh a by-shar
There's a strong current here	***Há aqui muita corrente**	Ah a-kee moo-ee-ta koo-ray^{n}t
You will be out of your depth	***Não há pé**	Now^n ah peh
Are you a strong swimmer?	***É bom nadador?**	Eh bo^n na-da-dor
Is it deep?	**É fundo?**	Eh foo^n-doo
Is the water cold?	**A água está fria?**	A a-gwa esh-ta free-a
It's warm	**Está morna**	Esh-ta mor-na
Can one swim in the lake/river?	**Pode-se nadar no lago/rio?**	Po-de-se na-dar noo la-goo/ree-oo
Is there an indoor/outdoor swimming pool?	**Há piscina coberta/ao ar livre?**	Ah peesh-see-na koo-ber-ta/a-oo ar lee-vre
Is it fresh or salt water?	**É água doce ou salgada?**	Eh a-gwa do-se oh sal-ga-da
Are there showers?	**Há duches?**	Ah doo-shesh

I want to hire a cabin	**Quero alugar uma barraca**	Ke-roo a-loo-gar oo-ma ba-ra-ka
for the day	**para todo o dia**	pa-ra toh-doh oo dee-a
for the morning	**pela manhã**	pay-la ma-nya^{n}
for two hours	**por duas horas**	poor doo-ash o-rash
Can we hire (deck) chairs/ sunshades?	**Podemos alugar cadeiras (de encosto)/chapéus de sol?**	Poo-day-moosh a-loo-gar ka-day-ee-rash (de ay^{n}-kosh-too)/sha-pe-oosh de sol
Where can I buy a snorkel/flippers?	**Onde posso comprar um respiradouro subaquático/ barbatanas?**	O^{n}-de po-soo ko^{n}-prar oo^{n} resh-pee-ra-do-roo soob-a-kwa-tee-koo/ bar-ba-ta-nash
Where's the harbour?	**Onde é o porto?**	O^{n}-de eh oo por-too
Can we go out in a fishing boat?	**Pode-se sair num barco de pesca?**	Po-de-se sa-eer noo^{n} bar-koo de pesh-ka
We want to go fishing	**Queremos ir à pesca**	Ke-ray-moosh eer ah pesh-ka
Can I hire a rowing boat/motor boat?	**Pode-se alugar um barco a remos/um barco a motor?**	Po-de-se a-loo-gar oo^{n} bar-koo a ray-moosh/ oo^{n} bar-koo a moo-tor
What does it cost by the hour?	**Quanto custa por hora?**	Kwa^{n}-too koosh-ta poor o-ra
ball	**a bola**	bola
bat	**a raquete**	ra-ket
beach bag	**o saco de praia**	sa-koo de pry-a

boat	**o barco**	bar-koo
sailing	**à vela**	ah ve-la
motor	**a motor**	a moo-tor
pedal	**a pedais**	a pe-da-eesh
rowing	**a remo**	a ray-moo
bucket and spade	**o balde e pá**	bald ee pa
crab	**o caranguejo**	ka-ran-gay-zhoo
first aid	**primeiros socorros**	pree-may-ee-roosh soo-ko-roosh
jellyfish	**a alforreca**	al-for-re-ka
lifebelt	**o cinto de salvação**	seen-too de sal-va-sow^n
lifebuoy	**a boia de salvação**	boy-a de sal-va-sow^n
lighthouse	**o farol**	fa-rol
rock	**a rocha**	ro-sha
sand	**a areia**	a-ray-ya
sandbank	**o banco de areia**	ban-koo de a-ray-ya
sandcastle	**o castelo de areia**	kash-te-loo de a-ray-ya
sun	**o sol**	sol
sunglasses	**os óculos de sol**	o-koo-loosh de sol
sunshade	**o toldo**	tol-doo
swimming suit	**o fato de banho**	fa-too de ba-nyoo
swimming trunks	**os calções de banho**	kal-soy^{n}sh de ba-nyoo
towel	**a toalha**	too-a-llya
water wings	**as braçadeiras**	bra-sa-dey-rash
wave	**as ondas**	o^n-dash

IN THE COUNTRY[1]

Is there a scenic route to ...?	**Há uma rota cénica para ...?**	Ah oo-ma ro-ta se-nee-ka pa-ra
Can you give me a lift to ...?	**Pode dar-me uma boleia até ...?**	Po-de dar-me oo-ma boo-lay-ee-a a-te
Is there a footpath to ...?	**Há um caminho para peões para ...?**	Ah oo^{n} ka-mee-nyoo pa-ra pee-oy^{n}sh pa-ra
Is it possible to go across country?	**É possível ir pelo campo?**	Eh poo-see-vel eer pay-loo ka^{n}-poo
Is there a shortcut?	**Há um atalho?**	Ah oo^{n} a-ta-llyoo
Is this a public footpath?	**Há um caminho público?**	Ah oo^{n} ka-mee-nyoo poo-blee-koo
Is there a bridge across the stream?	**Há uma ponte por cima da corrente/rio?**	Ah oo-ma po^{n}t poor see-ma da koo-ray^{n}t/ree-oo
Can we walk?	**Podemos ir a pé**	Po-day-moosh eer a pe

1. See also DIRECTIONS, p. 32.

How far is the next village?	**A que distância fica a próxima aldeia/ povoado/vila?**	A ke deesh-ta^{n}-see-a fee-ka a pro-see-ma al-day-ee-a/poo-voo-a-doo/vee-la

THE WEATHER

Is it usually as hot as this?	**Costuma ser assim tão quente?**	Koosh-too-ma ser a-see^{n} tow^{n} kay^{n}t
It's going to be hot/ cool today	**Vai estar calor/fresco hoje**	Vy esh-tar ka-lor/ fraysh-koo o-zhe
The mist will clear later	**A neblina vai clarear mais tarde**	A ne-blee-na vy kla-ree-ar ma-eesh tard
Will it be fine tomorrow?	**Estará bom amanhã?**	Esh-ta-ra bo^{n} a-ma-nya^{n}
What is the weather forecast?	**Qual é a previsão do tempo?**	Kwal eh a pre-vee-zow^{n} doo tay^{n}-poo

TRAVELLING WITH CHILDREN

Can you put a child's bed/cot in our room?	**Pode pôr uma cama/berço no quarto?**	**Po**-de por **oo**-ma **ka**-ma/**bayr**-soo noo **kwar**-too
Can you give us an adjoining room?	**Pode dar-nos quartos juntos?**	**Po**-de **dar**-noosh **kwar**-toosh **zhoo^n**-toosh
Does the hotel have a babysitting service?	**O hotel tem serviço de baby-sitting/ guardar crianças?**	Oo o-**tel** tay^n ser-**vee**-soo de be-**be**-see-**teeng**/ gwar-**dar** kree-**a^n**-sash
Can you find me a baby-sitter?	**Pode arranjar-me uma baby-sitter?**	**Po**-de a-ra^n-**zhar**-me oo-ma be-**be**-see-tair
We shall be out for a couple of hours	**Vamos sair por algumas horas**	**Va**-moosh sa-**eer** poor al-**goo**-mash **o**-rash
We shall be back at ...	**Nós voltamos às ...**	Nosh vol-**ta**-moosh ash
Is there a children's menu?	**Há um menu para crianças?**	Ah oo^n me-**noo** **pa**-ra kree-**a^n**-sash
Do you have half portions for children?	**Tem meias-doses para crianças?**	Tay^n **may**-ee-ash **do**-zesh **pa**-ra kree-**a^n**-sash

English	Portuguese	Pronunciation
Have you got a high chair?	**Tem uma cadeira alta?**	Tay^{n} oo-ma ka-day-ee-ra al-ta
Are there any organized activities/games for children?	**Há algumas actividades/jogos para crianças?**	Ah al-goo-mash a-tee-vee-da-desh/jo-goosh pa-ra kree-a^{n}-sash
Is there	**Há**	Ah
a paddling pool?	**uma piscina para patinhar?**	oo-ma peesh-see-na pa-ra pa-tee-nyar
a children's swimming pool?	**uma piscina para crianças?**	ooma peesh-see-na pa-ra kree-a^{n}-sash
a playground?	**um recinto para brincar?**	oo^{n} re-see^{n}-too pa-ra bree^{n}-kar
a games room?	**salas de jogos/para brincar?**	sa-lash de zho-goosh/pa-ra bree^{n}-kar
Is there an amusement park nearby?	**Há um parque de diversões?**	Ah oo^{n} park de dee-ver-soy^{n}sh
a zoo?	**um jardim zoológico?**	zhar-dee^{n} zoo-oo-lo-zhee-koo
a toyshop?	**uma loja de brinquedos?**	oo-ma lo-zha de bree^{n}-kay-doosh
I'd like	**Queria**	Ke-ree-a
a beach ball	**uma bola para a praia**	oo-ma bo-la pa-ra a pry-a
a bucket and spade	**um balde e pá**	oo^{n} bal-de ee pah
a doll	**uma boneca**	oo-ma boo-ne-ka
flippers	**barbatanas para nadar**	bar-ba-ta-nash pa-ra na-dar
goggles	**óculos de protecção**	o-koo-loosh de proo-te-sow^{n}
playing cards	**cartas de jogar**	kar-tash de zhoo-gar
roller skates	**patins de rodas**	pa-tee^{n}sh de ro-dash
a snorkel	**um respiradouro submarino**	oo^{n} resh-pee-ra-do-roo soob-ma-ree-noo

Where can I feed/ change my baby?	**Onde posso dar de comer/mudar as fraldas do bebé?**	O^n-de **po**-soo dar de koo-**mayr**/moo-**dar** ash **fral**-dash doo be-**be**
Can you heat this bottle for me?	**Pode aquecer este biberão?**	**Po**-de a-ke-**sayr** aysht bee-be-**row^n**
I want	**Quero**	**Ke**-roo
some disposable nappies	**fraldas de papel**	**fral**-dash de pa-**pel**
a feeding bottle	**um frasco biberão**	oo^n **frash**-koo bee-be-**row^n**
some baby food	**comida de bebé**	koo-**mee**-da de be-**be**
My daughter suffers from travel sickness	**A minha filha enjoa**	A **mee**-nya **fee**-llya ay^n-**zho**-a
She has hurt herself	**Ela maguou-se/ aleijou-se**	**E**-la ma-**goo**-oh-se/a-lay-ee-**zho**-se
My son is ill	**Meu filho está doente**	**May**-oo **fee**-llyoo esh-**ta** doo-**ay^{n}t**
He has lost his toy	**Ele perdeu o brinquedo**	**Ay**-le per-**day**-oo oo bree^n-**kay**-doo
I'm sorry if they have bothered you	**Desculpe se o incomodaram**	Desh-**kool**-pe se oo ee^n-koo-moo-**da**-row^n

BUSINESS MATTERS[1]

I would like to make an appointment with ...	**Gostava de ter uma reunião com ...**	Goosh-**ta**-va de tayr **oo**-ma ray-oo-nee-**ow**^{n} ko^{n}
I have an appointment with ...	**Tenho uma reunião com ...**	**Tay**^{n}-nyoo **oo**-ma ray-oo-nee-**ow**^{n} ko^{n}
My name is ...	**O meu nome é ...**	Oo **may**-oo **no**-me eh
Here is my card	**Aqui está o meu cartão**	A-**kee** esh-**ta** oo **may**-oo kar-**tow**^{n}
This is our catalogue	**Este é o nosso catálogo**	Aysht eh oo **no**-soo ka-ta-loo-goo
I would like to see your products	**Gostava de ver os seus produtos**	Goosh-**ta**-va de vayr oosh **say**-oosh pro-**doo**-toosh
Could you send me some examples?	**Pode enviar-me amostras?**	Po-de ayn-vee-**ar**-me a-**mosh**-trash

1. See also TELEPHONING (p. 139).

Can you provide an interpreter/a secretary?	**Pode arranjar um intérprete/uma secretária?**	Po-de a-ra^{n}-zhar oo^{n} ee^{n}-ter-pret/oo-ma se-kre-ta-ree-a
Where can I make some photocopies?	**Onde posso fazer fotocópias?**	O^{n}-de po-soo fa-zayr fo-to-ko-pee-ash

AT THE DOCTOR'S

Is there a doctor's surgery nearby?	**Há um consultório médico aqui perto?**	Ah oo^n ko^n-sool-to-ree-oo me-dee-koo a-kee per-too
I must see a doctor; can you recommend one?	**Preciso de ser visto por um médico; pode aconselhar-me um?**	Pre-see-zoo de sayr veesh-too poor oo^n me-dee-koo; po-de a-ko^n-se-llyar-me oo^n
Please call a doctor	**Chame um médico, por favor**	Sha-me oo^n me-dee-koo poor fa-vor
When can the doctor come?	**Quando pode vir o médico?**	Kwa^n-doo po-de veer oo me-dee-koo
Does the doctor speak English?	**O médico fala inglês?**	Oo me-dee-koo fa-la ee^n-glaysh
Can I make an appointment for as soon as possible?	**Posso marcar uma consulta o mais cedo possível?**	Po-soo mar-kar oo-ma ko^n-sool-ta oo ma-eesh say-doo poo-see-vel

AILMENTS

I am ill	**Estou doente**	Esh-to doo-**ay^{n}t**
I take ... can you give me a prescription please?	**Eu estou a tomar ... pode-me dar uma receita por favor?**	Ay-oo esh-to a too-**mar** ... po-de-me dar oo-ma re-**say**-ee-ta poor fa-**vor**
I have low/high blood pressure	**Tenho tensão baixa/ alta**	**Tay^{n}**-nyoo tay^{n}-**sow^{n}** **ba**-ee-sha/**al**-ta
I am pregnant	**Estou grávida**	Esh-to **gra**-vee-da
I am allergic to ...	**Sou alérgico a ...**	So a-**ler**-zhee-koo a
I think it is infected	**Creio que está infectado**	**Kray**-ee-oo ke esh-**ta** ee^{n}-fe-**ta**-doo
I've a pain in my right arm	**Dói-me o braço direito**	**Do**-ee-me oo **bra**-soo dee-**ray**-ee-too
My wrist hurts	**Dói-me o pulso**	**Do**-ee-me oo **pool**-soo
I think I've sprained/ broken my ankle	**Penso que desloquei/parti o tornozelo**	**Pay^{n}**-soo ke desh-loo-**kay**-ee/par-**tee** o toor-noo-**zay**-loo
I fell down and my back hurts	**Caí e doem-me as costas**	Ka-**ee** ee **do**-ay^{n}-me ash **kosh**-tash
My foot is swollen	**Tenho o pé inchado**	**Tay^{n}**-nyoo oo pe ee^{n}-**sha**-doo
I've burned/cut myself	**Queimei-me/cortei-me**	Kay-ee-**may**-ee-me/ koor-**tay**-ee-me
My stomach is upset	**Estou mal do estômago**	Esh-**to** mal doo esh-**to**-ma-goo
I have indigestion	**Estou com indigestão**	Esh-**to** ko^{n} ee^{n}-dee-zhesh-**tow^{n}**

My appetite's gone	**Não tenho apetite**	Now^n **tay^n**-nyoo a-pe-**teet**
I think I've got food poisoning	**Penso que estou intoxicado**	**Pay^n**-soo ke esh-**to** ee^n-tok-see-**ka**-doo
I can't eat/sleep	**Não consigo comer/ dormir**	Now^n kon-**see**-goo koo-**mayr**/door-**meer**
I am a diabetic	**Sou diabético**	So dee-a-**be**-tee-koo
My nose keeps bleeding	**Deito sangue do nariz frequentemente**	**Day**-ee-too sa^{n}g doo na-**reesh** fre-kway^n-te-**may^{n}t**
I have earache/ toothache	**Doem-me os ouvidos/dentes**	Do-**ay^n**-me oosh oh-**vee**-doosh/**day^n**-tesh
I have difficulty in breathing	**Tenho dificuldade em respirar/Não respiro bem**	Tay-nyoo dee-fee-kool-**dad** ayn resh-pee-**rar**/ now^n resh-**pee**-roo bay^n
I feel dizzy/shivery	**Sinto vertigens/Estou com arrepios**	**See^n**-too ver-tee-zhay^{n}sh/**esh**-to ko^n a-re-**pee**-oosh
I feel sick	**Estou enjoado**	Esh-**to** ay^n-zhoo-**a**-doo
I keep vomiting	**Estou com vómitos**	Esh-**to** ko^n vo-**mee**-tosh
I think I've caught flu	**Penso que estou com gripe**	**Pay^n**-soo ke esh-**to** ko^n greep
I've got a cold	**Estou constipado/ Tenho uma constipação**	Esh-**to** ko^{n}sh-tee-**pa**-doo/**tay^n**-nyoo **oo**-ma ko^{n}sh-tee-pa-**sow^n**
I've had it since yesterday/for a few hours	**Tenho-a desde ontem/há algumas horas**	**Tay^n**-nyoo-a **dayzh**-de o^n-**tay^n**/ah al-**goo**-mash **o**-rash
abscess	**o abcesso**	ab-**se**-soo
ache	**a dor**	dor
allergy	**a alergia**	a-ler-**zhee**-a

appendicitis	**a apendicite**	a-**pe**^{n}-dee-seet
asthma	**a asma**	**ash**-ma
back pain	**a dor nas costas**	dor nash **kosh**-tash
blister	**a bolha**	**bo**-llya
boil	**o furúnculo**	foo-**roo**^{n}-koo-lo
bruise	**a contusão**	ko^n-too-**zow**^{n}
burn	**a queimadura**	kay-ee-ma-**doo**-ra
cardiac condition	**a afecção cardíaca**	a-fe-**sow**^{n} kar-**dee**-a-ka
chill/cold	**o resfriamento/a constipação**	resh-free-a-**me**^{n}-too/ ko^{n}sh-tee-pa-**sow**^{n}
constipation	**a prisão de ventre**	pree-**zow**^{n} de **ve**^{n}-tre
cough	**a tosse**	tos
cramp	**a cãibra**	**ky**^{n}-bra
diabetic	**diabético**	dee-a-**be**-tee-koo
diarrhoea	**a diarreia**	dee-a-**re**-ya
earache	**a dor de ouvidos**	dor de oh-**vee**-doosh
fever	**a febre**	**fe**-bre
food poisoning	**a intoxicação**	ee^n-tok-see-ka-**sow**^{n}
fracture	**a fractura**	**fra**-too-ra
hay fever	**a febre dos fenos**	**fe**-bre doosh **fay**-noosh
headache	**a dor de cabeça**	dor de ka-**bay**-sa
heart condition	**a doença do coração**	doo-**ay**^{n}-sa doo koo-ra-**sow**^{n}
high blood pressure	**a pressão arterial alta**	pre-**sow**^{n} ar-te-ree-**al al**-ta
ill/sick	**doente**	doo-**e**^{n}t
illness	**a doença**	doo-**e**^{n}-sa

indigestion	**a indigestão**	ee^{n}-dee-zhesh-tow^{n}
infection	**a infecção**	ee^{n}-fe-**sow^{n}**
influenza	**a gripe**	greep
insect bite	**a mordedura de insecto**	moor-de-**doo**-ra de ee^{n}-se-too
insomnia	**a insónia**	ee^{n}-**so**-nee-a
nausea	**a náusea**	**now**-zee-a
nose bleed	**o sangrar do nariz**	sa^{n}-**grar** doo na-**reesh**
pain	**a dor**	dor
rheumatism	**o reumatismo**	ree-oo-ma-**teeszh**-moo
sore throat	**a dor de garganta**	dor de gar-**ga^{n}**-ta
sprain	**a entorse**	e^{n}-**tors**
sting	**a picada de insecto**	pee-**ka**-da de ee^{n}-**se**-too
stomach ache	**a dor de estômago**	dor de esh-**to**-ma-goo
sunburn	**a queimadura de sol**	kay-ee-ma-**doo**-ra de sol
sunstroke	**a insolação**	ee^{n}-soo-la-**sow^{n}**
swelling	**o inchaço**	ee^{n}-**sha**-soo
tonsillitis	**a dor de garganta**	dor de gar-**ga^{n}**-ta
toothache	**a dor de dentes**	dor de **de^{n}**-tesh
ulcer	**a úlcera**	**ool**-se-ra
wound	**a ferida**	fe-**ree**-da

TREATMENT

You're hurting me	**Está a magoar-me**	Esh-**ta** a ma-goo-**ar**-me

Must I stay in bed?	**Tenho que ficar na cama?**	Tay^{n}-nyoo ke fee-**kar** na **ka**-ma
Will you call again?	**Voltará?**	Vol-ta-**ra**
How much do I owe you?	**Quanto lhe devo?**	**Kwa**^{n}-too llye **day**-voo
When can I travel again?	**Quando posso novamente viajar?**	**Kwa**^{n}-doo **po**-soo no-va-**may**^{n}t vee-a-**zhar**
I feel better now	**Estou melhor**	Esh-**to** me-**llyor**
Do you have a temperature?	***Tem febre?**	Tay^{n} **fe**-bre
Does that hurt?	***Dói-lhe?**	**Do**-ee-llye
A lot?	***Muito?**	**Moo**-ee-too
A little?	***Um pouco?**	Oo^{n} **po**-koo
Where does it hurt?	***Onde lhe dói?**	O^{n}-de llye **do**-ee
Have you a pain here?	***Dói-lhe aqui?**	**Do**-ee-llye a-**kee**
How long have you had the pain?	***Há quanto tempo lhe dói?**	Ah **kwa**^{n}-too **tay**^{n}-poo llye **do**-ee
Open your mouth	***Abra a boca**	**A**-bra a **bo**-ka
Put out your tongue	***Ponha a língua de fora**	**Po**^{n}-nya a **lee**^{n}-gwa de **fo**-ra
Breathe in	***Respire fundo**	Resh-**pee**-re **foo**^{n}-doo
Breathe out	***Expire**	Esh-**pee**-re
Please lie down	***Deite-se, por favor**	**Day**-ee-te-se poor fa-**vor**
I will need a specimen	***Preciso duma análise**	Pre-**see**-zoo **doo**-ma a-**na**-lee-se
What medicines have you been taking?	***Que remédios tem tomado?**	Ke re-**me**-**dee**-oosh tay^{n} too-**ma**-doo

I take this medicine; could you give me another prescription?	**Tomo este remédio; pode dar-me outra receita?**	To-moo aysht re-**me**-dee-oo **po**-de **dar**-me o-tra re-**say**-ee-ta
I will give you an antibiotic	***Vou lhe dar um antibiótico**	Vo llye dar oo^{n} a^{n}-tee-bee-**o**-tee-koo
a painkiller	**um analgésico**	oo^{n} a-nal-**zhe**-zee-koo
a sedative	**um sedativo**	oo^{n} se-da-**tee**-voo
I'll give you some pills/medicine	***Vou dar-lhe uns comprimidos/um remédio**	Vo **dar**-llye oo^{n}sh ko^{n}-pree-**mee**-doosh/oo^{n} re-**me**-dee-oo
Take this prescription to the chemist's	***Leve esta receita à farmácia**	**Le**-ve **esh**-ta re-**say**-ee-ta ah far-**ma**-see-a
Take this three times a day	***Tome isto três vezes ao dia**	**To**-me **eesh**-too traysh **vay**-zesh **a**-oo **dee**-a
I'll give you an injection	***Vou dar-lhe uma injecção**	Vo **dar**-llye **oo**-ma ee^{n}-zhe-**sow**^{n}
Roll up your sleeve	***Levante a manga**	Le-**vant** a **ma**^{n}-ga
I'll put you on a diet	***Vou pô-lo a dieta**	Vo **po**-loo a dee-**e**-ta
Come and see me again in two days' time	***Volte dentro de dois dias**	**Vol**-te **day**^{n}-troo de **do**-eesh **dee**-ash
You must be X-rayed	***Tem que tirar uma radiografia**	Tay^{n} ke tee-**rar** **oo**-ma ra-dee-oo-gra-**fee**-a
You must go to the hospital	***Tem de ir a um hospital/a uma clínica**	Tay^{n} de eer a oo^{n} **osh**-pee-**tal**/a **oo**-ma **klee**-nee-ka
You must stay in bed	***Tem de ficar na cama**	Tay^{n} de fee-**kar** na **ka**-ma
You should not travel until ...	***Não deve viajar até ...**	Now^{n} **day**-ve vee-a-**zhar** a-**te**

Nothing to worry about	*Nada para preocupar	Nah-da pa-ra pray-o-koo-par
I'd like a receipt for the health insurance	Queria um recibo para o seguro de saúde	Ke-ree-a oo^n re-see-boo pa-ra oo se-goo-roo de sa-oo-de
ambulance	a ambulância	a^n-boo-la^n-see-a
anaesthetic	a anestesia	a-nesh-te-see-a
aspirin	a aspirina	ash-pee-ree-na
bandage	a ligadura	lee-ga-doo-ra
chiropodist	o pedicuro	pe-dee-koo-roo
hospital	o hospital	osh-pee-tal
injection	a injecção	ee^n-zhe-sow^n
laxative	o laxativo	la-sha-tee-voo
nurse	a enfermeira	en-fer-may-ee-ra
operation	a operação	o-pe-ra-sow^n
optician	o oculista	o-koo-leesh-ta
osteopath	o osteopata	os-te-o-pa-ta
pill	a pílula	pee-loo-la
(adhesive) plaster	o adesivo	a-de-see-voo
prescription	a receita	re-say-ee-ta
X-ray	a radiografia	ra-dee-oo-gra-fee-a

PARTS OF THE BODY

ankle	o tornozelo	tor-noo-ze-loo
arm	o braço	bra-soo
back	as costas	kosh-tash

blood	**o sangue**	sa^{n}g
body	**o corpo**	kor-poo
bone	**o osso**	o-soo
bowels	**os intestinos**	ee^{n}-tes-tee-noosh
brain	**o cérebro**	se-re-broo
breast	**o seio**	say-ee-oo
cheek	**a face**	fas
chest	**o peito**	pay-ee-too
chin	**o queixo**	kay-ee-shoo
ear	**o ouvido**	oh-vee-doo
elbow	**o cotovelo**	koo-too-vay-loo
eye	**o olho**	oh-llyoo
eyelid	**a pálpebra**	pal-pe-bra
face	**a cara**	ka-ra
finger	**o dedo**	day-doo
foot	**o pé**	peh
forehead	**a testa**	tesh-ta
gum	**a gengiva**	zhe^{n}-zhee-va
hand	**a mão**	mow^{n}
head	**a cabeça**	ka-bay-sa
heart	**o coração**	koo-ra-sow^{n}
heel	**o calcanhar**	kal-ka-nyar
hip	**a anca**	a^{n}-ka
jaw	**a mandíbula**	ma^{n}-dee-boo-la
joint	**a articulação**	ar-tee-koo-la-sow^{n}
kidney	**o rim**	ree^{n}

knee	**o joelho**	zhoo-ay-llyoo
knee-cap	**a rótula**	ro-too-la
leg	**a perna**	per-na
lip	**o lábio**	la-bee-oo
liver	**o fígado**	fee-ga-doo
lung	**o pulmão**	pool-mow^{n}
mouth	**a boca**	bo-ka
muscle	**o músculo**	moosh-koo-loo
nail	**a unha**	oo-nya
neck	**o pescoço**	pesh-ko-soo
nerve	**o nervo**	nair-voo
nose	**o nariz**	na-reesh
rib	**a costela**	koosh-te-la
shoulder	**o ombro**	o^{n}-broo
skin	**a pele**	pell
spine	**a espinha/a coluna**	esh-pee-nya/ko-loo-na
stomach	**o estômago**	es-to-ma-goo
throat	**a garganta**	gar-ga^{n}-ta
thumb	**o polegar**	poh-le-gar
toe	**o dedo do pé**	day-doo doo pe
tongue	**a língua**	lee^{n}-gwa
tonsils	**as amígdalas**	a-mee-da-lash
tooth	**o dente**	de^{n}t
vein	**a veia**	vay-ya
wrist	**o pulso**	pool-soo

AT THE DENTIST'S

I must see a dentist	**Tenho de ir ao dentista**	Tay^n-nyoo de eer a-oo day^n-teesh-ta
Can I make an appointment?	**Posso fazer uma marcação?**	Po-soo fa-zayr oo-ma mar-ka-sow^n
As soon as possible	**O mais depressa possível**	Oo ma-eesh de-pre-sa poo-see-vel
I have toothache	**Doem-me os dentes**	Do-ay^n-me oosh day^n-tesh
This tooth hurts	**Dói-me este dente**	Do-ee-me aysht day^{n}t
I have a broken tooth/ an abscess	**Tenho um dente partido/um abcesso**	Tay^n-nyoo oo^n day^{n}t par-tee-doo/oo^n ab-se-soo
I've lost a filling	**Caíu-me uma obturação/um chumbo**	Ka-ee-oo-me oo-ma ob-too-ra-sow^n/oo^n shoo^n-boo
Can you fill it?	**Pode obturar-mo?**	Po-de ob-too-rar-moo
Can you do it now?	**Pode fazê-lo agora?**	Po-de fa-zay-loo a-go-ra

Must you take the tooth out?	**Tem que tirar-me o dente?**	Tay^n ke tee-**rar**-me oo day^{n}t
I do not want the tooth taken out	**Não quero arrancar o dente**	Now^n **ke**-roo a-ra^n-**kar** oo day^{n}t
Please give me an anaesthetic/injection	**Dê-me primeiro uma anestesia/uma injecção**	**Day**-me pree-**may**-ee-roo oo-ma a-nesh-te-**see**-a/oo-ma een-zhe-**sow**^{n}
My gums are swollen	**Tenho as gengivas inflamadas**	**Tay**^{n}-nyoo ash zhay^n-**zhee**-vash ee^n-fla-**ma**-dash
My gums keep bleeding	**As gengivas deitam sangue**	Ash zhay^n-**zhee**-vash **day**-ee-tow^n sa^{n}g
I have broken my plate, can you repair it?	**Parti a dentadura, pode repará-la?**	Par-**tee** a day^n-ta-**doo**-ra **po**-de re-pa-**ra**-la
Can you fix it (temporarily)?	**Pode consertá-la (temporáriamente)?**	**Po**-de ko^n-ser-**ta**-la (tay^n-poo-**ra**-ree-a-**may**^{n}**t**)
You're hurting me	**Está a magoar-me**	Esh-**ta** a ma-**gwar**-me
How much do I owe you?	**Quanto lhe devo?**	**Kwa**^{n}-too llye **day**-voo
When should I come again?	**Quando tenho que voltar?**	**Kwa**^{n}-doo **tay**^{n}-nyoo ke vol-**tar**
Please rinse your mouth	***Lave a boca, por favor**	**La**-ve a **bo**-ka poor fa-**vor**
I will X-ray your teeth	***Tenho que tirar uma radiografia aos seus dentes**	**Tay**^{n}-nyoo ke tee-**rar** oo-ma ra-dee-oo-gra-**fee**-a a-**oosh** **say**-oosh **day**^{n}-tesh
You have an abscess	***Tem um abcesso**	Tay^n oo^n ab-**se**-soo

The nerve is exposed	***O nervo está exposto**	Oo **nayr**-voo esh-**ta** esh-**posh**-too
This tooth can't be saved	***Este dente não se pode salvar**	**Aysht day^{n}t now^n** se **po**-de sal-**var**
You need an antibiotic	***Precisa dum antibiótico**	Pre-**see**-za doo^n a^n-tee-bee-**o**-tee-koo

PROBLEMS & ACCIDENTS

Where's the police station?	**Onde é a esquadra da polícia?**	O^{n}-de eh a esh-**kwa**-dra da poo-**lee**-see-a
Call the police	**Chame a polícia**	**Sha**-me a poo-**lee**-see-a
Where is the British consulate?	**Onde é o consulado inglês?**	O^{n}-de eh oo ko^{n}-soo-**la**-doo ee^{n}-**glaysh**
Please let the consulate know	**Comuniquem com o consulado, por favor**	Koo-moo-**nee**-kay^{n} ko^{n} oo ko^{n}-soo-**la**-doo poor fa-**vor**
It's urgent	**É um caso urgente**	Eh oo^{n} **ka**-zoo oor-**zhay^{n}t**
There's a fire	**Há um fogo**	Ah oo^{n} **fo**-goo
My son/daughter is lost	**O meu filho/filha perdeu-se**	Oo **may**-oo **fee**-llyoo/ **fee**-llya per-**day**-oo-se
Our car has been broken into	**O nosso carro foi arrombado**	Oo **no**-soo **ka**-roo **fo**-ee ar-ro^{n}-**ba**-doo
I've been robbed/ mugged	**Eu fui roubado/ agredido**	**Ay**-oo **foo**-ee ro-**ba**-doo/a-gre-**dee**-doo

My bag has been stolen	**Roubaram-me o meu saco/a minha bolsa**	Ro-**ba**-row^n-me oo **may**-oo sa-koo/a **mee**-nya **bol**-sa
I found this in the street	**Encontrei isto na rua**	Ay^n-ko^n-**tray eesh**-too na **roo**-a
I have lost	**Perdi**	Per-**dee**
my luggage	**a minha bagagem**	a **mee**-nya ba-**ga**-zhay^n
my passport	**o meu passaporte**	oo **may**-oo pa-sa-**port**
my travellers' cheques	**o meu livro de cheques de viagem**	oo **may**-oo **lee**-vroo de **she**-ksh de vee-**a**-zhay^n
I have missed my train	**Perdi o comboio**	Per-**dee** oo ko^n-**boy**-oo
My luggage is on board	**A minha bagagem está no comboio**	A **mee**-nya ba-**ga**-zhay^n esh-**ta** noo ko^n-**boy**-oo
Call a doctor	**Chame um médico**	**Sha**-me oo^n **me**-dee-koo
Call an ambulance	**Chame uma ambulância**	**Sha**-me **oo**-ma a^n-boo-**la**^{n}-see-a
There has been an accident	**Houve um acidente**	**Oo**-ve oo^n a-see-**day**^{n}**t**
We've had an accident	**Tivemos um acidente**	Tee-**ve**-moosh oo^n a-see-**day**^{n}**t**
He's badly hurt	**Está bastante ferido**	Esh-**ta** bas-**ta**^{n}**t** fe-**ree**-doo
He has fainted	**Está desmaiado**	Esh-**ta** dezh-ma-ee-**a**-doo
He's losing blood	**Está a perder sangue**	Esh-**ta** a per-**der** sa^{n}g
Her arm is broken	**O braço dela está partido**	Oo **bra**-soo **de**-la esh-**ta** par-**tee**-doo
Please get some water/a blanket/some bandages	**Traga água/uma manta/ligaduras, por favor**	**Tra**-ga **a**-gwa/**oo**-ma **ma**^{n}-ta/lee-ga-**doo**-rash poor fa-**vor**

I've broken my glasses	**Parti os óculos**	Par-**tee** oosh **o**-koo-loosh
I can't see	**Não consigo ver**	Now^n ko^n-**see**-goo ver
A child has fallen in the water	**Caíu uma criança à água**	Ka-**ee**-oo **oo**-ma kree-**a^n**-sa ah **a**-gwa
A woman is drowning	**Está-se a afogar uma mulher**	Esh-**ta**-se a a-foo-**gar** oo-ma moo-**llyer**
May I see your insurance certificate/your driving licence?	***Posso ver o seu certificado de seguro/a sua carta de condução?**	**Po**-soo vayr oo **say**-oo ser-tee-fee-**ka**-doo de se-**goo**-roo/a soo-a **kar**-ta de ko^n-doo-**sow^n**
I didn't understand the sign	**Não compreendi o sinal**	Now^n ko^n-pre-ay^n-**dee** oo see-**nal**
How much is the fine?	**Quanto é a multa?**	**Kwa^n**-too eh a **mool**-ta
Apply to the insurance company	***Dirija-se à companhia de seguros**	Dee-**ree**-zha-se ah ko^n-pa-**nyee**-a de se-**goo**-roosh
I want a copy of the police report	**Quero uma cópia do relatório policial**	**Ke**-roo **oo**-ma **ko**-pee-a doo re-la-**to**-ree-o poo-lee-see-**al**
What are the name and address of the owner?	**Como se chama e qual é a morada do proprietário?**	**Ko**-moo se **sha**-ma ee kwal eh a moo-**ra**-da doo proo-pree-ay-**ta**-ree-oo
Are you willing to act as a witness?	**Está disposto a servir de testemunha?**	Esh-**ta** deesh-**posh**-too a ser-**veer** de tesh-te-**moo**-nya
Can I have your name and address please?	**Pode dar-me o seu nome e morada?**	**Po**-de **dar**-me oo **say**-oo **no**-me ee moo-**ra**-da
Can you help me?	**Pode ajudar-me?**	**Po**-de a-zhoo-**dar**-me

TIME & DATES

TIME

What time is it?	**Que horas são?**	Ke o-rash sow^n
It's one o'clock	**É uma hora**	Eh oo-ma o-ra
two o'clock	**São duas horas**	Sow^n **doo**-ash o-rash
quarter past five	**cinco e um quarto**	**see^n**-koo ee oo^n **kwar**-too
five past eight	**oito e cinco**	o-**ee**-too ee **see^n**-koo
twenty-five past eight	**oito e vinte cinco**	o-**ee**-too ee **vee^{n}t** **see^n**-koo
half past four	**quatro e meia**	**kwa**-troo ee **may**-ee-a
twenty to three	**três menos vinte**	traysh **may**-noosh **vee^{n}t**
quarter to ten	**dez menos um quarto**	desh **may**-noosh oo^n **kwar**-tro
Second	**Segundo**	Se-**goo^n**-doo
Minute	**Minuto**	Mee-**noo**-too

Hour	**Hora**	O-ra
It's early/late	**É cedo/tarde**	Eh **say**-doo/tard
My watch is slow/fast	**O meu relógio está atrasado/adiantado**	Oo **may**-oo re-**lo**-zhee-oo esh-**ta** a-tra-**za**-doo/a-dee-a^{n}-**ta**-doo
Sorry I am late	**Desculpe o atrazo**	Desh-**kool**-pe oo a-**tra**-zoo

DATE

What's the date?	**Que dia é hoje?**	Ke **dee**-a eh **o**-zhe
It's 9 December	**É nove de Dezembro**	Eh **no**-ve de de-**zay**^{n}-broo
We got here on 27 July	**Chegámos a vinte e sete de Julho**	She-**ga**-moosh a vee^{n}t ee set de **zhoo**-llyoo
We're leaving on 5 January	**Saímos a cinco de Janeiro**	Sa-**ee**-moosh a **see**^{n}-koo de zha-**nay**-ee-roo

DAY

morning	**a manhã**	ma-**nya**^{n}
this morning	**esta manhã**	**esh**-ta ma-**nya**^{n}
in the morning	**pela manhã**	**pe**-la ma-**nya**^{n}
midday, noon	**o meio-dia**	**may**-ee-oo-**dee**-a
at noon	**é meio-dia**	eh **may**-ee-oo-**dee**-a
afternoon	**a tarde**	tard
yesterday afternoon	**ontem à tarde**	**o**^{n}-te^{n} ah tard

evening	**o anoitecer**	a-no-ee-te-sair
tomorrow evening	**amanhã à noite**	a-ma-nya^{n} ah no-eet
midnight	**a meia-noite**	may-ee-a-no-eet
night	**a noite**	no-eet
sunrise	**o nascer do sol**	na-sayr doo sol
sunset	**o pôr do sol**	por doo sol
today	**hoje**	o-zhe
yesterday	**ontem**	o^{n}-te^{n}
day before yesterday	**anteontem**	an-te-o^{n}-te^{n}
tomorrow	**amanhã**	a-ma-nya^{n}
day after tomorrow	**depois de amanhã**	de-po-eesh de a-ma-nya^{n}
in ten days' time	**dentro de dez dias**	de^{n}-troo de desh dee-ash

WEEK

Sunday	**o Domingo**	Doo-mee^{n}-goo
Monday	**a Segunda-feira**	Se-goo^{n}-da-fay-ee-ra
Tuesday	**a Terça-feira**	Tair-sa-fay-ee-ra
Wednesday	**a Quarta-feira**	Kwar-ta-fay-ee-ra
Thursday	**a Quinta-feira**	Kee^{n}-ta-fay-ee-ra
Friday	**a Sexta-feira**	Saysh-ta-fay-ee-ra
Saturday	**o Sábado**	Sa-ba-doo
on Tuesday	**na Terça-feira**	na tair-sa-fay-ee-ra
on Sundays[1]	**aos Domingos**	a-osh doo-mee^{n}-goosh

1. In timetables the days from Monday to Friday are often abbreviated: *às* 2as – on Mondays; *às* 4as on Wednesdays.

fortnight	**a quinzena**	kee^{n}-zay-na

MONTH

January	**Janeiro**	Zha-nay-ee-roo
February	**Fevereiro**	Fe-ve-ray-ee-roo
March	**Março**	Mar-soo
April	**Abril**	A-breel
May	**Maio**	My-oo
June	**Junho**	Zhoo-nyoo
July	**Julho**	Zhoo-llyoo
August	**Agosto**	A-gosh-too
September	**Setembro**	Se-te^{n}-broo
October	**Outubro**	O-too-broo
November	**Novembro**	Noo-ve^{n}-broo
December	**Dezembro**	De-ze^{n}-broo

SEASON

spring	**a primavera**	pree-ma-vair-a
summer	**o verão**	ve-row^{n}
autumn	**o outono**	o-to-noo
winter	**o inverno**	ee^{n}-vair-noo
in spring	**na primavera**	na pree-ma-vair-a
during the summer	**durante o verão**	doo-ra^{n}t oo ve-row^{n}

YEAR

this year	**este ano**	aysht a-noo
last year	**o ano passado**	oo a-noo pa-sa-doo
next year	**o próximo ano**	oo pro-see-moo a-noo

PUBLIC HOLIDAYS

1 January (New Year's Day)	**O dia de Ano Novo**
1 May (Labour Day)	**O Primeiro de Maio**
10 June (Portuguese National Day)	**O dia de Camões/Portugal**
Corpus Christi (Thursday of 8th week after Easter)	**O dia do Corpo de Deus**
15 August (The Assumption)	**O dia da Assunção**
5 October (Republic Day)	**O dia da República**
1 November (All Saints' Day)	**O dia de Todos os Santos**
1 December (Independence Day)	**O Primeiro de Dezembro**
8 December (Immaculate Conception)	**O dia da Imaculada Conceição**
25 December (Christmas)	**O Natal**

Apart from these holidays every town and village celebrates its own holiday, which usually coincides with the day of its patron saint. Although not official holidays, many businesses, shops, etc. are closed on Shrove Tuesday, Good Friday and Maundy Thursday.

NUMBERS

CARDINAL

0	**zero**	**ze**-roo
1	**um**	oo^n
2	**dois**	**do**-eesh
3	**três**	traysh
4	**quatro**	**kwa**-troo
5	**cinco**	**see^n**-koo
6	**seis**	**say**-eesh
7	**sete**	set
8	**oito**	**o**-ee-to
9	**nove**	**no**-ve
10	**dez**	desh
11	**onze**	**o^n**-ze

12	**doze**	do-ze
13	**treze**	tray-ze
14	**catorze**	ka-tor-ze
15	**quinze**	kee^n-ze
16	**dezasseis**	de-za-saish
17	**dezassete**	de-za-set
18	**dezoito**	de-zoy-too
19	**dezanove**	de-za-no-ve
20	**vinte**	vee^{n}t
21	**vinte e um**	vee^{n}t ee oo^n
22	**vinte e dois**	vee^{n}t ee do-eesh
30	**trinta**	tree^n-ta
31	**trinta e um**	tree^n-ta ee oo^n
40	**quarenta**	kwa-re^n-ta
50	**cinquenta**	see^n-kwen-ta
60	**sessenta**	se-se^n-ta
70	**setenta**	se-te^n-ta
80	**oitenta**	oy-te^n-ta
90	**noventa**	no-ve^n-ta
100	**cem**	se^n
101	**cento e um**	se^n-too ee oo^n
200	**duzentos**	doo-ze^n-toosh
300	**trezentos**	tre-ze^n-toosh
1000	**mil**	meel
2000	**dois mil**	do-eesh meel
1,000,000	**um milhão**	un mee-llyow^n

ORDINAL

1st	**primeiro, -a**	pree-**may**-ee-roo
2nd	**segundo, -a**	se-**goo**^{n}-doo
3rd	**terceiro, -a**	ter-**say**-ee-roo
4th	**quarto, -a**	**kwar**-too
5th	**quinto, -a**	**kee**^{n}-too
6th	**sexto, -a**	**saysh**-too
7th	**sétimo, -a**	**se**-tee-moo
8th	**oitavo, -a**	oy-**ta**-voo
9th	**nono, -a**	**no**-noo
10th	**décimo, -a**	**de**-see-moo
half	**meio, -a/metade**	**may**-ee-oo/me-**tad**
quarter	**um quarto**	oo^{n} **kwar**-too
three quarters	**três quartos**	traysh **kwar**-toosh
a third	**um terço**	oo^{n} **ter**-soo
two thirds	**dois terços**	**do**-eesh **ter**-soosh

WEIGHTS & MEASURES

DISTANCE

kilometres – miles

km	*miles or km*	miles	km	*miles or km*	miles
1·6	*1*	0·6	14·5	*9*	5·6
3·2	*2*	1·2	16·1	*10*	6·2
4·8	*3*	1·9	32·2	*20*	12·4
6·4	*4*	2·5	40·2	*25*	15·3
8	*5*	3·1	80·5	*50*	31·1
9·7	*6*	3·7	160·9	*100*	62·1
11·3	*7*	4·3	804·7	*500*	310·7
12·9	*8*	5·0			

A rough way to convert from miles to km: divide by 5 and multiply by 8; from km to miles: divide by 8 and multiply by 5.

LENGTH AND HEIGHT

centimetres – inches

cm	*inch or cm*	inch	cm	*inch or cm*	inch
2·5	*1*	0·4	17·8	*7*	2·8
5·1	*2*	0·8	20·3	*8*	3·1
7·6	*3*	1·2	22·9	*9*	3·5
10·2	*4*	1·6	25·4	*10*	3·9
12·7	*5*	2·0	50·8	*20*	7·9
15·2	*6*	2·4	127	*50*	19·7

A rough way to convert from inches to cm: divide by 2 and multiply by 5; from cm to inches: divide by 5 and multiply by 2.

metres – feet

m	*ft or m*	ft	m	*ft or m*	ft
0·3	*1*	3·3	2·4	*8*	26·2
0·6	*2*	6·6	2·7	*9*	29·5
0·9	*3*	9·8	3	*10*	32·8
1·2	*4*	13·1	6·1	*20*	65·6
1·5	*5*	16·4	15·2	*50*	164
1·8	*6*	19·7	30·5	*100*	328·1
2·1	*7*	23			

A rough way to convert from ft to m: divide by 10 and multiply by 3; from m to ft: divide by 3 and multiply by 10.

metres – yards

m	*yds or m*	yds	m	*yds or m*	yds
0·9	*1*	1·1	7·3	*8*	8·8
1·8	*2*	2·2	8·2	*9*	9·8
2·7	*3*	3·3	9·1	*10*	10·9
3·7	*4*	4·4	18·3	*20*	21·9
4·6	*5*	5·5	45·7	*50*	54·7
5·5	*6*	6·6	91·4	*100*	109·4
6·4	*7*	7·7	457·2	*500*	546·8

A rough way to convert from yds to m: subtract 10 per cent from the number of yds; from m to yds: add 10 per cent to the number of metres.

LIQUID MEASURES

litres – gallons

litres	*galls or litres*	galls	litres	*galls or litres*	galls
4·6	*1*	0·2	36·4	*8*	1·8
9·1	*2*	0·4	40·9	*9*	2·0
13·6	*3*	0·7	45·5	*10*	2·2
18·2	*4*	0·9	90·9	*20*	4·4
22·7	*5*	1·1	136·4	*30*	6·6
27·3	*6*	1·3	181·8	*40*	8·8
31·8	*7*	1·5	227·3	*50*	11

1 pint = 0·6 litre   1 litre = 1·8 pint

A rough way to convert from galls to litres: divide by 2 and multiply by 9; from litres to galls: divide by 9 and multiply by 2.

WEIGHT

logrammes – pounds

kg	*lb or kg*	lb	kg	*lb or kg*	lb
0·5	*1*	2·2	3·2	*7*	15·4
0·9	*2*	4·4	3·6	*8*	17·6
1·4	*3*	6·6	4·1	*9*	19·8
1·8	*4*	8·8	4·5	*10*	22·1
2·3	*5*	11·0	9·1	*20*	44·1
2·7	*6*	13·2	22·7	*50*	110·2

rough way to convert from lb to kg: divide by 11 and multiply by 5; from ; to lb: divide by 5 and multiply by 11.

ammes – ounces

rammes	*oz.*	*oz.*	grammes
100	3·5	2	56·7
250	8·8	4	114·3
500	17·6	8	228·6
000 (1 kg)	35	16 (1 lb)	457·2

TEMPERATURE

centigrade (°C)	fahrenheit (°F)
°C	°F
– 10	14
– 5	23
0	32
5	41
10	50
15	59
20	68
25	77
30	86
35	95
37	98·4
38	100·5
39	102
40	104
100	212

To convert °F to °C: deduct 32, divide by 9 and multiply by 5; to convert °C to °F: divide by 5, multiply by 9 and add 32.

BASIC GRAMMAR

NOUNS

Nouns in Portuguese are either masculine or feminine.
Nouns denoting males, and most nouns ending in **-o** (except **-ção -são**) are masculine.

e.g. tio – uncle; castelo – castle

Nouns denoting females, and those ending in **-a, -ção, -são, -dade** are feminine.

e.g. tia – aunt; cidade – city

There are exceptions to these rules.

e.g. o coração – heart

Plural
The plural is formed by adding **-s** if the word ends in a vowel.
Most words ending in a consonant add **-es** to form the plural.

e.g. mulher (woman) – mulheres; luz (light) – luzes.

As a general rule nouns ending in **-al** become **-ais** in the plural.

e.g. metal (metal) – metais; material (material) – materiais.

Nouns ending in **-ão** have varied forms in the plural.
e.g. limão (lemon) – limões; instrução (instruction) – instruções; but pão (bread) – pães; cão (dog) – cães.

DEFINITE ARTICLE

o before a masculine singular noun	o banco (the bank)
os before a masculine plural noun	os bancos
a before a feminine singular noun	a mulher (the woman)
as before a feminine plural noun	as mulheres

INDEFINITE ARTICLE

um before a masculine singular noun	um barco (a ship)
uns before a masculine plural noun	uns barcos (some ships)
uma before a feminine singular noun	uma cadeira (a chair)
umas before a feminine plural noun	umas cadeiras (some chairs)

ADJECTIVES

Adjectives agree in gender and number with the noun.
Those ending in **-o** change to **-a** in the feminine.
e.g. fresco – fresca (fresh, cool); cansado *of a man* – cansada *of a woman* (tired).

Those ending in **-e** and most of those ending in a consonant are the same in the masculine and the feminine.
e.g. o castelo grande; a cadeira grande.

The plural is formed by adding **-s** if the word ends in a vowel, and **-es** in most cases when it ends in a consonant.
e.g. fresco – frescos; grande – grandes; inglês – ingleses.

Adjectives ending in **-l** change the **-l** to **-is** or **-eis**.
e.g. subtil – subtis (subtle).

The comparative and superlative are formed by putting **mais** before the adjective.

e.g.	um hotel barato	a cheap hotel
	um hotel mais barato	a cheaper hotel
	o hotel mais barato	the cheapest hotel

There are, however, exceptions to this rule; e.g. grande (big, great) becomes maior (bigger, greater).

POSSESSIVE ADJECTIVES

	m s	***m pl***	***f s***	***f pl***
my	meu	meus	minha	minhas
your *fam.*	teu	teus	tua	tuas
his, hers	seu/dele	seus/deles	sua/dela	suas/delas
our	nosso	nossos	nossa	nossas
your *fam.*	vosso	vossos	vossa	vossas
their, your *polite*	seu	seus	sua	suas

These adjectives agree with the thing possessed, e.g. meu pai (my father); meus pais (my parents); minha casa (my house), minhas casas (my houses); vosso livro (your book); vossas cartas (your letters).

PERSONAL PRONOUNS

	subject	***object***		***subject***	***object***
I	eu	me	we	nós	nos
you *fam.*	tu	te	you *fam.*	vós	vos
you *polite*	o senhor *m*	o	you *polite*	os senhores *m*	os
	a senhora *f*	a		as senhoras *f*	as
he	ele	o	they *m*	eles	os
she	ela	a	they *f*	elas	as

Personal pronouns are usually omitted before the verb.
e.g. vou – I go; vem – he (or she) comes.

Direct object pronouns are usually placed after the verb.
e.g. tenho-o – I have it.

Indirect object pronouns are the same as direct object pronouns except that **lhe** is used to mean to it, to him, to her, to you (*polite*), and **lhes** means to them, to you (*polite*). The third person reflexive pronoun is always **se**.
e.g. dar-lhe – to give to him etc.; dar-lhes – to give to them.

If a direct and an indirect object pronoun are used together, the indirect one is placed first.
e.g. damo-vo-lo – we give it to you (vos+o becomes vo-lo).

Lhe and **lhes** combine with the direct object pronoun to give the forms **lho, lha, lhos, lhas.**
e.g. dar-lho – to give it to him, her, you (*polite*).

When speaking to strangers always use the form **o senhor, a senhora** and **os senhores, as senhoras**, with the verb in the third person. **Tu** and **você** are used to close friends and to children.

DEMONSTRATIVE PRONOUNS

this one, that one

	m	*f*
this (*one*)	este	esta
these	estes	estas
that (*one*)	esse	essa
those	esses	essas
that (*one*) over there	aquele	aquela
those over there	aqueles	aquelas

'hey agree in gender and number with the nouns they represent.

e.g. **este** é o meu bilhete – this is my ticket.
quero **este** livro, **esse**, e **aquele** – I want this book,
that one and that one over there.

'he demonstrative adjectives have the same form as the pronouns.

'ERBS

To be' is translated by **ser** and **estar**.
Vhen it is followed by a noun, or when it indicates an origin, or a
ermanent or inherent quality, **ser** is used.

e.g.	a neve **é** fria e branca	snow is cold and white
	sou Britanico	I am British
	a Inglaterra **é** parte duma ilha	England is part of an island

Vhen it indicates position or a temporary state, **estar** is used.

e.g.	o carro **está** na rua principal	the car is in the main street
	estamos em Portugal	we are in Portugal

resent tense of **ser** and **estar**

	ser	**estar**
am	sou	estou
ou are *fam.*	és	estás
ou are *polite*	é	está
e, she is	é	está
'e are	somos	estamos
ou are	sois	estais
ey, you are	são	estão

n Portuguese there are three types of regular verbs, distinguished by the ndings of the infinitives.

e.g.
-ar falar – to speak **-er** vender – to sell

-ir partir – to leave, go away

The ***present tense*** is formed as follows:

falar	vender	partir
falo	vendo	parto
falas	vendes	partes
fala	vende	parte
falamos	vendemos	partimos
falais	vendeis	partis
falam	vendem	partem

The ***imperfect tense***

falar		**vender**	
falava –	*I spoke, have spoken, was speaking, etc.*	vendia –	*I sold, have sold, was selling, etc.*
falavas		vendias	
falava		vendia	
falávamos		vendíamos	
faláveis		vendíeis	
falavam		vendiam	

Verbs ending in **-ir** (partir) have the same endings in the imperfect as those in **-er** (vender).

The ***irregular imperfect tense*** of **ser** – to be
era
eras
era
éramos
éreis
eram

The present and imperfect tenses of some common irregular verbs:

dar – *to give*		**dizer** – *to say*		**fazer** – *to do, make*	
dou	dava	digo	dizia	faço	fazia
dás	davas	dizes	dizias	fazes	fazias
dá	dava	diz	dizia	faz	fazia
damos	dávamos	dizemos	dizíamos	fazemos	fazíamos
dais	dáveis	dizeis	dizíeis	fazeis	fazíeis
dão	davam	dizem	diziam	fazem	faziam

ir – *to go*		**poder** – *can, to be able*		**saber** – *to know*	
vou	ia	posso	podia	sei	sabia
vais	ias	podes	podias	sabes	sabias
vai	ia	pode	podia	sabe	sabia
vamos	íamos	podemos	podíamos	sabemos	sabíamos
ides	íeis	podeis	podíeis	sabeis	sabíeis
vão	iam	podem	podiam	sabem	sabiam

ter – *to have*		**ver** – *to see*		**vir** – *to come*	
tenho	tinha	vejo	via	venho	vinha
tens	tinhas	vês	vias	vens	vinhas
tem	tinha	vê	via	vem	vinha
temos	tínhamos	vemos	víamos	vimos	vínhamos
tendes	tínheis	vêdes	víeis	vindes	vínheis
têm	tinham	vêem	viam	vêm	vinham

The ***future*** is formed by adding the following endings to the infinitives of all regular verbs:

falar	vender	partir
falar**ei**	vender**ei**	partir**ei**
falar**ás**	vender**ás**	partir**ás**
falar**á**	vender**á**	partir**á**
falar**emos**	vender**emos**	partir**emos**
falar**eis**	vender**eis**	partir**eis**

falarão venderão partirão

The present tense of **ir** – to go, can also be used to form the future, as in English.

e.g. **vou** comprar um guia – I'm going to buy a guide book, I shall buy a guide book.

The ***negative*** is formed by putting **não** before the verb.
e.g. **não** falo português – I don't speak Portuguese.

VOCABULARY

Various groups of specialized words are given elsewhere in this book and these words are not usually repeated in the vocabulary:

A

a/an	**um/uma**	oo^{n}/**oo**-ma
abbey	**a abadía**	a-ba-**dee**-a
able (to be)	**poder**	poo-**dair**
about	**cerca de**	**sair**-ka de
above	**em cima de**	e^{n} **see**-ma de
abroad	**estrangeiro**	esh-tra^{n}-**zhay**-ee-roo
accept (to)	**aceitar**	a-say-ee-**tar**
accident	**o acidente**	a-see-**de^{n}t**
accommodation	**o alojamento**	a-loo-zha-**me^{n}**-too
account	**a conta**	**ko^{n}**-ta
ache (to)	**doer**	dwer
acquaintance	**o conhecido**	koo^{n}-nye-**see**-doo
across	**através**	a-tra-**vesh**
act (to)	**actuar/agir**	a-**twar**/a-**zheer**
add (to)	**unir**	oo-**neer**
address	**a direcção**	dee-re-**sow^{n}**
admire (to)	**admirar**	ad-mee-**rar**
admission	**a admissão**	ad-mee-**sow^{n}**
adventure	**a aventura**	a-ven-**too**-ra
advertisement	**o anúncio**	a-**noon**-see-oo
advice	**o conselho**	ko^{n}-**say**-llyoo
aeroplane	**o avião**	a-vee-**ow^{n}**
afford (to)	**comportar**	ko^{n}-por-**tar**
afraid (to be)	**ter medo**	tayr **may**-doo
after	**depois**	de-**po**-eesh

afternoon	**a tarde**	tard
again	**outra vez**	**oh**-tra vaysh
against	**contra**	**ko^{n}**-tra
age	**a idade**	ee-**dad**
agree (to)	**concordar**	ko^{n}-koor-**dar**
air	**o ar**	ar
airbed	**o colchão de ar**	kol-**show^{n}** de ar
air-conditioning	**o ar condicionado**	ar ko^{n}-dee-see-oo-**na**-doo
alarm clock	**o despertador**	desh-per-ta-**dor**
alcoholic (drink)	**a bebida alcoólica**	be-**bee**-da al-koo-**o**-lee-ka
alike	**igual/parecido**	ee-**gwal**/pa-re-**see**-doo
alive	**vivo**	**vee**-voo
all	**todo**	**toh**-doo
all right	**está bem**	esh-ta be^{n}
allow (to)	**permitir**	per-mee-**teer**
almost	**quase**	**kwa**-ze
alone	**só**	so
along	**ao longo**	ow **lo^{n}**-goo
already	**já**	zhah
alter (to)	**modificar**	moo-dee-fee-**kar**
alternativc	**a alternativa**	al-ter-na-**tee**-va
although	**embora**	e^{n}-**bo**-ra
always	**sempre**	**se^{n}**-pre
ambulance	**a ambulância**	a^{n}-boo-**la^{n}**-see-a
America	**América**	a-**me**-ree-ka

American	**o americano**	a-me-ree-**ka**-noo
among	**entre**	**e^n**-tre
amuse (to)	**divertir**	dee-ver-**teer**
amusement park	**o parque de diversões**	park de dee-ver-**soy^{n}sh**
amusing	**divertido**	dee-ver-**tee**-doo
ancient	**antigo**	a^n-**tee**-goo
and	**e**	ee
angry	**zangado**	za^n-**ga**-doo
animal	**o animal**	a-nee-**mal**
anniversary	**o aniversário**	a-nee-ver-**sa**-ree-oo
annoy (to)	**incomodar**	ee^n-koo-moo-**dar**
another	**outro**	**oh**-troo
answer	**a resposta**	resh-**posh**-ta
answer (to)	**responder**	resh-po^n-**dair**
antique	**a antiguidade**	a^n-tee-gwee-**dad**
any	**algum**	al-**goo^n**
anyone, someone	**alguém**	al-**ge^n**
anything, something	**algo**	**al**-goo
anyway	**de qualquer modo**	de kwal-**kair mo**-doo
anywhere, somewhere	**em qualquer parte**	e^n kwal-**kair** part
apartment	**o apartamento**	a-par-ta-**me^n**-too
apologize (to)	**pedir desculpa**	pe-**deer** desh-**kool**-pa
appetite	**o apetite**	a-pe-**teet**
appointment	**a entrevista**	e^n-tre-**veesh**-ta
architect	**o arquitecto**	ar-kee-**te**-too

architecture	**a arquitectura**	ar-kee-te-too-ra
area	**a área**	a-ree-a
area code	**o código da área**	ko-dee-goo da a-ree-a
arm	**o braço**	bra-soo
armchair	**a cadeira de braços**	ka-day-ee-ra de bra-soosh
army	**o exército**	e-zer-see-too
around	**em volta de**	e^{n} vol-ta de
arrange (to)	**arranjar**	ar-ra^{n}-zhar
arrival	**a chegada**	she-ga-da
arrive (to)	**chegar**	she-gar
art	**a arte**	art
art gallery	**a galeria de arte**	ga-le-ree-a dart
artist	**o artista**	ar-teesh-ta
as	**como**	ko-moo
as much as	**tanto como**	ta^{n}-too ko-moo
as soon as	**logo que**	lo-goo ke
as well	**também**	ta^{n}-bc^{n}
ashtray	**o cinzeiro**	see^{n}-zay-ee-roo
ask (to)	**perguntar**	per-goo^{n}-tar
asleep	**adormecido**	a-door-me-see-doo
at	**em**	e^{n}
at last	**por fim**	poor fee^{n}
at once	**em seguida**	e^{n} see-gee-da
atmosphere	**a atmosfera**	at-moosh-fair-a
attention	**a atenção**	a-te^{n}-sow^{n}

attractive **atractivo** a-tra-tee-voo
auction **o leilão** le-ee-low^n
audience **a audiência** ow-dee-ay^n-see-a
aunt **a tia** tee-a
Australia **Austrália** owsh-tra-lee-a
Australian **australiano/a** owsh-tra-lee-a-noo/a
author **o autor** ow-tor
autumn **o outono** o-to-no
available **disponível** deesh-poo-nee-vel
avenue **a avenida** a-ve-nee-da
average **médio** me-dee-oo
avoid (to) **evitar** ee-vee-tar
awake **acordado** a-koor-da-doo
away **fora** fo-ra

B

baby **o, a bebé** be-be
baby food **a comida de bebé** ko-mee-da de be-be
baby-sitter **baby-sitter** be-be-see-tair
bachelor **o solteiro** sol-tay-ee-roo
back *returned* **de volta** de vol-ta
bad **mau** mow
bag **o saco** sa-koo
baggage **a bagagem** ba-ga-zhay^n
baggage cart **a carrinha de bagagens** kar-ree-nya de ba-ga-zhe^{n}sh

baggage check	**o balcão de bagagens**	bal-kow^{n} de ba-ga-zhe^{n}sh
bait	**a isca**	ees-ka
balcony	**o balcão**	bal-kow^{n}
ball *sport*	**a bola**	bo-la
ballet	**o bailado**	by-la-doo
balloon	**o balão**	ba-low^{n}
band *music*	**a orquestra**	or-kesh-tra
bank	**o banco**	ba^{n}-koo
bank account	**a conta bancária**	ko^{n}-ta ba^{n}-ka-ree-a
bare	**nu/nua**	noo/noo-a
barn	**o celeiro**	se-lay-ee-roo
basket	**o cesto**	saysh-too
bath	**o banho**	ba-nyoo
bath essence	**os sais de banho**	sy-eesh de ba-nyoo
bathe (to)	**banhar-se**	ba-nyar-se
bathing cap	**a touca**	to-ka
bathing costume	**o fato de banho**	fa-too de ba-nyoo
bathing trunks	**os calções de banho**	kal-soy^{n}sh de ba-nyoo
bathroom	**a casa de banho**	ka-za de ba-nyoo
battery	**a bateria**	ba-te-ree-a
bay	**a baía**	ba-ee-a
be (to)	**ser/estar**	sayr/esh-tar
beach	**a praia**	pry-a
beard	**a barba**	bar-ba
beautiful	**bonito**	boo-nee-too
because	**porque**	poor-ke

become (to)	**tornar**	toor-**nar**
bed	**a cama**	**ka**-ma
bedroom	**o quarto**	**kwar**-too
before *in time*	**antes**	**an**-tesh
begin (to)	**começar**	koo-me-**sar**
beginning	**o começo**	koo-**may**-soo
behind	**atrás**	a-**trash**
believe (to)	**crer**	krair
bell	**a campaínha**	ka^n-pa-**ee**-nya
belong (to)	**pertencer**	per-te^n-**sair**
below	**em baixo**	e^n **ba**-ee-shoo
belt	**o cinto**	**see^n**-too
bench	**o banco**	**ba^n**-koo
bend	**a curva**	**koor**-va
beneath	**debaixo**	de-**ba**-ee-shoo
berth	**o beliche**	be-**leesh**
best	**o melhor**	me-**lyor**
bet	**a aposta**	a-**posh**-ta
better	**melhor**	me-**lyor**
between	**entre**	**en**-tre
bicycle	**a bicicleta**	bee-see-**kle**-ta
big	**grande**	gra^{n}d
bill	**a conta**	**ko^n**-ta
binoculars	**os binóculos**	bee-**no**-koo-loosh
bird	**o pássaro**	**pa**-sa-roo
birthday	**o aniversário**	a-nee-ver-**sa**-ree-oo

bite (to)	**morder**	moor-dair
bitter	**amargo**	a-mar-goo
blanket	**a manta**	ma^{n}-ta
bleed (to)	**sangrar**	sa^{n}-grar
blind	**cego**	sey-goo
blister	**a bolha**	bo-lya
blond	**louro/loiro**	loh-roo/loy-roo
blood	**o sangue**	sa^{n}g
blouse	**a blusa**	bloo-za
blow	**o sôpro**	so-proo
blow (to)	**soprar**	soo-prar
(on) board	**a bordo**	a bor-doo
boarding house	**a pensão**	pe^{n}-sow^{n}
boat	**o barco**	bar-koo
body	**o corpo**	kor-poo
bolt	**o ferrolho**	fer-ro-llyoo
bone	**o osso**	o-soo
bone *fish*	**a espinha**	esh-pee-nya
bonfire	**a fogueira**	foo-gey-ra
book	**o livro**	lee-vroo
book (to)	**reservar**	re-zer-var
boot	**a bota**	bo-ta
border	**a fronteira**	fro^{n}-tay-ee-ra
bored	**aborrecido**	a-boo-re-see-doo
boring (to be)	**aborrecer**	a-boo-re-sayr
borrow (to)	**pedir emprestado**	pe-deer e^{n}-presh-ta-doo

both	**ambos**	a^{n}-boosh
bother (to) *annoy*	**irritar**	ee-ree-tar
bottle	**a garrafa**	ga-ra-fa
bottle opener	**o saca-rolhas**	sa-ka-ro-llyash
bottom	**o fundo**	foo^{n}-doo
bow tie	**o laço de homem**	la-soo de o-me^{n}
bowl	**a tigela**	tee-zhe-la
box *container*	**a caixa**	ka-ee-sha
box *theatre*	**o camarote**	ka-ma-rot
box office	**a bilheteira**	bee-llye-tay-ee-ra
boy	**o rapaz**	ra-pash
bracelet	**a pulseira**	pool-say-ee-ra
braces	**os suspensórios**	soos-pe^{n}-so-ree-osh
brain	**o cérebro**	se-re-broo
branch *office*	**a filial**	fee-lee-al
branch *tree*	**o ramo**	ra-moo
brand	**a marca**	mar-ka
brassière	**o soutien**	soo-tee-a^{n}
Brazil	**o Brasil**	bra-zeel
Brazilian	**brasileiro**	bra-zee-lay-ee-roo
break (to)	**romper**	ro^{n}-pair
breakfast	**o pequeno almoço**	pe-kay-noo al-mo-soo
breathe (to)	**respirar**	resh-pee-rar
brick	**o tijolo**	tee-zho-loo
bridge	**a ponte**	po^{n}t
bright *colour*	**viva**	vee-va

bring (to)	**trazer**	tra-**zair**
British	**britânico**	bree-**ta**-nee-koo
broken	**partido**	par-**tee**-doo
brooch	**o broche**	brosh
brother	**o irmão**	eer-**mow**^{n}
bruise (to)	**contundir/pisar**	ko^n-too^n-**deer**/pee-**zar**
brush	**a escova**	esh-**ko**-va
brush (to)	**escovar**	esh-koo-**var**
bucket	**o balde**	bald
buckle	**a fivela**	fee-**ve**-la
build (to)	**construir**	ko^{n}sh-troo-**eer**
building	**o edifício**	e-dee-**fee**-see-oo
bullfight	**a tourada**	to-**ra**-da
bullring	**a praça de touros**	**pra**-sa de **to**-roosh
bunch *flowers*	**o ramo de flores**	**ra**-moo de florsh
bunch *keys*	**o molho de chaves**	**mo**-llyoo de **sha**-**vesh**
buoy	**a boia**	**boy**-a
burn (to)	**queimar**	kay-ee-**mar**
burst (to)	**rebentar**	re-be^n-**tar**
bus	**o autocarro**	ow-to-**ka**-roo
bus stop	**a paragem**	pa-**ra**-zhay^n
business	**o negócio**	ne-**go**-see-oo
busy	**ocupado**	o-koo-**pa**-doo
but	**mas**	mash
butterfly	**a borboleta**	boor-boo-**lay**-ta
button	**o botão**	boo-**tow**^{n}

buy (to)	**comprar**	ko^{n}-prar
by	**por**	poor

C

cab	**o taxi**	tak-see
cabin	**o camarote**	ka-ma-rot
calculator	**o calculador**	kal-koo-la-dor
calendar	**o calendário**	ka-len-da-ree-oo
call *telephone*	**a chamada telefónica**	sha-ma-da te-le-fo-nee-ka
call *visit*	**a visita**	vee-see-ta
call (to) *summon*	**chamar**	sha-mar
call (to) *telephone*	**chamar/telefonar**	sha-mar/te-le-fo-nar
call (to) *visit*	**visitar**	vee-see-tar
camp (to)	**acampar**	a-ka^{n}-par
camp site	**o acampamento**	a-ka^{n}-pa-me^{n}-too
can (to be able)	**poder**	poo-dair
can *tin*	**a lata**	la-ta
can opener	**o abre-latas**	a-bre-la-tash
Canada	**o Canadá**	ka-na-da
Canadian	**canadiano**	ka-na-dee-a-noo
cancel (to)	**anular**	a-noo-lar
candle	**a vela**	ve-la
canoe	**a canoa**	ka-no-a
cap	**o gorro**	gor-roo
capable of	**capaz**	ka-pash

capital city	**a capital**	ka-pee-tal
car	**o carro**	kar-roo
car park	**o parque de estacionamento**	park desh-ta-see-oo-na-may^{n}-too
carafe	**a jarra**	zhar-ra
caravan	**a caravana**	ka-ra-va-na
card	**o cartão**	kar-tow^{n}
care	**cuidado**	kwee-da-doo
careful	**cuidadoso**	kwee-da-do-zoo
careless	**descuidado**	des-kwee-da-doo
caretaker	**o porteiro**	poor-tay-ee-roo
carpet	**a carpete**	kar-pet
carry (to)	**levar**	le-var
cash (to)	**trocar**	troo-kar
cashier	**caixa**	ka-ee-sha
casino	**o casino**	ka-zee-noo
cassette	**a cassete**	ka-set
cassette recorder	**o leitor de cassetes**	lay-ee-tor de ka-se-tesh
castle	**o castelo**	kash-te-loo
cat	**o gato**	ga-too
catalogue	**o catálogo**	ka-ta-loo-goo
catch (to)	**apanhar**	a-pa-nyar
cathedral	**a catedral**	ka-te-dral
catholic	**católico**	ka-to-lee-koo
cause	**a causa**	kow-za
cave	**a caverna**	ka-vair-na

cement	o cimento	see-me^n-too
central	central	se^n-tral
centre	o centro	se^n-troo
century	o século	se-koo-loo
ceremony	a cerimónia	se-ree-mo-nee-a
certain	certo	sair-too
chain *jewellery*	o fio/colar	fee-oo/ko-lar
chair	a cadeira	ka-day-ee-ra
chambermaid	a criada de quarto	kree-a-da de kwar-too
chance	a oportunidade	o-por-too-nee-dad
(small) change	o dinheiro trocado	dee-nyay-ee-roo troo-ka-doo
change (to)	trocar	troo-kar
chapel	a capela	ka-pe-la
charge	a tarifa/o preço	ta-ree-fa/pray-soo
charge (to)	cobrar	koo-brar
cheap	barato	ba-ra-too
check (to)	examinar	ee-za-mee-nar
chef	o cozinheiro chefe	koo-zee-nyay-ee-roo shef
cheque	o cheque	shek
chess	o xadrez	sha-draysh
chess set	o jogo de xadrez	zho-go de sha-draysh
child	a criança	kree-a^n-sa
chill (to)	arrefecer	a-re-fe-sayr
china	a porcelana	por-se-la-na
choice	a escolha	esh-ko-llya

hoose (to)	**escolher**	esh-ko-**llyer**
hurch	**a igreja**	ee-**gray**-zha
igarette case	**a cigarreira**	see-ga-**ray**-ee-ra
inema	**o cinema**	see-**nay**-ma
ircle *theatre*	**o balcão**	bal-**kow**^{n}
ircus	**o circo**	**seer**-koo
ity	**a cidade**	see-**dad**
lass	**a classe**	**klass**
lean	**limpo**	**lee**^{n}-poo
lean (to)	**limpar**	lee^n-**par**
leansing cream	**o creme de limpeza**	**krem** de lee^n-**pay**-za
lear *substance*	**claro**	**kla**-roo
lerk	**o empregado**	e^n-pre-**ga**-doo
liff	**o rochedo**	roo-**shay**-doo
limb (to)	**subir**	soo-**beer**
loakroom	**o vestiário**	vesh-tee-**a**-ree-oo
lock	**o relógio**	re-**lo**-zhee-oo
lose (to)	**fcchar**	fe-**shar**
losed	**fechado**	fe-**sha**-doo
loth	**o tecido**	te-**see**-doo
lothes	**o vestuário**	vesh-too-**a**-ree-oo
loud	**a nuvem**	**noo**-ve^n
oach *bus*	**a camioneta**	ka-mee-o-**ne**-ta
oach *train*	**a carruagem**	ka-roo-**a**-zhe^n
oast	**a costa**	**kosh**-ta
oat	**o casaco**	ka-**sa**-koo

coat hanger	**o cabide**	ka-**beed**
coin	**a moeda**	moo-**e**-da
cold	**frio**	**free**-oo
collar	**o colarinho**	koo-la-**ree**-nyoo
collect (to)	**cobrar**	ko-**brar**
colour	**a cor**	kor
comb	**o pente**	pe^{n}t
come (to)	**vir**	veer
come in	**entre**	e^{n}-tre
comfortable	**confortável**	ko^{n}-foor-**ta**-vel
common	**comum**	ko-**moo^{n}**
compact disc	**o disco compacto**	**deesh**-koo ko^{n}-**pak**-too
company	**a companhia**	ko^{n}-pa-**nyee**-a
compartment *train*	**o compartimento**	ko^{n}-par-tee-**me^{n}**-too
compass	**o compasso**	ko^{n}-**pa**-soo
compensation	**a compensação**	ko^{n}-pe^{n}-sa-**sow^{n}**
complain (to)	**queixar-se**	kay-ee-**shar**-se
complaint	**a queixa**	**kay**-sha
complete	**completo**	ko^{n}-**ple**-too
computer	**o computador**	ko^{n}-poo-ta-**dor**
concert	**o concerto**	ko^{n}-**sair**-too
concert hall	**o salão de concerto**	sa-**low^{n}** de ko^{n}-**sair**-too
concrete	**o cimento armado**	see-**me^{n}**-too ar-**ma**-doo
condition	**a condição**	kon-dee-**sow^{n}**
conductor *bus*	**o cobrador**	koo-bra-**dor**
conductor *orchestra*	**o maestro**	ma-**esh**-troo

congratulations	**felicitações/parabéns**	fe-lee-see-ta-**soy^{n}sh**/pa-ra-**be^{n}sh**
connect (to)	**ligar**	lee-**gar**
connection *train, etc.*	**a ligação**	lee-ga-**sow^{n}**
consul	**o cônsul**	**ko^{n}**-sool
consulate	**o consulado**	ko^{n}-soo-**la**-doo
contact lenses	**as lentes de contacto**	**le^{n}**-tesh de ko^{n}-**tak**-too
contain (to)	**conter**	ko^{n}-**tair**
contraceptive	**o contraceptivo**	ko^{n}-tra-se-**tee**-voo
contrast	**o contraste**	kon-**trast**
convenient	**conveniente**	ko^{n}-ve-nee-**e^{n}t**
convent	**o convento**	ko^{n}-**ve^{n}**-too
conversation	**a conversação**	ko^{n}-ver-sa-**sow^{n}**
cook	**o cozinheiro**	koo-zee-**nyay**-ee-roo
cook (to)	**cozinhar**	koo-zee-**nyar**
cool	**fresco**	**fraysh**-koo
copper	**o cobre**	**ko**-bre
copy *book*	**o exemplar**	ee-zem-**plar**
copy *dup.*	**a cópia**	ko-**pee-a**
copy (to)	**copiar**	ko-pee-**ar**
cork	**a rolha**	**ro**-llya
corkscrew	**o saca-rolhas**	sa-ka-**ro**-llyash
corner	**o canto**	**ka^{n}**-too
correct	**correcto**	koo-**re**-too
corridor	**o corredor**	koo-re-**dor**
cosmetics	**os cosméticos**	koosh-**me**-tee-koosh

cost	**o custo**	**koosh**-too
cost (to)	**custar**	koosh-**tar**
costume jewellery	**as jóias de imitação**	zhoy-ash de ee-mee-ta-**sow^n**
cot	**a cama de bebé**	ka-ma de be-**be**
cottage	**a casa de campo**	ka-sa de **ka^n**-poo
cotton	**o algodão**	al-goo-**dow^n**
cotton wool	**o algodão em rama**	al-goo-**dow^n** e^n **ra**-ma
count (to)	**contar**	ko^n-**tar**
country	**o país**	pa-**eesh**
countryside	**o campo**	**ka^n**-poo
course *dish*	**o prato**	**pra**-too
courtyard	**o quintal**	keen-**tal**
cousin	**o primo**	**pree**-moo
cover	**a cobertura**	koo-ber-**too**-ra
cover (to)	**cobrir**	koo-**breer**
crash *collision*	**o acidente/choque**	a-see-**de^{n}t**/shok
cream *face*	**o creme**	krem
credit	**o crédito**	**kre**-dee-too
credit card	**o cartão de crédito**	kar-**tow^n** de **kre**-dee-too
crew	**a tripulação**	tree-poo-la-**sow^n**
cross	**a cruz**	kroosh
cross (to)	**atravessar**	a-tra-ve-**sar**
crossroads	**o cruzamento**	kroo-za-**me^n**-too
crowd	**a multidão**	mool-tee-**dow^n**
cry (to) *shout*	**gritar**	gree-**tar**

cry (to) *weep*	**chorar**	shoo-rar
crystal	**o cristal**	kreesh-tal
cufflinks	**os botões de punho**	bo-toy^{n}sh de poo-nyoo
cup	**a chávena**	sha-ve-na
cupboard	**o armário**	ar-ma-ree-oo
cure (to)	**curar**	koo-rar
curious	**curioso**	koo-ree-o-so
curl (to)	**frisar**	free-zar
current	**a corrente**	koo-ray^{n}t
curtain	**a cortina**	kor-tee-na
curve	**a curva**	koor-va
cushion	**a almofada**	al-moo-fa-da
customs	**a alfândega**	al-fa^{n}-de-ga
customs officer	**o funcionário aduaneiro**	foo^{n}-see-oo-na-ree-oo a-doo-a-nay-ee-roo
cut (to)	**cortar**	koor-tar
cycling	**o ciclismo**	see-kleesh-moo
cyclist	**o ciclista**	see-kleesh-ta

D

daily	**diário**	dee-a-ree-oo
damaged	**danificado**	da-nee-fee-ka-doo
damp	**húmido**	oo-mee-doo
dance	**a dança**	da^{n}-sa
dance (to)	**dançar**	da^{n}-sar
danger	**o perigo**	pe-ree-goo

dangerous	**perigoso**	pe-ree-**go**-zoo
dark	**escuro**	esh-**koo**-roo
date *calendar*	**a data**	**da**-ta
daughter	**a filha**	**fee**-llya
day	**o dia**	**dee**-a
dead	**morto**	**mor**-too
deaf	**surdo**	**soor**-doo
dealer	**o negociante**	ne-goo-see-**ant**
dear	**querido/caro**	ke-**ree**-doo/**ka**-roo
decanter	**a garrafa de cristal**	gar-**ra**-fa de kreesh-**tal**
decide (to)	**decidir**	de-see-**deer**
deck	**a coberta**	koo-**bair**-ta
deckchair	**a cadeira de praia**	ka-**day**-ee-ra de **pry**-a
declare (to)	**declarar**	de-kla-**rar**
deep	**profundo**	proo-**foo**^{n}-doo
delay	**o atraso**	a-**tra**-zoo
deliver (to)	**entregar**	e^n-tre-**gar**
delivery	**a entrega**	e^n-**tre**-ga
dentures	**a dentadura postiça**	den-ta-**doo**-ra posh-**tee**-sa
deodorant	**o desodorizante**	de-zoh-doo-ree-**za**^{n}**t**
depart (to)	**partir**	par-**teer**
department	**o departamento**	de-par-ta-**me**^{n}-too
departure	**a partida**	par-**tee**-da
dessert	**a sobremesa**	soo-bre-**may**-za
detour	**o desvio**	dezh-**vee**-oo

dial (to) *telephone*	**marcar**	mar-**kar**
dialling code	**o código de ligação**	**ko**-dee-go de lee-ga-**sow**^{n}
diamond	**o diamante**	dee-a-**ma**^{n}**t**
dice	**os dados**	**da**-doosh
dictionary	**o dicionário**	dee-see-oo-**na**-ree-oo
diet	**a dieta**	dee-**e**-ta
diet (to)	**fazer dieta**	fa-**zair** dee-**e**-ta
different	**diferente**	dee-fe-**re**^{n}**t**
difficult	**difícil**	dee-**fee**-seel
dine (to)	**jantar**	zha^n-**tar**
dining room	**a sala de jantar**	**sa**-la de zha^n-**tar**
dinner	**o jantar**	zha^n-**tar**
dinner jacket	**o smoking**	**smo**-keeng
direct	**directo**	dee-**re**-too
direction	**a direcção**	dee-re-**sow**^{n}
dirty	**sujo**	**soo**-zhoo
disappointed	**desapontado**	des-a-pon-**ta**-doo
discothéque	**a discoteca**	deesh-koo-**te**-ka
discount	**o desconto**	desh-**ko**^{n}-too
dish	**o prato**	**pra**-too
disinfectant	**o desinfectante**	de-see^n-fe-**ta**^{n}**t**
distance	**a distância**	deesh-**ta**^{n}-see-a
disturb (to)	**perturbar**	per-toor-**bar**
ditch	**a vala**	**va**-la
dive (to)	**mergulhar**	mer-goo-**llyar**
diving board	**o trampolim**	tra^n-poo-**lee**^{n}

divorced	**divorciado**	dee-voor-see-a-doo
do (to)	**fazer**	fa-zair
dock (to)	**atracar**	a-tra-kar
doctor	**o médico**	me-dee-koo
dog	**o cão**	kow^n
doll	**a boneca**	boo-ne-ka
door	**a porta**	por-ta
double	**dobro**	do-broo
double bed	**a cama de casal**	ka-ma de ka-zal
double room	**o quarto de casal**	kwar-too de ka-zal
down (stairs)	**abaixo**	a-ba-ee-shoo
dozen	**a dúzia**	doo-zee-a
draught	**a corrente de ar**	koo-ray^{n}t de ar
draw (to)	**desenhar**	de-ze-nyar
drawer	**a gaveta**	ga-vay-ta
drawing	**o desenho**	de-ze-nyoo
dream	**o sonho**	so-nyoo
dress	**o vestido**	vesh-tee-doo
dressing gown	**o roupão**	ro-pow^n
dressmaker	**a modista**	moo-deesh-ta
drink (to)	**beber**	be-bair
drinking water	**a água potável**	a-gwa poo-ta-vel
drive (to)	**conduzir/guiar**	ko^n-doo-zeer/gee-ar
driver	**o condutor**	ko^n-doo-tor
driving licence	**a carta de condução**	kar-ta de kon-doo-sow^n
drop (to)	**cair**	ka-eer

drunk	**bêbado/embriegado**	**be**-ba-doo/e^{n}-bree-a-**ga**-doo
dry (to)	**secar**	se-**kar**
dry *adj.*	**seco**	**say**-koo
during	**durante**	doo-**ra^{n}t**
duvet	**o duvet**	doo-**ve**
dye (to)	**tingir**	tee^{n}-**zheer**

E

each	**cada**	**ka**-da
early	**cedo**	se-**doo**
earrings	**os brincos**	**bree^{n}**-koosh
east	**o este/leste**	esht/lesht
Easter	**a Páscoa**	**pash**-kwa
easy	**fácil**	**fa**-seel
eat (to)	**comer**	koo-**mair**
edge	**a beira**	**bey**-ra
EEC	**a CEE**	se e e
elastic	**o elástico**	ee-**lash**-tee-koo
electric light bulb	**a lâmpada**	**la^{n}**-pa-da
electric point	**a tomada**	too-**ma**-da
electricity	**a electricidade**	e-le-tree-see-**dad**
elevator	**o elevador**	ee-le-va-**dor**
embarrass (to)	**embaraçar**	e^{n}-ba-ras-**sar**
embassy	**a embaixada**	e^{n}-ba-ee-**sha**-da

emergency exit	**a saída de emergência**	sa-ee-da de ee-mer-zhen-see-a
empty	**vazio**	va-zee-oo
end	**o fim**	fee^n
engaged *people*	**noivo**	noy-voo
engaged *telephone, toilet*	**ocupado**	o-koo-pa-doo
engine	**a máquina**	ma-kee-na
England	**a Inglaterra**	ee^n-gla-te-ra
English	**inglês**	ee^n-glaysh
enjoy (to)	**gozar**	go-zar
enough	**bastante**	bash-ta^{n}t
enquiries	**as informações**	ee^n-foor-ma-soy^{n}sh
enter (to)	**entrar**	en-trar
entrance	**a entrada**	e^n-tra-da
entrance fee	**o custo de entrada**	koosh-too de e^n-tra-da
envelope	**o envelope**	e^n-ve-lop
equipment	**o equipamento**	ee-kee-pa-me^n-too
escalator	**a escada rolante**	esh-ka-da roo-lant
escape (to)	**escapar**	esh-ka-par
estate agent	**o agente de propriedades**	a-zhe^{n}t de proo-pree-e-dadesh
Europe	**a Europa**	ay-oo-ro-pa
even *not odd*	**par**	par
evening	**a tardinha**	tar-dee-nya
event	**o acontecimento**	a-ko^n-te-see-me^n-too
every	**cada**	ka-da
everybody	**todos**	to-doosh

everything	**tudo**	**too**-doo
everywhere	**em toda a parte**	e^{n} **to**-da a **part**
example	**o exemplo**	ee-**ze^{n}**-ploo
excellent	**excelente**	esh-se-**le^{n}t**
except	**excepto**	esh-**se**-too
excess	**o excesso**	esh-**se**-soo
exchange bureau	**a casa de câmbio**	**kah**-za de **ka^{n}**-bee-oo
exchange rate	**o câmbio**	**ka^{n}**-bee-oo
excursion	**a excursão**	esh-koor-**sow^{n}**
excuse	**a desculpa**	des-**kool**-pa
exhausted	**exausto**	ez-**ows**-too
exhibition	**a exposição**	esh-poo-zee-**sow^{n}**
exit	**a saída**	sa-**ee**-da
expect (to)	**esperar**	esh-pe-**rar**
expensive	**caro**	**ka**-roo
explain (to)	**explicar**	esh-plee-**kar**
express	**expresso**	esh-**pre**-soo
express train	**o rápido**	**ra**-pee-doo
eye shadow	**a sombra para os olhos**	**so^{n}**-bra **pa**-ra osh **oh**-llyoosh

F

fabric	**o tecido**	te-**see**-doo
face	**a cara/o rosto**	**ka**-ra/**rosh**-too
face cloth	**a toalha de rosto**	too-**a**-lya de **rosh**-too
face cream	**o creme de rosto**	**krem** de **rosh**-too

face powder	**o pó de arroz**	po da-rosh
fact	**o facto**	fak-too
factory	**a fábrica**	fah-bree-ka
fade (to)	**desbotar**	dezh-boo-tar
faint (to)	**desmaiar**	dezh-my-yar
fair	**a feira**	fay-ee-ra
fair *blond*	**loiro**	lo-ee-roo
fall (to)	**cair**	ka-eer
family	**a família**	fa-mee-lee-a
far	**longe**	lo^{n}zh
fare	**o bilhete**	bee-llyayt
farm	**a quinta**	kee^{n}-ta
farmer	**o agricultor**	agree-kool-tor
farmhouse	**a casa de quinta/ herdade**	ka-za de kee^{n}-ta/er-dad
farther	**mais longe**	ma-eesh lo^{n}zh
fashion	**a moda**	mo-da
fast	**rápido**	ra-pee-doo
fat	**gordo**	gor-doo
father	**o pai**	py
fault	**a culpa**	kool-pa
fear	**o medo**	me-doo
feed (to)	**alimentar**	a-lee-me^{n}-tar
feeding bottle	**o biberão**	bee-be-row^{n}
feel (to)	**sentir**	se^{n}-teer
felt-tip pen	**a caneta de ponta de feltro**	ka-nay-ta de po^{n}-ta de fel-troo

female *adj.*	**fêmea**	fe-mee-a
ferry	**o barco de travessia**	bar-koo de tra-ves-see-a
fetch (to)	**buscar**	boosh-kar
few	**pouco**	po-koo
fiancé(e)	**o noivo/a noiva**	noy-voo/noy-va
field	**o campo**	ka^{n}-poo
fight (to)	**combater**	ko^{n}-ba-ter
fill (to)	**encher**	e^{n}-shayr
fill in (to)	**preencher**	pree-e^{n}-shayr
film	**a película**	pe-lee-koo-la
find (to)	**encontrar**	e^{n}-ko^{n}-trar
fine	**a multa**	mool-ta
finish (to)	**acabar**	a-ka-bar
finished	**acabado**	a-ka-ba-doo
fire	**o fogo**	fo-goo
fire escape	**a saída de emergência**	sa-ee-da de ee-mer-zhe^{n}-see-a
fire extinguisher	**o extintor de incêndio**	esh-tee^{n}-tor de een-se^{n}-dee-oo
fireworks	**o fogo de artifício**	fo-goo de ar-tee-fee-see-oo
first	**primeiro**	pree-may-ee-roo
first aid	**os primeiros socorros**	pree-mey-roosh soo-ko-roosh
fish	**o peixe**	pay-eesh
fish (to)	**pescar**	pesh-kar
fisherman	**o pescador**	pesh-ka-dor

fit (to)	**assentar**	as-se^{n}-**tar**
flag	**a bandeira**	ba^{n}-**day**-ee-ra
flat	**plano**	**pla**-noo
flat	**o apartamento**	a-par-ta-**me**^{n}-too
flavour	**o sabor**	sa-**bor**
flea market	**a feira da ladra**	fay-**ee**-ra da **la**-dra
flight	**o vôo**	**vo**-oo
float (to)	**flutuar**	floo-too-**ar**
flood	**a inundação**	ee-noo^{n}-da-**sow**^{n}
floor	**o chão**	show^{n}
floor *storey*	**o andar**	a^{n}-**dar**
floor show	**o espectáculo**	esh-pe-**ta**-koo-loo
flower	**a flor**	flor
fly	**a mosca**	**mosh**-ka
fly (to)	**voar**	voo-**ar**
fog	**o nevoeiro**	ne-voo-**ey**-roo
fold (to)	**dobrar**	doo-**brar**
follow (to)	**seguir**	se-**geer**
food	**a comida**	koo-**mee**-da
foot	**o pé**	pe
football	**o futebol**	foot-**bol**
footpath	**o caminho**	ka-**mee**-nyoo
for	**por/para**	poor/**pa**-ra
forbid (to)	**proibir**	proo-ee-**beer**
foreign	**estrangeiro**	esh-tran-**zhay**-roo
forest	**a floresta**	floo-**resh**-ta

forget (to)	**esquecer**	esh-ke-**sair**
fork	**o garfo**	**gahr**-foo
forward	**adiante**	a-dee-**a^{n}t**
fountain	**a fonte**	fo^{n}t
fragile	**frágil**	**fra**-zheel
free	**livre**	**lee**-vre
freight	**a carga**	**kar**-ga
fresh	**fresco**	**fraysh**-koo
fresh water	**a água fresca**	**a**-gwa **fraysh**-ka
friend	**o amigo/a amiga**	a-**mee**-goo/a-**mee**-ga
friendly	**amigável**	a-mee-**ga**-vel
from	**de**	de
(in) front	**frente**	fre^{n}t
frontier	**a fronteira**	fro^n-**tay**-ee-ra
frost	**a geada**	zhee-**a**-da
frozen	**congelado**	ko^n-zhe-**la**-doo
fruit	**a fruta**	**froo**-ta
full	**cheio**	**shay**-ee-yoo
full board	**a pensão completa**	pe^n-**sow^n** ko^n-**ple**-ta
fun	**o gozo**	**go**-zoo
funny	**engraçado**	e^n-gra-**sa**-doo
fur	**a pele**	pel
furniture	**a mobília**	moo-**bee**-lya

G

gallery	**a galeria**	ga-le-**ree**-a

gamble (to)	**jogar**	zhoo-**gar**
game	**o jogo**	**zho**-goo
game reserve	**a reserva de caça**	re-**zer**-va de **ka**-sa
garage	**a garagem**	ga-**ra**-zhay^{n}
garbage	**o lixo**	**lee**-shoo
garden	**o jardim**	zhar-**dee**^{n}
gate	**a entrada**	e^{n}-**tra**-da
gentleman	**o cavalheiro/senhor**	ka-va-**llyey**-ee-roo/se-**nyor**
genuine	**genuino/autêntico**	zhe-noo-**ee**-noo/ow-**te**^{n}-tee-koo
get (to)	**obter**	ob-**tair**
get off (to)	**sair**	sa-**eer**
get on (to)	**montar em**	mo^{n}-**tar** e^{n}
gift	**o presente**	pre-**ze**^{n}**t**
gift wrapping	**o papel de embalagem**	pa-**pel** de e^{n}-ba-**la**-zhe^{n}
girdle	**a cinta**	**see**^{n}-ta
girl	**a rapariga**	ra-pa-**ree**-ga
give (to)	**dar**	dar
glad	**contente**	ko^{n}-**te**^{n}**t**
glass	**o copo**	**ko**-poo
glasses	**os óculos**	**o**-koo-loosh
gloomy	**depressivo**	de-pre-**see**-voo
gloves	**as luvas**	**loo**-vash
go (to)	**ir**	eer
goal	**o golo/a meta**	**go**-loo/**me**-ta

god	**deus**	day-oosh
gold	**o ouro**	oh-roo
gold plate	**dourado**	doh-rah-doo
golf course	**o campo de golfe**	ka^{n}-poo de golf
good	**bom**	bo^{n}
government	**o governo**	goo-vair-noo
granddaughter	**a neta**	ne-ta
grandfather	**o avô**	a-voh
grandmother	**a avó**	a-voo
grandson	**o neto**	ne-too
grass	**a relva**	rel-va
grateful	**agradecido**	a-gra-de-see-doo
gravel	**o cascalho**	kas-ka-llyo
great	**grande**	gra^{n}d
groceries	**os artigos de mercearia**	ar-tee-goosh de mer-see-a-ree-a
ground *sports*	**o campo**	ka^{n}-poo
grow (to)	**crescer**	kresh-ser
grow (to) *plant*	**cultivar**	kool-tee-var
guarantee	**a garantia**	ga-ra^{n}-tee-a
guest	**o hóspede**	osh-ped
guest house	**a pensão**	pe^{n}-sow^{n}
guide	**o guia**	gee-a
guide book	**o guia**	gee-a
guided tour	**a excursão com guia**	esh-koor-sow^{n} ko^{n} gee-a

H

hair	o cabelo	ka-bay-loo
hair brush	a escova de cabelo	esh-ko-va de ka-bay-loo
hair dryer	o secador de cabelo	se-ka-dor de ka-bay-loo
hair spray	o pulverisador	pool-ve-ree-za-dor
hairgrips, hairpins	os ganchos	ga^{n}-shoosh
half	metade	me-tad
half board	a meia pensão	may-ee-a pen-sow^{n}
half fare	meio bilhete	may-ee-oo be-llyayt
hammer	o martelo	mar-te-loo
hand	a mão	mow^{n}
handbag	a carteira	kar-tay-ee-ra
handkerchief	o lenço	le^{n}-soo
handmade	feito à mão	fay-ee-too ah mow^{n}
hang (to)	pendurar	pen-doo-rar
hanger	o cabide	ka-beed
happen (to)	acontecer	a-ko^{n}-te-sair
happy	feliz	fe-leesh
happy birthday	feliz aniversário	fe-leesh a-nee-ver-sa-ree-oo
harbour	o porto	por-too
hard *difficult*	difícil	dee-fee-seel
hardly	dificilmente	dee-fee-seel-me^{n}t
harmful	prejudicial	pre-zhoo-dee-see-al
harmless	inofensivo	ee-noo-fe^{n}-see-voo
hat	o chapéu	sha-pe-oo

have (to)	**ter**	tair
have to (to)	**ter obrigação de**	tair o-bree-ga-**sow**^{n} de
haversack	**a mochila**	moo-**shee**-la
he	**ele**	ayl
head	**a cabeça**	ka-**bay**-sa
headphones	**os auscultadores**	owsh-kool-ta-**dorsh**
health	**a saúde**	sa-**ood**
hear (to)	**ouvir**	oh-**veer**
heart	**o coração**	koo-ra-**sow**^{n}
heat	**o calor**	ka-**lor**
heating	**o aquecimento**	a-ke-see-**may**^{n}-too
heavy	**pesado**	pe-**za**-doo
hedge	**a sebe**	**se**-be
heel *shoe*	**o tacão**	ta-**kow**^{n}
height	**a altura**	al-**too**-ra
helicopter	**o helicóptero**	e-lee-**kop**-te-roo
help	**a ajuda**	a-**zhoo**-da
help (to)	**ajudar**	a-zhoo-**dar**
hem	**a baínha**	ba-**ee**-nya
her/hers	**seu** *m*/**sua** *f*/**seus/ suas/dela**	**say**-oo/**soo**-a/**say**-oosh/ **soo**-ash/**de**-la
here	**aqui**	a-**kee**
high	**alto**	**al**-too
hill	**a colina**	koo-**lee**-na
hire (to)	**alugar**	a-loo-**gar**
his	**seu** *m*/**sua** *f*/**seus/ suas/dele**	**say**-oo/**soo**-a/**say**-oosh/ **soo**-ash/**de**-le

history	**a história**	ish-to-ree-a
hitch hike (to)	**ir à boleia**	eer ah boo-le-ya
hobby	**o passatempo**	pa-sa-tay^{n}-poo
hold (to)	**segurar**	se-goo-rar
hole	**o furo/o buraco**	foo-roo/boo-ra-koo
holiday	**o feriado**	fe-ree-a-doo
holidays	**as férias**	fe-ree-ash
hollow	**vazio**	va-zee-oo
(at) home	**em casa**	e^{n} ka-za
honeymoon	**a lua de mel**	loo-a de mel
hope	**a esperança**	esh-pe-ra^{n}-sa
hope (to)	**ter esperança**	ter esh-pe-ra^{n}-sa
horse	**o cavalo**	ka-va-loo
horse riding	**a equitação**	e-kee-ta-sow^{n}
hose	**a mangueira**	ma^{n}-gay-ee-ra
hospital	**o hospital**	osh-pee-tal
hostel	**o abrigo/albergue**	a-bree-goo/al-bairg
hot	**quente**	kay^{n}t
hot water bottle	**a botija**	boo-tee-zha
house	**a casa**	kah-za
how?	**como?**	ko-moo
how much?	**quanto?**	kwa^{n}-too
hungry	**esfomeado**	esh-fo-mee-a-doo
hunt (to) *game*	**caçar**	ka-sar
hurry (to)	**ter pressa**	tair pre-sa
hurt (to)	**doer**	doo-air

husband	**o marido**	ma-**ree**-doo

I

I	**eu**	**ay**-oo
ice	**o gêlo**	**zhay**-loo
ice cream	**o gelado/sorvete**	zhay-**la**-doo/soor-**vet**
identify (to)	**identificar**	ee-de^{n}-tee-fee-**kar**
if	**se**	se
imagine (to)	**imaginar**	ee-ma-zhee-**nar**
immersion heater	**o aquecedor de imersão**	a-ke-se-**dor** de ee-mer-**sow^{n}**
important	**importante**	ee^{n}-poor-**ta^{n}t**
in	**dentro**	**de^{n}**-troo
include (to)	**incluir**	ee^{n}-kloo-**eer**
included	**incluído**	ee^{n}-kloo-**ee**-doo
inconvenient	**incómodo**	ee^{n}-**ko**-moo-doo
incorrect	**incorrecto**	ee^{n}-koo-**re**-too
independent	**independente**	cc^{n}-dc-pe^{n}-**de^{n}t**
indoors	**dentro de casa**	**de^{n}**-troo de **ka**-sa
industry	**a indústria**	ee^{n}-**doosh**-tree-a
inexpensive	**barato**	ba-**ra**-too
inflammable	**inflamável**	ee^{n}-fla-**ma**-vel
inflatable	**de encher**	de e^{n}-**shayr**
inflation	**a inflação**	ee^{n}-fla-**sow^{n}**
information	**a informação**	ee^{n}-foor-ma-**sow^{n}**
ink	**a tinta**	**tee^{n}**-ta

inn	**a pensão/o albergue**	pe^{n}-sow^{n}/al-berg
insect	**o insecto**	ee^{n}-se-too
insect bite	**a picada de insecto**	pee-ka-da de ee^{n}-se-too
insect repellant	**o repelente de insectos**	re-pe-le^{n}t de ee^{n}-se-toosh
inside	**dentro (de)**	de^{n}-troo (de)
instead	**em vez de**	e^{n} vesh de
instructor	**o instructor**	ee^{n}-stroo-tor
insurance	**o seguro**	se-goo-roo
insure (to)	**segurar**	se-goo-rar
interested	**interessado**	ee^{n}-te-res-sa-doo
interesting	**interessante**	ee^{n}-te-re-sa^{n}t
interpreter	**o intérprete**	ee^{n}-tair-pret
into	**dentro/em**	de^{n}-troo/e^{n}
introduce	**introduzir**	ee^{n}-troo-doo-zeer
invitation	**o convite**	ko^{n}-veet
invite (to)	**convidar**	ko^{n}-vee-dar
Ireland	**a Irlanda**	eer-la^{n}-da
Irish	**irlandês**	eer-la^{n}-daysh
iron (to)	**passar a ferro**	pa-sar a fe-roo
island	**a ilha**	ee-llya
it	**ele** *m*/**ela** *f*	ayl/e-la
Italian	**italiano**	ee-ta-lee-a-noo
Italy	**a Itália**	ee-ta-lee-a

J

jacket	**o casaco**	**ka-za-koo**
jar	**o jarro**	**zha-roo**
jellyfish	**a alforreca**	**al-for-re-ka**
Jew	**o Judeu**	**zhoo-day-oo**
jewellery	**a joalharia, as jóias**	**zho-a-llya-ree-a, zhoy-ash**
Jewish	**judaico**	**zhoo-da-ee-koo**
job	**o emprego**	**een-pre-goo**
journey	**a viagem**	**vee-a-zhay^n**
jug	**a jarra**	**zhar-ra**
jump (to)	**saltar**	**sal-tar**
jumper	**a blusa**	**bloo-za**

K

keep (to)	**guardar**	**gwar-dar**
key	**a chave**	**shahv**
kick (to)	**chutar**	**shoo-tar**
kind	**o género**	**zhe-ne-roo**
kind *adj.*	**amável**	**a-ma-vel**
king	**o rei**	**ray-ee**
kiss	**o beijo**	**bey-zhoo**
kiss (to)	**beijar**	**bey-zhar**
kitchen	**a cozinha**	**koo-zee-nya**
knickers, briefs	**as cuecas**	**koo-e-kash**
knife	**a faca**	**fa-ka**

knock (to)	**bater (à porta)**	ba-**tair** (ah **por**-ta)
know (to) *fact*	**saber**	sa-**bair**
know (to) *person*	**conhecer**	koo-nye-**sair**

L

label	**a etiqueta**	ee-tee-**kay**-ta
lace	**a renda**	**re^n**-da
lady	**a senhora**	se-**nyo**-ra
lake	**o lago**	**la**-goo
lamp	**a lâmpada**	**la^n**-pa-da
land	**a terra**	**ter**-ra
landlord	**o proprietário**	proo-pree-e-**ta**-ree-oo
landmark	**o marco**	**mar**-koo
landscape	**a paisagem**	pa-ee-**zah**-zhayn
lane	**o caminho**	ka-**mee**-nyoo
language	**a língua/o idioma**	**lee^n**-gwa/ee-dee-**o**-ma
large	**grande**	**gra^{n}d**
last	**último**	**ool**-tee-moo
late	**tarde**	**tard**
laugh (to)	**rir**	**reer**
launderette	**a lavandaria**	la-va^n-da-**ree**-a
lavatory	**a retrete**	re-**trayt**
lavatory paper	**o papel higiénico**	pa-**pel** ee-zhee-**e**-nee-koo
law	**a lei**	**lay**
lawn	**o campo de relva**	**ka^n**-poo de **rel**-va
lawyer	**o advogado**	ad-voo-**ga**-doo

ead (to)	**conduzir**	ko^{n}-doo-zeer
eaf	**a folha**	fo-llya
eak (to)	**escapar/verter**	esh-ka-par/ver-tair
earn (to)	**aprender**	a-pre^{n}-dair
east	**mínimo**	mee-nee-moo
t least	**pelo menos**	pe-loo me-noosh
eather	**o couro/o cabedal**	koh-oo-roo/ka-be-dal
eave (to) *abandon*	**deixar**	day-ee-shar
eave (to) *go out*	**sair**	sa-eer
eft *opp. right*	**esquerdo**	esh-kayr-doo
eft luggage	**o depósito de bagagem**	de-po-zee-too de ba-ga-zhay^{n}
eg	**a perna**	pair-na
end (to)	**emprestar**	e^{n}-presh-tar
ength	**o comprimento**	ko^{n}-pree-men-too
ess	**menos**	me-noosh
esson	**a lição**	lee-sow^{n}
et (to) *allow*	**consentir**	ko^{n}-se^{n}-teer
et (to) *rent*	**arrendar**	a-re^{n}-dar
etter	**a carta**	kar-ta
evel crossing	**a passagem de nível**	pa-sa-zhay^{n} de nee-vel
brary	**a biblioteca**	bee-blee-oo-te-ka
cence	**a licença**	lee-se^{n}-sa
fe	**a vida**	vee-da
febelt	**o cinto de salvação**	see^{n}-too de sal-va-sow^{n}
feboat	**o barco de salva-vidas**	bar-koo de sal-va-vee-dash

lifeguard	**o salva-vidas**	sal-va-vee-dash
lift	**o elevador**	ee-le-va-dor
light	**a luz**	loosh
light *colour*	**claro**	kla-roo
light *weight*	**leve**	le-ve
lighthouse	**o farol**	fa-rol
lightning	**o relâmpago**	re-la^{n}-pa-goo
like (to)	**gostar**	goosh-tar
line	**a linha**	lee-nya
linen	**o linho/lençóis**	lee-nyoo/lay^{n}-soysh
lingerie	**a roupa interior**	ro-pa een-te-ree-or
lipsalve	**a pomada para os lábios**	poo-ma-da pa-ra osh la-bee-oosh
lipstick	**o baton**	ba-to^{n}
liquid *adj.*	**líquido**	lee-kee-doo
liquid *noun*	**o líquido**	lee-kee-doo
listen (to)	**escutar**	esh-koo-tar
little	**pouco**	poh-koo
live (to)	**viver**	vee-vair
local	**local**	loo-kal
lock (to)	**fechar à chave**	fe-shar ah shahv
long	**longo**	lo^{n}-goo
look (to) *at*	**olhar**	o-llyar
look (to) *for*	**procurar**	pro-koo-rar
look (to) *like*	**parecer**	pa-re-sair
loose	**solto/folgado**	sol-too/fool-ga-doo

lorry	**a camioneta**	ka-mee-oo-**nay**-ta
lose (to)	**perder**	pair-**dair**
lost property office	**a secção de objectos perdidos**	sek-**sow^n** de ob-**zhe**-toosh pair-**dee**-doosh
(a) lot	**muito**	**mwee**-too
loud	**ruidoso**	roo-ee-**do**-zoo
love (to)	**amar**	a-**mar**
low	**baixo**	bay-**ee**-shoo
lucky	**com sorte**	ko^n sort
luggage	**a bagagem**	ba-**ga**-zhay^n
lunch	**o almoço**	al-**mo**-soo

M

magazine	**a revista**	re-**veesh**-ta
maid	**a moça/empregada doméstica**	**moh**-sa/e^n-pre-**ga**-da doo-**mesh**-tee-ka
mail	**o correio**	koo-**ray**-yoo
main street	**a rua principal**	**roo**-a pree^n-see-**pal**
make (to)	**fazer**	fa-**zair**
make-up	**a maquilhagem**	ma-kee-**llyah**-zhe^n
male *adj.*	**macho**	**ma**-shoo
man	**o homem**	**o**-me^n
man-made	**artificial**	ar-tee-fee-see-**al**
manage (to)	**gerir/dirigir**	zhe-**reer**/dee-ree-**zheer**
manager	**o director/gerente**	dee-re-**tor**/zhe-**re^{n}t**
manicure	**a manicura**	ma-nee-**koo**-ra

many	**muitos**	**mwee**-toosh
map	**o mapa**	**ma**-pa
marble	**o mármore**	**mar**-moor
market	**o mercado**	mer-**ka**-doo
married	**casado**	ka-**za**-doo
marsh	**o pântano**	**pa**^{n}-ta-noo
Mass	**a missa**	**mee**-sa
massage	**a massagem**	ma-**sa**-ge^{n}
match *light*	**o fósforo**	**fosh**-foo-roo
match *sport*	**o desafio**	de-za-**fee**-oo
material	**o material**	ma-te-ree-**al**
matinee	**a matiné**	ma-tee-**nay**
mattress	**o colchão**	kol-**show**^{n}
maybe	**talvez**	tal-**vesh**
meal	**a refeição**	re-fay-ee-**sow**^{n}
mean (to)	**significar**	seeg-nee-fee-**kar**
measurements	**as medidas**	me-**dee**-dash
meat	**a carne**	karn
meet (to)	**encontrar**	e^{n}-ko^{n}-**trar**
mend (to)	**reparar**	re-pa-**rar**
menstruation	**a menstruação**	me^{n}sh-troo-a-**sow**^{n}
mess	**a confusão/desordem**	con-fu-**sow**^{n}/de-**sor**-de^{n}
message	**o recado**	re-**ka**-doo
messenger	**o mensageiro**	me^{n}-sa-**zhey**-roo
metal	**o metal**	me-**tal**
midday	**o meio-dia**	may-ee-oo-**dee**-a

middle	**médio/meio**	**me-dee-oo/may-ee-oo**
middle-aged	**a meia-idade**	me-ya-ee-**dad**
middle-class *adj.*	**a classe média**	klass **me-dee-a**
midnight	**a meia-noite**	may-ee-a-**no**-eet
mild	**suave**	**swa**-ve
mill	**o moínho**	moo-**ee**-nyoo
mine *pron.*	**meu/minha**	may-oo/**mee**-nya
mirror	**o espelho**	esh-**pe**-llyoo
Miss	**Menina**	me-**nee**-na
miss (to) *train, etc.*	**perder**	pair-**dair**
mistake	**o erro**	**ay**-roo
mix (to)	**misturar**	meesh-too-**rar**
mixed	**misto**	**meesh**-too
modern	**moderno**	moo-**dair**-noo
moisturizer	**o creme hidratante**	krem ee-dra-**ta^{n}t**
moment	**o momento**	moo-**me^{n}**-too
monastery	**o mosteiro/o convento**	moosh-**tay**-ee-ro/ko^{n}-**ve^{n}**-too
money	**o dinheiro**	dee-**nyay**-ee-roo
monk	**o monge**	**mo^{n}**-zhe
month	**o mês**	**maysh**
monument	**o monumento**	moo-noo-**me^{n}**-too
moon	**a lua**	**loo**-a
moorland	**a charneca**	shar-**ne**-ka
moped	**a motoreta**	mo-to-**re**-ta
more	**mais**	**ma**-eesh

morning	**a manhã**	ma-**nya**^{n}
mortgage	**a hipoteca**	ee-poo-**te**-ka
mosque	**a mesquita**	mesh-**kee**-ta
mosquito	**o mosquito**	moosh-**kee**-too
most	**o/a mais**	oo/a **ma**-eesh
mother	**a mãe**	**my**^{n}
motor	**o motor**	mo-**tor**
motor bike	**a motocicleta**	mo-to-see-**kle**-ta
motor boat	**o barco a motor**	**bar**-koo a mo-**tor**
motor racing	**a corrida de automóveis**	koo-**ree**-da de ow-to-**mo**-vaysh
motorway	**a auto-estrada**	ow-to-esh-**tra**-da
mountain	**a montanha**	mo^n-**ta**-nya
mouse	**o rato**	**ra**-too
mouth	**a boca**	**bo**-ka
move (to)	**mover**	mo-**vair**
Mr	**Senhor**	se-**nyor**
Mrs	**Senhora**	se-**nyo**-ra
much	**muito**	**mwee**-too
museum	**o museu**	moo-**zay**-oo
music	**a música**	**moo**-zee-ka
must (to have to)	**dever**	de-**vair**
my/mine	**meu** *m*/**minha** *f*	**may**-oo/**mee**-nya

N

nail *carpentry*	**o prego**	**pre**-goo

ail polish	**o verniz de unhas**	ver-**neesh** de **oo**-nyash
ailbrush	**a escova de unhas**	esh-**ko**-va de **oo**-nyash
ailfile	**a lima**	**lee**-ma
ame	**o nome**	nom
apkin	**o guardanapo**	gwar-da-**na**-poo
appy	**a fralda**	**fral**-da
arrow	**estreito**	esh-**tray**-ee-too
atural	**natural**	na-too-**ral**
ear	**perto**	**per**-too
ecessary	**necessário**	ne-se-**sa**-ree-oo
ecklace	**o colar**	koo-**lar**
eed (to)	**necessitar**	ne-se-see-**tar**
eedle	**a agulha**	a-**goo**-lya
ephew	**o sobrinho**	soo-**bree**-nyoo
et	**a rêde**	**rayd**
ever	**nunca**	**noo^{n}**-ka
ew	**novo**	**no**-voo
New Zealand	**a Nova Zelandia**	**no**-va ze-**land**-dee-a
ews	**as notícias**	noo-**tee**-see-ash
ewspaper	**o jornal**	zhoor-**nal**
ext	**próximo**	**pro**-see-moo
ice	**bonito**	boo-**nee**-too
iece	**a sobrinha**	soo-**bree**-nya
ightclub	**a boîte**	bwat
ightdress	**a camisa de noite**	ka-**mee**-za de **no**-eet
o one	**ninguém**	nee^{n}-**ge^{n}**

nobody	**ninguém**	nee^{n}-**ge^{n}**
noisy	**ruidoso**	roo-ee-**do**-zoo
non-alcoholic	**não-alcoólico**	now^{n}-al-koo-**o**-lee-koo
none	**nenhum**	ne-**nyoo^{n}**
normal	**normal**	nor-**mal**
north	**o norte**	nort
not	**não**	now^{n}
note *money*	**a nota**	**no**-ta
notebook	**o livro de notas**	**lee**-vroo de **no**-tash
nothing	**nada**	**na**-da
notice	**o aviso**	a-**vee**-zoo
notice (to)	**notar**	no-**tar**
novel	**o romance/a novela**	roo-**ma^{n}s**/noo-**ve**-la
now	**agora**	a-**go**-ra
number	**o número**	**noo**-me-roo
nylon	**o nylon**	**ny**-lo^{n}

O

obtain (to)	**obter**	ob-**tayr**
occasion	**a ocasião**	o-ka-see-**ow^{n}**
occupation	**a ocupação**	o-koo-pa-**sow^{n}**
occupied	**ocupado**	o-koo-**pa**-doo
odd *not even*	**ímpar**	**ee^{n}**-par
odd *strange*	**raro**	**ra**-roo
of	**de**	de
of course	**é claro**	eh **kla**-roo

offer	**a oferta**	o-**fer**-ta
offer (to)	**oferecer**	o-fe-re-**ser**
office	**o escritório**	esh-kree-**to**-ree-oo
official *adj.*	**oficial**	o-fee-see-**al**
official *noun*	**o funcionário**	foon-see-oo-**na**-ree-oo
often	**muitas vezes**	**mwee**-tash **vay**-zesh
oily	**oleoso**	o-lee-**o**-zoo
ointment	**a pomada**	poo-**ma**-da
old	**velho**	**ve**-lyoo
on	**em**	**e**^{n}
on foot	**a pé**	a **pe**
on time	**a tempo**	a **tay**^{n}-poo
once	**uma vez**	**oo**-ma vaysh
only	**somente**	so-**me**^{n}**t**
open (to)	**abrir**	a-**breer**
open	**aberto**	a-**bair**-too
open-air	**ar livre**	ar **lee**-vre
opening	**a abertura**	a-ber-**too**-ra
opportunity	**a oportunidade**	o-por-too-nee-**dad**
opposite	**oposto**	o-**posh**-too
optician	**o oculista**	o-koo-**leesh**-ta
or	**ou**	**oh**
orchard	**o pomar**	po-**mar**
orchestra	**a orquestra**	or-**kesh**-tra
order (to)	**encomendar**	e^n-koo-me^n-**dar**
ordinary	**vulgar**	vool-**gar**

other	**outro/a**	oh-troo/tra
ought	**dever**	de-vair
our, ours	**nosso** *m*, **nossa** *f*	no-soo, no-sa
out, outside	**fora**	fo-ra
out of order	**avariado**	a-va-ree-a-doo
out of stock	**esgotado**	esh-goo-ta-doo
over	**sobre**	soh-bre
over there	**ali**	a-lee
overcoat	**o sobretudo**	soo-bre-too-doo
owe (to)	**dever**	de-vair
owner	**o proprietário**	proo-pree-e-ta-ree-o

P

pack (to)	**arrumar as malas**	a-roo-mar ash mal-ash
packet	**o pacote**	pa-kot
paddle	**o remo**	re-moo
paddling pool	**a piscina para crianças**	peesh-see-na pa-ra kree-a^{n}-sash
page	**a página**	pa-zhee-na
paid	**pago**	pa-goo
pain	**a dor**	dor
painkiller	**o analgésico**	a-nal-zhe-zee-koo
paint (to)	**pintar**	pee^{n}-tar
painting	**a pintura**	pee^{n}-too-ra
pair	**o par**	par
palace	**o palácio**	pa-la-see-oo

pale	**pálido**	**pa**-lee-doo
paper	**o papel**	pa-**pel**
parcel	**o pacote**	pa-**kot**
park	**o parque**	park
park (to)	**estacionar**	esh-ta-see-oo-**nar**
parking meter	**o parquímetro**	par-**kee**-me-troo
parking ticket	**a multa de estacionamento**	**mool**-ta de esh-ta-see-oo-na-**may^{n}**-too
parliament	**o parlamento**	par-la-**me^{n}**-too
part	**a parte**	part
party *fête*	**a festa**	**fesh**-ta
party *political*	**o partido político**	par-**tee**-doo poo-**lee**-tee-koo
pass (to)	**passar**	pa-**sar**
passenger	**o passageiro**	pa-sa-**zhay**-ee-roo
passport	**o passaporte**	pa-sa-**port**
path	**o caminho**	ka-**mee**-nyoo
patient	**o doente**	doo-**e^{n}t**
pavement	**o passeio**	pa-**say**-yoo
pay (to)	**pagar**	pa-**gar**
payment	**o pagamento**	pa-ga-**me^{n}**-too
peace	**a paz**	pash
peak	**o cimo**	**see**-moo
pearl	**a pérola**	**pe**-roo-la
pebble	**o seixo**	**se**-ee-shoo
pedal	**o pedal**	pe-**dal**
pedestrian	**o peão**	pee-**ow^{n}**

pedestrian crossing	**o cruzamento de peões**	kru-za-me^{n}-too de pe-oy^{n}sh
pedestrian precinct	**a área para peões**	a-re-a pa-ra pe-oy^{n}sh
pen	**a caneta**	ka-ne-ta
pencil	**o lápis**	la-pesh
penknife	**o canivete**	ka-nee-vet
pensioner	**o pensionista**	pe^{n}-see-oo-neesh-ta
people	**a gente**	zhe^{n}t
per person	**por pessoa**	por pe-so-a
perfect	**perfeito**	per-fey-too
performance	**o espectáculo**	es-pe-ta-koo-loo
perfume	**o perfume**	per-foo^{n}
perhaps	**talvez**	tal-vaysh
perishable	**deteriorável**	de-te-ryoo-ra-vel
permit	**a autorização**	ow-too-ree-za-sow^{n}
permit (to)	**permitir**	per-mee-teer
person	**a pessoa**	pe-so-a
personal	**pessoal**	pe-soo-al
petticoat	**a combinação**	ko^{n}-bee-na-sow^{n}
photograph	**a fotografia**	foo-too-gra-fee-a
photographer	**o fotógrafo**	foo-to-gra-foo
pick (to) *choose*	**escolher**	es-ko-llyair
piece	**a peça**	pe-sa
pier	**o molhe**	mo-llye
pillow	**a almofada**	al-moo-fa-da
(safety) pin	**o alfinete (de ama)**	al-fee-nayt de a-ma

pipe	**o cachimbo**	ka-**shee**^{n}-boo
pipe *tube*	**o cano**	**ka**-no
place	**o lugar**	loo-**gar**
plan	**o plano**	**pla**-noo
plant	**a planta**	**pla**^{n}-ta
plastic	**o plástico**	**plash**-tee-koo
plate	**o prato**	**pra**-too
play	**a peça de teatro**	**pe**-sa de tee-**a**-troo
play (to)	**jogar**	zhoo-**gar**
player	**o jogador**	zhoo-ga-**dor**
please	**por favor/faz favor**	poor fa-**vor**/fash fa-**vor**
pleased	**satisfeito**	sa-tees-**fey**-too
pliers	**o alicate**	a-lee-**kat**
plug *bath*	**o tampão**	ta^n-**pow**^{n}
plug *electric*	**a tomada**	too-**ma**-da
pocket	**o bolso**	**bol**-soo
point	**a ponta**	**po**^{n}-ta
poisonous	**venenoso**	ve-ne-**no**-zoo
policeman	**o polícia**	poo-**lee**-see-a
police station	**a esquadra de polícia**	esh-**kwad**-ra de poo-**lee**-see-a
political	**político**	poo-**lee**-tee-koo
politician	**o político**	poo-**lee**-tee-koo
politics	**a política**	poo-**lee**-tee-ka
pollution	**a poluição**	poo-loo-ee-**sow**^{n}
pond	**a lagoa**	la-**go**-a

poor	**pobre**	**po**-bre
pope	**o papa**	**pa**-pa
popular	**popular**	poo-poo-**lar**
porcelain	**a porcelana**	poor-se-**la**-na
port	**o porto**	**por**-too
Portugal	**Portugal**	poor-too-**gal**
Portuguese	**português**	poor-too-**gaysh**
possible	**possível**	poo-**see**-vel
post (to)	**remeter**	re-me-**tair**
post box	**o marco postal**	**mar**-koo poosh-**tal**
postcard	**o (bilhete) postal**	(bee-**llyayt**) poosh-**tal**
postman	**o correio**	ko-**ray**-ee-oo
post office	**os correios**	koo-**ray**-yoosh
postpone (to)	**adiar/protelar**	a-dee-**ar**/pro-te-**lar**
pound	**a libra**	**lee**-bra
prefer (to)	**preferir**	pre-fe-**reer**
pregnant	**grávida**	**gra**-vee-da
prepare (to)	**preparar**	pre-pa-**rar**
present *gift*	**o presente**	pre-**ze**^{n}**t**
president	**o presidente**	pre-zee-**de**^{n}**t**
press (to)	**passar a ferro**	pa-**sar** a **fe**-roo
pretty	**bonito**	boo-**nee**-too
price	**o preço**	**pray**-soo
priest	**o padre**	**pa**-drey
prime minister	**o primeiro ministro**	pree-**may**-ee-roo mee-**neesh**-troo

print	**a estampa/a gravura**	es-**tan**-pa/gra-**voo**-ra
print (to)	**imprimir**	ee^{n}-pree-**meer**
print (to) *photo*	**revelar**	re-ve-**lar**
private	**particular**	par-tee-koo-**lar**
problem	**o problema**	proo-**ble**-ma
profession	**a profissão**	proo-fee-**sow**^{n}
programme	**o programa**	proo-**gra**-ma
promise	**a promessa**	proo-**mes**-sa
promise (to)	**prometer**	proo-me-**tair**
prompt	**pronto**	**pro**^{n}-to
protestant	**protestante**	pro-tesh-**ta**^{n}**t**
provide (to)	**fornecer**	foor-ne-**sair**
public	**público**	**poo**-blee-koo
public holiday	**o feriado**	fe-ree-**a**-doo
pull (to)	**puxar**	poo-**shar**
pump	**a bomba motriz**	**bo**^{n}-ba mo-**treesh**
pure	**puro**	**poo**-roo
purse	**a bolsa**	**bol**-sa
push (to)	**empurrar**	e^{n}-poo-**rar**
put (to)	**pôr**	por
pyjamas	**o pijama**	pee-**zha**-ma

Q

quality	**a qualidade**	kwa-lee-**dad**
quantity	**a quantidade**	kwa^{n}-tee-**dad**
quarter	**o quarto**	**kwar**-too

queen	**a raínha**	ra-**ee**-nya
question	**a pergunta**	per-**goo**^{n}-ta
queue	**a bicha**	**bee**-sha
queue (to)	**estar na bicha**	esh-**tar** na **bee**-sha
quick	**rápido**	**ra**-pee-doo
quiet	**tranquilo**	tra^n-**kwee**-loo

R

race	**a corrida**	koo-**ree**-da
radiator	**o radiador**	ra-dee-a-**dor**
radio	**o rádio**	**ra**-dee-oo
railway	**o caminho de ferro**	ka-**mee**^{n}-nyoo de **fe**-roo
rain	**a chuva**	**shoo**-va
raincoat	**a gabardina/o impermeável**	ga-bar-**dee**-na/ee^n-per-mee-**a**-vel
(it is) raining	**chove**	shov
rare *unusual*	**raro**	**ra**-roo
rash	**a erupção na pele**	ee-roop-**sow**^{n} na pel
raw	**cru**	kroo
razor	**a navalha de barba**	na-**va**-lya de **bar**-ba
razor blades	**as lâminas de barbear**	**la**-mee-nash de bar-bee-**ar**
reach (to)	**atingir**	a-tee^n-**zheer**
read (to)	**ler**	layr
ready	**pronto**	**pro**^{n}-too
real	**real**	ree-**al**

really	**realmente**	ree-al-**me^{n}t**
reason	**a razão**	ra-**sow^{n}**
receipt	**o recibo**	re-**see**-boo
receive (to)	**receber**	re-se-**bair**
recent	**recente**	re-**se^{n}t**
recipe	**a receita**	re-**sey**-ta
recognize (to)	**reconhecer**	re-ko-nye-**sair**
recommend (to)	**recomendar**	re-koo-me^{n}-**dar**
record *music*	**o disco**	**deesh**-koo
record *sport*	**o recorde**	re-**kord**
refrigerator	**o frigorífico**	free-goo-**ree**-fee-ko
refund	**a restituição**	res-tee-too-ee-**sow^{n}**
regards	**os cumprimentos**	koo^{n}-pree-**men**-tosh
register (to)	**registar**	re-zheesh-**tar**
relatives	**os parentes**	pa-**re^{n}**-tesh
religion	**a religião**	re-lee-zhee-**ow^{n}**
remember (to)	**recordar**	re-koor-**dar**
rent	**a renda**	**re^{n}**-da
rent (to)	**alugar**	a-loo-**gar**
repair (to)	**reparar**	re-pa-**rar**
repeat (to)	**repetir**	re-pe-**teer**
reply (to)	**responder**	res-po^{n}-**dair**
reservation	**a reserva**	re-**zair**-va
reserve (to)	**reservar**	re-zer-**var**
reserved	**reservado**	re-zer-**va**-doo
restaurant	**o restaurante**	resh-tow-**ra^{n}t**

return (to)	**regressar**	re-gre-sar
reward	**o prémio**	pre-myoo
ribbon	**a fita**	fee-ta
rich	**rico**	ree-ko
right *not left*	**direito**	dee-ray-ee-too
right *not wrong*	**certo**	ser-too
right (to be)	**ter razão**	ter ra-sow^{n}
ring	**o anel**	a-nel
ripe	**maduro/pronto**	ma-doo-roo/pro^{n}-too
rise (to)	**levantar**	le-va^{n}-tar
river	**o rio**	ree-oo
road	**a estrada**	esh-tra-da
road map	**o mapa de estrada**	ma-pa de esh-tra-da
road sign	**o sinal de estrada**	see-nal de esh-tra-da
road works	**os trabalhos de estrada**	tra-ba-llyoosh de esh-tra-da
rock	**a rocha**	ro-sha
roll (to)	**rolar**	roo-lar
roof	**o telhado**	te-llya-doo
room	**o quarto**	kwar-too
rope	**a corda**	kor-da
rotten	**pôdre**	po-dre
rough	**áspero**	ash-pe-roo
round	**redondo**	re-do^{n}-doo
rowing boat	**o barco de remos**	bar-koo de ray-moosh
rubber	**a borracha**	boo-ra-sha

rubbish	**o lixo**	**lee**-shoo
rucksack	**a mochila**	moo-**shee**-la
rude	**mal educado**	mal ee-doo-**ka**-doo
ruin	**a ruína**	roo-**ee**-na
rug	**o tapête**	ta-**pet**
rule (to)	**governar**	goo-ver-**nar**
run (to)	**correr**	koo-**rair**

S

sad	**triste**	treest
saddle	**a cela**	**se**-la
safe *noun*	**o cofre**	**ko**-fre
sail	**a vela**	**ve**-la
sailing boat	**o barco à vela**	**bar**-koo ah **ve**-la
sailor	**o marinheiro**	ma-ree-**nyey**-roo
sale *clearance*	**a liquidação**	lee-kee-da-**sow**^{n}
(for) sale	**(para) venda**	**pa**-ra **ve**^{n}-da
saleswoman	**a vendedora**	ve^{n}-de-**dor**-a
salesman	**o vendedor**	ve^{n}-de-**dor**
salt	**o sal**	sal
salt water	**a água salgada**	**a**-gwa sal-**ga**-da
same	**mesmo**	**mayzh**-moo
sand	**a areia**	a-**ray**-ya
sandals	**as sandálias**	sa^{n}-**da**-lee-ash
sanitary towels	**os pensos higiénicos**	**pen**-soosh ee-zee-e-nee-koos

satisfactory	**satisfatório**	sa-tees-fa-**to**-ree-oo
saucer	**o pires**	**pee**-resh
save (to)	**poupar**	po-**par**
save (to) *rescue*	**salvar**	sal-**var**
say (to)	**dizer**	dee-**zair**
scald (to)	**queimar-se**	kay-ee-**mar**-se
scarf	**o cachecol**	kash-**kol**
scent	**o perfume**	per-**foo**^{n}
school	**a escola**	esh-**ko**-la
scissors	**a tesoura**	te-**zoh**-ra
Scotland	**a Escócia**	esh-**ko**-see-a
Scottish	**escocês**	esh-koo-**saysh**
sculpture	**a esculptura**	esh-kool-**too**-ra
sea	**o mar**	mar
sea food	**o marisco**	ma-**reesh**-koo
seasick	**enjoado**	e^{n}-zhoo-**a**-do
season (*of year*)	**a estação**	esh-ta-**sow**^{n}
seat	**o assento**	a-**se**^{n}-too
seat belt	**o cinto de segurança**	**see**^{n}-too de se-goo-**ra**^{n}-sa
second hand	**usado**	oo-**sa**-doo
see (to)	**ver**	vair
seem (to)	**parecer**	pa-re-**sair**
sell (to)	**vender**	ve^{n}-**dair**
send (to)	**enviar**	e^{n}-vee-**ar**
separate	**separado**	se-pa-**ra**-doo
serious	**sério**	**sair**-ee-oo

serve (to)	**servir**	ser-**veer**
service	**o serviço**	ser-**vee**-soo
several	**vários**	**var**-ee-oosh
sew (to)	**coser**	koo-**zair**
shade *colour*	**o matiz**	ma-**teesh**
shade/shadow	**a sombra**	**so^{n}**-bra
shallow	**pouco profundo**	**po**-koo proo-**foo^{n}**-doo
shampoo	**o shampô**	sha^{n}-**poh**
shape	**a forma**	**for**-ma
share (to)	**repartir**	re-par-**teer**
sharp	**agudo**	a-**goo**-doo
shave (to)	**barbear**	bar-bee-**ar**
shaving brush	**o pincel de barba**	pee^{n}-**sel** de **bar**-ba
shaving cream	**o creme de barbear**	**krem** de bar-bee-**ar**
she	**ela**	**e**-la
sheet	**o lençol**	le^{n}-**sol**
shelf	**a prateleira**	pra-te-**ley**-ra
shell	**a concha**	**ko^{n}**-sha
shelter	**o abrigo**	a-**bree**-goo
shine (to)	**brilhar**	bree-**llyar**
shingle *beach*	**as pedrinhas**	pe-**dree**-nyash
ship	**o barco**	**bar**-koo
shirt	**a camisa**	ka-**mee**-za
shock	**o choque**	shok
shoe polish	**a graxa de sapatos**	**gra**-sha de sa-**pa**-toosh
shoelaces	**os atacadores**	a-ta-ka-**dor**-esh

shoes	**os sapatos**	sa-pa-toosh
shop	**a loja**	lo-zha
shopping centre	**o centro comercial**	sen-troo koo-mer-see-al
shore	**a costa/a praia**	kosh-ta/pry-a
short	**curto**	koor-too
shorts	**os calções**	kal-soy^{n}sh
shoulder	**o ombro**	o^n-broo
show	**o espectáculo**	esh-pe-ta-koo-loo
show (to)	**mostrar**	moosh-trar
shower	**o duche**	doosh
shut (to)	**fechar**	fe-shar
shut	**fechado**	fe-sha-doo
side	**o lado**	la-doo
sights	**os lugares de interêsse**	loo-garsh de ee^n-te-rays
sightseeing	**a excursão/visita**	esh-koor-sow^n/vee-zee-ta
sign	**o sinal**	see-nal
sign (to)	**assinar**	a-see-nar
signpost	**o marco de sinalisação**	mar-koo de see-na-lee-za-sow^n
silver	**a prata**	pra-ta
simple	**simples**	see^n-plesh
since	**desde**	dayzh-de
sing (to)	**cantar**	ka^n-tar
single	**único**	oo-nee-koo
single room	**o quarto individual**	kwar-too ee^n-dee-vee-doo-al

sister	**a irmã**	eer-ma^{n}
sit, sit down (to)	**sentar-se**	se^{n}-tar-se
size	**o tamanho**	ta-ma-nyoo
skate (to)	**patinar**	pa-tee-nar
skirt	**a saia**	sa-ee-a
sky	**o céu**	se-oo
sleep (to)	**dormir**	door-meer
sleeping bag	**o saco de dormir**	sa-koo de door-meer
sleeve	**a manga**	ma^{n}-ga
slice	**a porção**	poor-sow^{n}
slip	**a combinação**	ko^{n}-bee-na-sow^{n}
slippers	**os chinelos**	shee-ne-loosh
slow	**lento**	lay^{n}-too
small	**pequeno**	pe-kay-noo
smart	**elegante**	ee-le-ga^{n}t
smell	**o cheiro**	shey-roo
smell (to)	**cheirar**	shay-ee-rar
smile (to)	**sorrir**	soor-reer
smoke (to)	**fumar**	foo-mar
(no) smoking	**(proibido) fumar**	proo-ee-bee-doo foo-mar
smoking compartment	**reservado a fumadores**	re-ser-va-doo a foo-ma-do-resh
snow	**a neve**	nev
(it is) snowing	**está a nevar**	esh-ta a ne-var
so	**assim**	a-see^{n}
soap	**o sabão**	sa-bow^{n}

soap powder	**o sabão em pó**	sa-**bow**^{n} e^n po
sober	**sóbrio**	**so**-bryoo
socks	**as peúgas**	pee-**oo**-gash
soft	**mole**	**mo**-le
sold	**vendido**	ve^n-**dee**-doo
sold out	**esgotado**	ezh-goo-**ta**-doo
sole *shoe*	**a sola**	**so**-la
solid	**sólido**	**so**-lee-doo
some	**alguns**	al-**goo**^{n}**sh**
somebody	**alguém**	al-**ge**^{n}
something	**algo**	**al**-goo
sometimes	**algumas vezes**	al-**goo**-mash **vay**-zesh
somewhere	**em algum sítio**	e^n **al-goo**^{n} **see**-tee-oo
son	**o filho**	fee-**llyoo**
song	**a canção**	ka^n-**sow**^{n}
soon	**em breve**	e^n brev
sort	**o género**	**zhe**-ne-roo
sound	**o som**	so^n
sound and light show	**o espectáculo de som e luz**	esh-pe-**ta**-koo-loo de so^n ee loosh
sour	**azedo**	a-**ze**-doo
south	**o sul**	sool
souvenir	**a recordação**	re-koor-da-**sow**^{n}
space	**o espaço**	esh-**pa**-soo
spanner	**a chave de porcas**	shahv de **por**-kash
spare	**poupar**	poh-**par**

speak (to)	**falar**	fa-**lar**
speciality	**a especialidade**	esh-pe-see-a-lee-**dad**
spectacles *glasses*	**os óculos**	**o**-koo-loosh
speed	**a velocidade**	ve-loo-see-**dad**
speed limit	**o limite de velocidade**	lee-**meet** de ve-loo-see-**dad**
spend (to)	**gastar**	gas-**tar**
spice	**o condimento**	ko^n-dee-**me^n**-too
spoon	**a colher**	koo-**llyair**
sports	**o desporto**	desh-**por**-too
sprain (to)	**deslocar**	dezh-loo-**kar**
spring *season*	**a primavera**	pree-ma-**ve**-ra
spring *water*	**a nascente**	nash-**se^{n}t**
square *adj.*	**quadrado**	kwa-**dra**-doo
square *noun*	**a praça**	**pra**-sa
stage	**o palco**	**pal**-koo
stain	**a mancha**	**ma^n**-sha
stained	**manchado**	ma^n-**sha**-doo
stairs	**as escadas**	esh-**ka**-dash
stalls *theatre*	**a plateia**	pla-**tay**-ee-a
stamp	**o selo**	**say**-loo
stand (to)	**estar de pé**	esh-**tar** de pe
star	**a estrela**	esh-**tre**-la
start (to)	**começar**	koo-me-**sar**
station	**a estação**	esh-ta-**sow^n**
statue	**a estátua**	esh-**ta**-too-a

stay (to)	**ficar**	fee-**kar**
steward	**o criado**	kree-**a**-doo
stewardess	**a criada**	kree-**a**-da
stick	**a bengala**	be^{n}-**ga**-la
stiff	**rígido/teso**	**ree**-zhee-doo/**te**-soo
still *not moving*	**imóvel**	ee-**mo**-vel
sting	**a picada**	pee-**ka**-da
stockings	**as meias**	**may**-yash
stolen	**roubado**	roh-**ba**-doo
stone	**a pedra**	**pe**-dra
stool	**o banco**	**ba**^{n}-koo
stop (to)	**parar**	pa-**rar**
store	**a loja**	**lo**-zha
stove	**o fogão**	foo-**gow**^{n}
straight	**direito**	dee-**ray**-ee-too
straight on	**a direito**	a dee-**ray**-ee-too
strange	**estranho**	esh-**tra**-nyoo
strap	**a correia**	koo-**ray**-ee-a
stream	**a corrente**	koo-**re**^{n}**t**
street	**a rua**	**roo**-a
street map	**a planta da cidade**	**pla**^{n}-ta da see-**dad**
string	**o cordel**	kor-**del**
strong	**forte**	fort
student	**o estudante**	esh-too-**da**^{n}t
style	**o estilo**	esh-**tee**-loo
suburb	**o subúrbio**	soo-**boor**-bee-oo

subway	**o caminho subterrâneo**	ka-**mee**-nyoo soob-te-**ra**-nee-oo
suddenly	**de repente/ subitamente**	de re-**pe**^{n}**t**/soo-bee-ta-**me**^{n}**t**
suede	**a camurça**	ka-**moor**-sa
suit	**o fato**	**fa**-too
suitcase	**a mala**	**ma**-la
summer	**o verão**	ve-**row**^{n}
sun	**o sol**	sol
sunbathing	**o banho de sol**	**ba**-nyoo de sol
sunglasses	**os óculos de sol**	**o**-koo-loosh de sol
sunhat	**o chapéu de sol**	sha-**pe**-oo de sol
sunshade	**o guarda sol**	**gwar**-da sol
suntan oil	**o óleo para bronzear**	**o**-lee-oo **pa**-ra bro^{n}-zee-**ar**
supper	**a ceia**	**say**-a
sure	**seguro**	se-**goo**-roo
surface mail	**o correio ordinário**	koo-**ray**-oo or-dee-**na**-ree-oo
surgery	**a clínica**	**klee**-nee-ka
surgery hours	**as horas de consulta**	**o**-rash de kon-**sool**-ta
surprise	**a surpresa**	soor-**pre**-za
surprise (to)	**surpreender**	soor-pree-en-**der**
sweat	**o suor**	soo-**or**
sweater	**o pulover**	poo-lo-**vair**
sweet	**doce**	**do**-se
swell (to)	**inchar**	ee^{n}-**shar**

swim (to)	**nadar**	na-dar
swimming pool	**a piscina**	peesh-see-na
swing	**o baloiço**	ba-loy-soo
switch *light*	**o interruptor**	ee^{n}-te-roop-tor
synagogue	**a sinagoga**	see-na-go-ga

T

table	**a mesa**	may-za
tablecloth	**a toalha de mesa**	too-a-llya de may-za
tablet	**o comprimido**	ko^{n}-pree-mee-doo
tailor	**o alfaiate**	al-fy-yat
take (to)	**tomar**	too-mar
talk (to)	**falar**	fa-lar
tall	**alto**	al-too
tampon	**o tampão**	ta^{n}-pow^{n}
tank	**o tanque**	ta^{n}k
tanned	**bronzeado**	bro^{n}-zee-a-doo
tap	**a torneira**	toor-nay-ee-ra
tapestry	**a tapeçaria**	ta-pe-sa-ree-a
taste	**o gôsto**	gosh-too
tax	**o impôsto**	ee^{n}-posh-too
taxi (rank)	**(a praça de) taxis**	pra-sa de tak-seesh
teach (to)	**ensinar**	e^{n}-see-nar
tear (to)	**rasgar**	razh-gar
telegram	**o telegrama**	te-le-gra-ma
telephone	**o telefone**	te-le-fon

telephone (to)	**telefonar**	te-le-foo-nar
telephone call	**a chamada**	sha-ma-da
television	**a televisão**	te-le-vee-zow^{n}
tell (to)	**dizer**	dee-zair
temperature	**a temperatura**	te^{n}-pe-ra-too-ra
temple	**o templo**	te^{n}-ploo
temporary	**temporário**	te^{n}-poor-ra-ree-oo
tennis	**o ténis**	te-neesh
tent	**a tenda de campismo**	te^{n}-da de ka^{n}-peezh-moo
tent peg	**a estaca**	esh-ta-ka
tent pole	**o prumo**	proo-moo
terrace	**o terraço**	te-ra-soo
than	**do que**	doo ke
thank you *said by a man*	**obrigado**	ob-ree-ga-doo
thank you *said by a woman*	**obrigada**	ob-ree-ga-da
theatre	**o teatro**	tee-a-troo
their, theirs	**seu** *m*/**sua** *f*	say-oo/soo-a
them	**eles/elas**	aylsh/e-lash
then	**então**	en-tow^{n}
there	**ali**	a-lee
there is/are	**há**	ah
thermometer	**o termómetro**	ter-mo-me-troo
these	**estes**	ayshtsh
they	**eles** *m*/**elas** *f*	aylsh/e-lash
thick	**grosso**	gro-soo

thief	**o ladrão**	la-drow^{n}
thin	**magro/fino**	ma-groo/fee-noo
thing	**a coisa**	ko-ee-za
think (to)	**pensar**	pe^{n}-sar
thirsty (to be)	**ter sede**	tair sayd
this	**este**	aysht
those	**aqueles**	a-kel-sh
thread	**o fio**	fee-oo
through	**por**	poor
throw (to)	**atirar**	a-tee-rar
thunder	**o trovão**	tro-vow^{n}
thunderstorm	**a trovoada**	troo-voo-a-da
ticket	**o bilhete**	bee-llyayt
ticket office	**a bilheteira**	bee-llyay-te-ee-ra
tide	**a maré**	ma-re
tie	**a gravata**	gra-va-ta
tight	**apertado**	a-pair-ta-doo
tights	**as meias colantes**	mey-ash ko-la^{n}-tesh
time	**o tempo/a hora**	te^{n}-poo/o-ra
timetable	**o horário**	oo-ra-ree-oo
tin	**a lata**	la-ta
tin opener	**o abre-latas**	a-bre-la-tash
tip	**a gorjeta**	goor-zhay-ta
tip (to)	**gratificar**	gra-tee-fee-kar
tired (to be)	**estar cansado**	esh-tar ka^{n}-sa-doo
to	**a**	a

tobacco	**o tabaco**	ta-ba-koo
tobacco pouch	**a tabaqueira**	ta-ba-kay-ee-ra
together	**juntos**	zhoo^{n}-toosh
toilet	**o lavatório/a retrete**	la-va-to-ree-o/re-trayt
toilet paper	**o papel higiénico**	pa-pel ee-zhee-e-nee-koo
toll	**a portagem**	poor-ta-zhay^{n}
tomorrow	**amanhã**	a-ma-nya^{n}
tongue	**a língua**	lee^{n}-gwa
too *also*	**também**	ta^{n}-be^{n}
too much/many	**demasiado**	de-ma-zee-a-doo
toothbrush	**a escova de dentes**	esh-ko-va de day^{n}-tesh
toothpaste	**a pasta de dentes**	pash-ta de day^{n}-tesh
toothpick	**o palito**	pa-lee-too
top	**o topo**	to-poo
torch	**a lanterna**	la^{n}-tair-na
torn	**roto**	ro-too
touch (to)	**tocar**	too-kar
tough	**forte/duro**	fort/doo-roo
tour	**o passeio**	pas-sey-oo
tourist	**o turista**	too-reesh-ta
tourist office	**o departamento de turismo**	de-par-ta-me^{n}-too de too-reesh-moo
towards	**para/em direcção de**	pa-ra/e^{n} dee-re-sow^{n} de
towel	**a toalha**	too-a-llya
tower	**a torre**	tor
town	**a cidade**	see-dad

town hall	**a camara municipal**	ka-ma-ra moo-nee-see-**pal**
toy	**o brinquedo**	bree^{n}-**kay**-doo
traffic	**o tráfego**	**tra**-fe-goo
traffic jam	**o engarrafamento**	e^{n}-gar-ra-fa-**me^{n}**-too
traffic lights	**os semáforos**	se-**ma**-fo-roosh
trailer	**o atrelado**	a-tre-**la**-doo
train	**o comboio**	ko^{n}-**boy**-oo
transfer (to)	**transferir**	tra^{n}zh-fe-**reer**
transit	**trânsito**	**tra^{n}**-see-too
translate (to)	**traduzir**	tra-doo-**zeer**
travel (to)	**viajar**	vee-a-**zhar**
travel agent	**o agente de viagens**	a-**zhe^{n}t** de vee-**a**-zhe^{n}sh
traveller	**o viajante**	vee-a-**zha^{n}t**
travellers' cheque	**o cheque de viagem**	shek de vee-**a**-zhe^{n}
treat (to)	**tratar**	tra-**tar**
treatment	**o tratamento**	tra-ta-**me^{n}**-too
tree	**a árvore**	**ar**-voor
trip	**a viagem**	vee-**a**-zhe^{n}
trouble	**a dificuldade**	dee-fee-kool-**dad**
trousers	**as calças**	**kal**-sash
true	**verdadeiro**	ver-da-**day**-ee-roo
trunk *luggage*	**o baú**	ba-**oo**
trunks *bathing*	**os calções de banho**	kal-**soy^{n}sh** de ba-**nyoo**
truth	**a verdade**	ver-**dad**
try (to)	**tentar**	te^{n}-**tar**

try on (to)	**provar**	proo-var
tunnel	**o túnel**	too-nel
turn (to)	**virar**	vee-rar
turning	**a curva/a viragem**	koor-va/vee-ra-zhay^{n}
tweezers	**a pinça**	pee^{n}-sa
twin beds	**as camas gémeas**	ka-mash zhe-mee-ash
twisted	**torcido**	toor-see-doo
typewriter	**a máquina de escrever**	ma-kee-na de esh-kre-vair

U

ugly	**feio**	fayee-oo
umbrella	**o guarda-chuva**	gwar-da-shoo-va
(beach) umbrella	**a sombrinha**	so^{n}-bree-nya
uncle	**o tio**	tee-oo
uncomfortable	**incómodo**	ee^{n}-ko-moo-doo
unconscious	**desmaiado**	dezh-may-a-doo
under	**debaixo**	de-ba-ee-shoo
underground	**o metropolitano**	me-troo-poo-lee-ta-noo
underneath	**debaixo**	de-ba-ee-shoo
understand	**entender**	e^{n}-te^{n}-dair
underwater fishing	**a pesca submarina**	pesh-ka soob-ma-ree-na
underwear	**a roupa interior**	roh-pa ee^{n}-te-ree-or
university	**a universidade**	oo-nee-ver-see-dad
until	**até**	a-te
unusual	**raro**	ra-roo

up, upstairs	**em cima**	e^{n} **see**-ma
urgent	**urgente**	oor-**ge^{n}t**
us	**nós**	nosh
USA	**os EUA/Estados Unidos da América**	es-**ta**-doosh oo-**nee**-doosh da a-**me**-ree-ka
use (to)	**usar**	oo-**zar**
useful	**útil**	**oo**-teel
useless	**inútil**	een-**oo**-teel
usual	**usual**	oo-zoo-**al**

V

vacancies	**as vagas**	**va**-gash
vacant	**vago**	**va**-goo
valid	**válido**	**va**-lee-doo
valley	**o vale**	vall
valuable	**valioso**	va-lee-**o**-zoo
value	**o valor**	va-**lor**
vase	**o vaso**	**va**-zoo
VAT	**o IVA**	**ee**-va
vegetable	**o legume**	le-**goom**
vegetarian	**o vegetariano**	ve-zhe-ta-ree-**a**-noo
velvet	**o veludo**	ve-**loo**-doo
ventilation	**a ventilação**	ve^{n}-tee-la-**sow^{n}**
very	**muito**	**moo**-ee-too
very little	**muito pouco**	moo-ee-**too** **po**-koo
very much	**muitíssimo**	moo-ee-**tee**-see-moo

vest	**a camisola interior**	ka-mee-zo-la een-te-ree-or
video recorder	**o gravador de cassetes**	gra-va-dor de ka-se-tesh
view	**a vista**	vees-ta
villa	**a vila**	vee-la
village	**a vila/a aldeia**	vee-la/al-day-ya
vineyard	**a vinha**	vee-nya
violin	**o violino**	vee-oo-lee-noo
visa	**o visto**	vee-shtoo
visibility	**a visibilidade**	vee-zee-bee-lee-dad
visit	**a visita**	vee-zee-ta
visit (to)	**visitar**	vee-zee-tar
voice	**a voz**	vosh
voltage	**a voltagem**	vol-ta-zhay^{n}
voucher	**o cupão**	koo-pow^{n}
voyage	**a viagem**	vee-a-zhay^{n}

W

wait (to)	**esperar**	esh-pe-rar
waiter	**o criado de mesa**	kree-a-doo de may-za
waiting room	**a sala de espera**	sa-la de esh-pe-ra
waitress	**a criada de mesa**	kree-a-da de may-za
wake (to)	**despertar/acordar**	des-per-tar/a-koor-dar
Wales	**o País de Gales**	pa-eesh de galsh
walk	**o passeio**	pa-say-yoo

walk (to)	**caminhar**	ka-mee-**nyar**
wall	**a parede**	pa-**re**-de
wall plug	**a tomada de parede**	too-**ma**-da de pa-**re**-de
wallet	**a carteira**	kar-**tay**-ee-ra
want (to)	**querer**	ke-**rair**
wardrobe	**o guarda-roupa**	**gwar**-da-**roh**-pa
warm	**quente/morno**	**ke**^{n}**t/mor**-noo
wash (to)	**lavar**	la-**var**
washbasin	**o lavatório**	la-va-**to**-ree-oo
waste	**o desperdício/o lixo**	des-per-**dee**-see-oo/**lee**-shoo
waste (to)	**desperdiçar/perder**	des-per-dee-**sar**/per-**der**
watch	**o relógio**	re-**lo**-zhee-oo
water	**a água**	**a**-gwa
water ski-ing	**a esqui aquático**	es-**kee** a-**kwa**-tee-koo
waterfall	**a cascata**	kas-**ka**-ta
wave	**a onda**	**o**^{n}-da
way	**o caminho**	ka-**mee**-nyoo
we	**nós**	nosh
wear (to)	**vestir**	vesh-**teer**
weather	**o tempo**	**te**^{n}-poo
weather forecast	**a previsão do tempo**	pre-vee-**zow**^{n} do **tay**^{n}-poo
wedding ring	**a aliança**	a-lee-**a**^{n}-sa
weigh (to)	**pesar**	pe-**sar**
weight	**o peso**	**pe**-zoo
well	**bem**	bay^{n}

well *water*	**o poço (de água)**	po-soo
Welsh	**galês**	ga-laysh
west	**o oeste**	oo-esht
wet	**molhado**	mo-llya-doo
what?	**o quê?**	oo ke
wheel	**a roda**	ro-da
wheelchair	**a cadeira de rodas**	ka-day-ee-ra de ro-dash
when?	**quando?**	kwa^n-doo
where?	**onde?**	o^n-de
which?	**qual?**	kwal
while	**enquanto**	e^n-kwa^n-too
who?	**quem?**	ke^n
whole	**inteiro**	ee^n-tay-roo
whose?	**de quem?**	de ke^n
why?	**porquê?**	poor-ke
wide	**largo**	lar-goo
widow	**a viúva**	vee-oo-va
widower	**o viúvo**	vee-oo-voo
wife	**a esposa**	esh-po-za
wild	**selvagem**	sel-va-zhay^n
win (to)	**ganhar**	ga-nyar
wind	**o vento**	ve^n-too
window	**a janela**	zha-ne-la
wine merchant	**o negociante de vinhos**	ne-goo-see-a^{n}t de vee-nyoosh
winter	**o inverno**	een-vair-noo

wish (to)	**desejar**	de-ze-**zhar**
with	**com**	**ko**^{n}
within	**dentro/entre**	**de**^{n}-troo/**e**^{n}-tre
without	**sem**	se^{n}
woman	**a mulher**	moo-**llyair**
wonderful	**maravilhoso**	ma-ra-vee-**llyo**-zoo
wood	**a madeira**	ma-**dey**-ra
wool	**a lã**	la^{n}
word	**a palavra**	pa-**la**-vra
work	**o trabalho**	tra-**ba**-llyoo
work (to)	**trabalhar**	tra-ba-**llyar**
worry (to)	**preocupar**	pray-o-koo-**par**
worse	**pior**	pee-**or**
worth (to be)	**valer**	va-**lair**
wrap (to)	**envolver/embrulhar**	e^{n}-vol-**vair**/e^{n}-broo-**lyar**
write (to)	**escrever**	esh-kre-**vair**
writing paper	**o papel de escrever**	pa-**pel** de esh-kre-**vair**
wrong	**equivocado**	ee-kee-voo-**ka**-doo
wrong (to be)	**estar equivocado**	esh-**tar** ee-kee-voo-**ka**-doo

X

xerox	**a fotocópia**	fo-to-**ko**-pee-a
X-ray	**os raios X**	**ry**-osh sheesh

Y

yacht	**o iate**	yat
year	**o ano**	**a**-noo
yesterday	**ontem**	**o**^{n}-te^{n}
you	**o senhor** *m*/**a senhora** *f*	se-**nyor**/se-**nyo**-ra
young	**jovem**	**zho**-ve^{n}
your	**seu** *m*/ **sua** *f*	**say**-oo/**soo**-a
youth hostel	**o albergue da juventude**	al-**bairg** da zhoo-vay^{n}-**tood**

Z

zip	**o fecho éclair**	**fay**-shoo ay-**klair**
zoo	**o jardim zoológico**	zhar-**dee**^{n} zoo-oo-**lo**-zhee-koo

INDEX